REACHING FOR THE DREAM

The **Nordic Institute of Asian Studies** (NIAS) is funded by the governments of Denmark, Finland, Iceland, Norway and Sweden via the Nordic Council of Ministers, and works to encourage and support Asian studies in the Nordic countries. In so doing, NIAS has been publishing books since 1969, with more than one hundred titles produced in the last decade.

The **Institute of Southeast Asian Studies** (ISEAS) was established as an autonomous organization in 1968. It is a regional research centre for scholars and other specialists concerned with modern Southeast Asia, particularly the many-faceted issues and challenges of stability and security, economic development, and political and social change.

The Institute's research programmes are Regional Economic Studies (RES, including ASEAN and APEC), Regional Strategic and Political Studies (RSPS), and Regional Social and Cultural Studies (RSCS).

The Institute is governed by a twenty-two-member Board of Trustees comprising nominees from the Singapore Government, the National University of Singapore, the various Chambers of Commerce, and professional and civic organizations. An Executive Committee oversees day-to-day operations; it is chaired by the Director, the Institute's chief academic and administrative officer.

Reaching for the Dream

Challenges of Sustainable Development in Vietnam

EDITED BY
MELANIE BERESFORD AND
TRAN NGOC ANGIE

INSTITUTE OF SOUTHEAST ASIAN STUDIES
Singapore

First published in 2004 by NIAS Press
Nordic Institute of Asian Studies
Leifsgade 33, DK–2300 Copenhagen S, Denmark
tel: (+45) 3532 9501 • fax: (+45) 3532 9549
E–mail: books@nias.ku.dk • Website: http://www.niaspress.dk

First published in 2004 in Singapore by
Institute of Southeast Asian Studies (ISEAS)
30 Heng Mui Keng Terrace, Pasir Panjang, Singapore 119614
E-mail: publish@iseas.edu.sg • Website: http://bookshop.iseas.edu.sg
for distribution in the ASEAN countries, Japan, Korea, Taiwan,
Australia and New Zealand.

British Library Cataloguing in Publication Data
Reaching for the dream : challenges of sustainable
development in Vietnam. - (Studies in Asian topics ; 33)
1.Sustainable development - Vietnam 2.Vietnam - Economic
conditions - 1975- 3.Vietnam - Economic policy - 1975-
4.Vietnam - Social conditions - 1975-
I.Beresford, Melanie II.Tran, Angie Ngoc III.Nordic
Institute of Asian Studies
338.9'597

ISBN 87-91114-19-5 (NIAS hbk edition)
ISBN 87-91114-48-9 (NIAS pbk edition)
ISBN 981-230-228-X (ISEAS edition)

Typesetting by Translations ved LJ
Produced by SRM Production Services Sdn. Bhd.
and printed in Malaysia

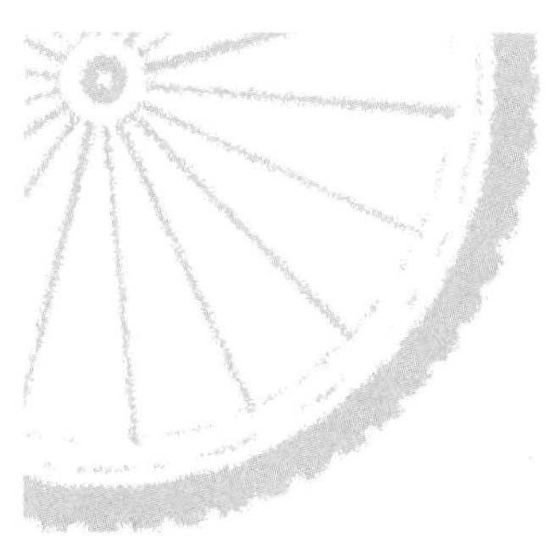

Contents

FIGURES

APPENDICES

TABLES

Preface

The gestation of this book began long ago at the Euroviet III Conference in Amsterdam in July 1997. As co-ordinator and discussant for the Economics Panel of that conference we were struck by the theme, which emerged in several of the papers and in the discussion, of how Vietnam could sustain its then rapid rate of growth in order to 'catch up' to its Southeast Asian neighbours. Even at that time, before the Asian crisis struck, questions were being raised about Vietnamese market institutions, in particular, and their suitability to support long-term development. Some of these papers are more explicitly acknowledged in our Introduction. We would, however, like to thank all the participants of that panel for providing us with the initial inspiration for this book.

The topic acquired a new urgency in light of the Asian crisis, and we then set about finding authors. Macquarie University's Research Grant programme generously provided us with funds to hold a workshop in Darwin, Australia, where several of the authors were able to gather to discuss the overall concept of the book and some early draft chapters. Hoang Thi Thu Ha provided us with valuable research assistance in the preparation for that workshop.

California State University at Monterey Bay provided excellent technical facilities and spiritual support from faculty and staff at the Social and Behavioral Sciences Department, which contributed significantly to the completion of this book.

Finally, the editors would like to acknowledge many wonderful people, inside and outside of Vietnam, who have inspired, supported, provided advice and insights, and sustained us throughout this long gestation process. In particular, we thank our kind-hearted and hardworking landlady, Ms. Hanh, whose life story inspired us both while we did our fieldwork in Hanoi (her photo graces the cover of this book).

Notes on contributors

REGINA ABRAMI is an assistant professor at the Harvard Business School, Boston, USA.

BACH TAN SINH is senior research fellow and deputy-director, Department of Science Policy Studies, National Institute for Science and Technology Policy and Strategy Studies, Ministry of Science, Technology and Environment, Hanoi, Vietnam.

MELANIE BERESFORD is associate professor in economics at Macquarie University, Sydney, Australia.

BUI VAN HUNG is lecturer in economics in the Post-graduate Faculty of the National Economics University, Hanoi, Vietnam.

DANG PHONG is professor of economics at the Hanoi University of Business Management and director of research for the project '55 years of the Vietnamese Economy' at the Institute of Economics, National Centre for Social Sciences and Humanities, Hanoi, Vietnam.

NOLWEN HENAFF is a researcher in economics at the Institute for Research on Development (formerly ORSTOM), Paris, France.

WILLIAM SMITH was working for the Vietnam–Sweden Mountain Rural Development Programme at the time his research was carried out. He is now director of the World Council of Credit Associations in Vietnam.

TRAN NGOC ANGIE is associate professor in political economy at California State University, Monterey Bay, USA.

TECHNICAL NOTE

All references to dollars are to US dollars unless otherwise stated.

CHAPTER 1

Introduction

Melanie Beresford and Tran Ngoc Angie

Since the failure of centrally planned economies to produce sustainable growth over the long term, it has become conventional wisdom that market economies produce better results, from the points of view of both individual and social welfare. What remains controversial, however, are questions such as: how, exactly, do markets function to produce such superior results? Mainstream economic theory has long assumed that markets are better, but it is largely an ideological assertion. There is plenty of evidence that some capitalist economies, the early industrialisers, have performed better in the long-term growth stakes, but there is debate about why this should be so. Equally many capitalist economies have performed dismally, and the social welfare and environmental outcomes are patchy in all of them. Moreover, there is now a voluminous literature indicating that 'market failure' has been at least as important, if not more pervasive, than 'government failure' in some of the East Asian late industrialisers (the classic examples are Amsden 1989; Wade 1990). So how do markets work? What are the essential relationships between social institutions of the state and markets which tend to promote long-term and equitable growth rather than hinder it?

These are relatively old questions in the social sciences. The new setting to which the essays in this book address these old questions is the transitional economy of Vietnam. Transition economies give us the opportunity to study some fundamental questions about the nature of markets. How do they arise and do they necessarily follow the same *modus operandi* as markets in other countries? How does the state influence the development of markets through its policies and institutions? How does the opening of the economy to global market influences affect the processes of institutional change and human development? How do people respond to both internal and external influences? How do the various cultural practices and expectations within a society explain the dynamics of development politics? And how, in the context of an underdeveloped transitional economy like Vietnam, do such influences affect the prospects for sustainable and equitable development?

THE MEANING OF SUSTAINABLE DEVELOPMENT

Generally the literature on sustainable development is very broad, though tending to fall into a range of fairly specialised categories including feminism (Beneria and Roldan 1987, Beneria *et al.* 2000; Waring 1999; Harcourt 1994; Sen 1994 and Hausler 1994), environmental politics (Shiva 1991; Hajer and Fischer 1999), environmental economics (Daly 1996; Pearce 1985; Norgaard 1985) and the global political economy perspective of Redclift (1987). For the environmental economists the focus is on the relations between economic activities, finite natural resources and the possibilities for achieving environmental justice.

The literature generally provides a 'technological critique' of existing capitalist practice. Feminist perspectives concentrate on accounting for women's work (productive and reproductive), arguing for inclusion of gender equity and a greater voice for women in the definition of development. Similarly, the environmental politics' approach focuses on 'cultural critique', arguing for more respect for cultural diversity. The global political economy version argues that both the gender and environmental issues need to be considered in the context of the global economic system and sheds light on how environmental degradation and social inequity are not natural but historical processes linked to economic and political structures.

Mainstream economic analysis, on the other hand, considers the question of sustainability largely from the point of view of maintaining macroeconomic stability and growth of national income. Although new fields, such as environmental economics, have arisen in recent years, these generally do not consider externalities for which there is no market valuation or for which such a valuation cannot be imputed, such as women's reproductive work at home. 'The system cannot respond to values it refuses to recognise' (Waring 1999: 3). Therefore mainstream analysis does not consider many of the issues, such as power and conflicting cultural traditions, that are incorporated into the political economy approach to sustainable development.

Political economists share the common assumption that development cannot be defined solely in terms of economic growth. For them, sustainable development involves qualitative improvement beyond the singular focus on quantitative growth (with its common indicator, GNP) that characterises much of development economics.[1] They are critical of orthodox development theory in its tendency to assume that (1) growth, the main feature of development, can be achieved in a linear fashion (all countries proceed through the same stages); (2) growth is unlimited; (3) the use of resources is infinite; (4) profit maximisation at the expense of environmental degradation is possible. Further, they are sensitive to differences in cultural practice and the needs and priorities of the poor, and seek to analyse sustainable development within a framework which incorporates the interrelated dimensions of gender, class, levels of income and culture. From a practical and policy perspective they tend to be allied with those opposed to mainstream economic analysis and the institutions associated with maintenance of global capitalism such as the World Bank and the IMF. As elaborated below, our framework is broadly in agreement with the concerns of the global political economy perspective.

A principal insight provided by this literature is into the contradictions implied in the concept of sustainable development. Redclift (1987), for example, identifies three dimensions of sustainability: the social, the environmental and the ethical. Within these, he sees environmental, distributional and ethical rationalities as socially constructed and supported by different social groups having varying degrees of power as well as conflicting economic interests. In this approach, therefore, 'cultural critique' can be understood as encompassing differences in power within a given society that inevitably lead to different political agenda and methods of carrying them out.

First, unequal power is expressed, for example, by the benefits to transnational corporations from free trade and technological advantages which give them the scope to create and exploit consumer markets in the advanced industrial and newly industrialised countries, using raw materials and cheap labour from the low-income, 'less developed countries (LDCs)'. LDCs, on the other hand, are dependent upon industrial inputs and technologies (such as pesticides, fertilisers, bio-engineered seeds) for intensive farming practices which, although detrimental to the land, are required to earn foreign exchange for debt repayment. Where national governments in the Third World are co-opted and supported by global capitalism, ordinary people lose control over the management of their economic environment and their own labour. Production for global markets both undervalues the labour of women and impacts adversely on them through their dependence on a degraded environment for sources of fuel wood, water, or industrial inputs from developed countries, etc.

Second, sustainability is conceived in terms of different objectives and rationalities. For the industrialised countries, environmental preservation, biological diversity, conservation of rural space and aesthetic values are emphasised, while in the Third World economic survival is more important. Sustainability should, however, be conceptualised so that it supports basic needs and doesn't counterpose nature against the survival needs of the most vulnerable. The population question is a case in point (Sen 1994). While it is often argued that limitation of family size is the key to overcoming the Malthusian spectre of insufficient food, distributional factors are now widely accepted as being at least, if not more, important than population growth in sustaining hunger. Skewed land distribution, unequal access to development resources and commercialisation processes have produced uneven growth, leading to plenty in one location alongside dearth in another. For those who lack resources other than labour power, high fertility may be the only means of obtaining hands to work the fields and social security for illness and old age.

While there are clear similarities between Redclift's political economy approach and those used by the authors in this book, our definition of sustainability differs in some important respects. In the first place, we go far beyond the conventional focus on environmental issues, that is only one dimension of sustainable development for a country like Vietnam. While environmental issues are important, and are explicitly dealt with in Chapter 8, the chapters here examine economic, political and institutional sustainability, especially with regard to equitable income distribution and social welfare (people's well-being) as major consequences of Vietnam's *doi moi* [renovation] process. The Vietnamese Communist Party (VCP) has, since the early 1990s, set itself to achieve the goals of 'rich people, strong country, civilised and equitable society', and we find it hard to disagree with such objectives, especially in so far as they refer to the combination of rapid growth with equity. Where our approach differs from more conventional conceptions of sustainability is that we use specific issues, such as environment, gender, poverty, labour market segmentation, industrialisation and global integration, as windows through which to examine these larger issues of economic, political and institutional sustainability for the achievement of those goals.

For very poor transition economies like Vietnam, unequal power and differences in objectives and rationalities can be expressed in various ways. First, there is the struggle at the national level to catch up with its neighbours, a struggle which takes place within certain patterns of international and regional economic integration characterised by unequal power relations. Second, there are internal contradictions between those who have benefited most from the market economy (largely urban-based residents with significant capital accumulation and links to international capital) and those whose livelihoods remain vulnerable, not only to vicissitudes of the business cycle but to natural and environmental disaster, poor health status, restricted educational and employment opportunities, lack of access to and control over economic resources, and and to production and distribution decision making processes. Certainly, in such a context, economic growth is one of the keys to attaining sustainable lives and livelihoods. The distributional aspects of such growth as well as its environmental impacts, however, will determine whether sustainable development becomes something restricted to a wealthy minority (globally or nationally) or is shared by a broad cross-section of Vietnamese society. Third, the contradictory effects of state flexibility are reflected in its responses to the severe crises of the late 1970s and 1980s, and in its current struggle to regain coherence in the process of further integration into the world capitalist economy with the blurred lines between public and private sectors. These issues are discussed further in the next section.

Some of the contradictory aspects of the development process were canvassed in a paper by Dang Hoang Giang (1997). He tackled the question of development strategies at the macro level, using a systems analysis approach to weigh up the advantages and disadvantages of pursuing three alternative strategies – a 'growth pole' strategy emphasising continued allocation of resources to existing wealthier and high growth areas, an 'agricultural-led' strategy focusing on the sector where most Vietnamese are currently employed, and a 'rural industrialisation' strategy, emphasising resource allocation to rural industries such as food processing, handicraft, construction materials and machinery. These were cross-tabulated with different scenarios of population growth, internal migration and environmental policies. Since each of these strategies and scenarios would produce quite different outcomes in terms of growth rates, income distribution, employment and environmental effects, he argued that the choice of strategy depends mainly on political factors. While he neither discussed the interests and rationalities associated with each strategy nor speculated about how such political decisions might be reached, these are precisely the issues on which a shift from the current strategy (growth poles)[2] to a more equitable strategy hinge. Bui Van Hung (Chapter 6), also captures these contradictory aspects by showing state intermediate goals to ensure rapid growth with significant reduction in poverty and greater equity, while the current realities of physical and human infrastructure investment, structure of the credit market, mixed impacts of large state-owned enterpries (SOEs) and other institutional arrangements appear to be not amenable to a balanced, sustainable and equitable development, as is clearly reflected in a widening gap between incomes and living standards of urban and rural residents. Moreover, Abrami and Henaff, in Chapter 4, capture the subtle ways in which the interactions of different groups, exercising unequal power, may produce unintended results.

Indeed the lack of concrete analyses of sustainable development in specific institutional settings is a major shortcoming of the literature which this book attempts to redress. Much of the existing literature locates the problem of sustainable development within a dichotomous North–South (or developed and developing country) framework (Beneria and Roldan 1987, Beneria et al. 2000; Redclift 1987) and does not, therefore, shed light on the specific problems of a socialist transition economy like Vietnam. Moreover, despite the evidence of East Asia in past decades, this sustainable development literature tends to discount the role of national governments as weak and co-opted. National states, however, clearly do have an influence both on the patterns of integration into the global economy and the ways in which these patterns are experienced by the population as a whole. Local transformations can be achieved at the national and subnational levels which, while they may not upset the overall balance of global economic power, may significantly affect the terms on which social classes, ethnic minorities or men and women can achieve sustainable development.

THE ROLE OF THE STATE IN VIETNAM

An important difference between the emerging market economy in Vietnam and that of the overtly capitalist countries in the region is the continued existence of a Communist Party regime. At its national congresses since it formally adopted the policy of renovation in 1986, the VCP has consistently stated that it still considers the country to be undergoing a 'transition to socialism'. Since many in the party hold different, and perhaps uncertain, views on what 'socialism' might mean in the context of a market economy, the official pronouncements have been deliberately vague. However, some consistent themes have emerged. These themes are encapsulated in two slogans: the first, 'rich people, strong country, civilised and equitable society' in many ways continues the old emphases on national independence, rapid development and egalitarianism, while the second, 'socialist market-oriented economy under state guidance', expresses a continuity with the traditional socialist model in its stress on state-led development.

Since centrally directed allocation of resources had all but disappeared by the 1990s, the latter goal has usually been linked to continued domination of the 'commanding heights' of the economy by the state-owned enterprise (SOE) sector. To achieve this objective, SOEs in strategic sectors, such as electricity, coal, oil, food processing, textiles and garments, telecommunications and the national airline, have been consolidated into large general corporations (*tổng công ty*). At the same time, the emergence of a vibrant private sector has led to measures aimed at increasing the visibility of private activity in order to bring it more closely under state management. Clearly the VCP is not looking towards Western models of relatively laissez-faire market relations: its ideological stance has more in common with the highly interventionist development programmes favoured elsewhere in East Asia. Unlike its capitalist neighbours, however, the VCP also emphasises the need for such intervention to accommodate the goal of a 'civilised and equitable society'.

How well has this vision been translated into reality during the past decade and a half? If we try to answer this question, a certain ambiguity emerges. On the one hand, the continuing strength of the Vietnamese party-state has been exhibited by its ability to retain power throughout the difficult years of transition. Faced with a series of severe crises in the late 1970s and throughout the 1980s, the state demonstrated a high degree of flexibility in its response. As Dang Phong shows in Chapter 4 on the historical roots of the transformation, the phenomenon of 'fence breaking', or going outside the constraints imposed by central planning, was not entirely due to spontaneous grassroots actions occurring without sanction from the higher levels of authority. Local authorities and enterprise managers were able to gain endorsement from high-level party leaders for 'experiments' in market-orientated reforms (as, for example, in the case of the Long An provincial authorities using market prices within the state trading system as early as 1980, or the rice price 'fence breaking' in An Giang in 1978). In some cases the transformation process was initiated at very high levels (as in the case of the partial price reform of 1981). As has been noted elsewhere (Beresford and Fforde 1997), there was a symbiotic relation rather than an oppositional one between state action and grassroots change as well as between state and non-state sectors. Flexible state management of the reform process enabled the Vietnamese state to avoid the consequence, the eventual demise of the party-state, of more oppositional stances taken by Communist regimes in some East European countries. This capacity of the state apparatus to manage the transformation helps to explain not only why the Communist Party has remained firmly in power in the post-central planning era but also the continuing dominance of the state sector in economic life.[3]

On the other hand, the very flexibility of state management and the 'bottom up' nature of many changes meant that there was no blueprint for reform. The transition process itself has led to a weakening of state influence over the direction of economic development. Given a state apparatus deeply imbued with the traditions of administrative planning and control, the process of transforming state institutions into market managers has been protracted and difficult, providing many opportunities for both citizens and state officials to evade the rules and engage in self-interested activities. Rent-seeking,[4] corruption and smuggling increased alongside legitimate market production and distribution, leading to a common characterisation, during the earlier stages of transition of many state-owned enterprises as 'black boxes' that the government could not penetrate. Social power derived from a position within the state apparatus enabled individuals to accumulate capital and allocate resources to unplanned uses. As the lines between 'public' and 'private' became more blurred, state action lost much of its coherence and ability to impose central priorities on the changing structure of the economy. Even today, the government often lacks the capacity to evaluate the effectiveness of SOEs based on clearly defined performance criteria as conditions for state assistance and co-ordination with relevant ministries in implementation of centrally determined policies. As illustrated in several chapters, the issue gravitates towards the varying degrees and quality of state intervention that would facilitate sustainable development. For instance, state capacity to formulate and implement diversification strategies is inadequate in various sectors of the economy. As a consequence of this weakness, the state cannot intervene effectively to ensure that enterprises perform to desired standards.

Integration into the capitalist world economy has, if anything, enhanced this weakness. As Beresford argues in Chapter 3 on the impact of the Asian crisis in the late 1990s, the massive influx of often speculative foreign capital prior to the crisis, combined with the priorities of Western aid donors, has had a large impact on the economic structure and blunted the capacity of the government to use SOEs as leaders of the development process. Tran also shows in Chapter 5 how global influences on the Vietnamese textile and garment industry, although contributing to the rapid and important increase in export income, have led to difficulties in developing backward and forward linkages that would bring more value added to the economy. Moreover, as has been noted elsewhere (Tran, 2001, 2002), the fact that Vietnam has been caught in a bind of capital shortage and the need for global integration to attract foreign investment has resulted in contradictions between export-oriented policies that promote cheap, compliant and docile labour, and progressive labour policies that are intended to protect workers' rights and to promote labour representation through labour unions. The multi-level subcontracting and piece-rate remuneration structure of global production not only afford flexibility for foreign corporate buyers and subcontractors, requiring workers to bear the burden of adjustment and lose control over their own labour, but also render Vietnamese labour policies to protect workers ineffective and unimplementable. In terms of the gender division of labour, women workers bear the greatest burden because of expectations of docility, dexterity, passivity and flexibility on the shopfloor to raise productivity for global capitalist production. In the process of transition, therefore, the state has struggled to regain coherence and to become the 'developmental state' implied in its socialist vision.

In the past, the strength of the Vietnamese state was established on two main foundations: first, its broad legitimacy derived from success in the struggle for independence and national reunification, and, second, membership of the socialist bloc that, crucially, made available large quantities of aid giving it immense, though not absolute, power over the allocation of resources (see Chapter 2). The advent of peacetime, however, reduced the appeal of nationalism relative to material well-being among people of all social strata, while the termination of Soviet aid and the end of the cold war opened the economy to new international influences with a different set of strings attached. This transition has produced massive changes in economic structure, institutions and culture as well as new political pressures on the state.

THE MAJOR THEMES OF THIS BOOK

Such political considerations enter strongly into the definition of what is considered sustainable development. As noted above, the concept varies according to institutional and social imperatives. It is usually defined by governments in terms of long-term growth of the national income, though such a definition may also be constrained by the need to maintain national independence or preserve national integrity. For business, sustainability is most likely to be defined in terms of profitability and capital accumulation, while for households or individuals it may mean sustainable livelihoods and communities (social networks, basic infrastructure or cultural communities, for example). Sustainable development is therefore normally a highly contested notion which ultimately depends on the resolution of differences by political means. In the contemporary world, conflicting notions of sustainability are often fought out at a global level in, for example, the on-going debates over the benefits of free trade within the WTO framework or over IMF solutions to the Asian crisis. The nation state, however, remains a key locus of such debates since it is within national frameworks that positions in the global discourse are negotiated (Hirst and Thompson 1996).

Political and economic power are therefore central to the question of sustainability of development. In any development process there are winners and losers as people are forced to adapt to changes in economic structure, institutions and cultural norms. Changes in the balance of power within a given social formation make the difference between sustainability and non-sustainability of different communities and social practices. The extent to which the state is able to retain its legitimacy, by accommodating the interests of a broad range of social groups, and retain its strength and coherence *vis-à-vis* powerful sectional interests is thus not a trivial issue. It is central to the state's relative autonomy and capacity to avoid the sort of social instability that might threaten the development process as a whole.

As noted above, one of the key features of the Vietnamese transition has been the flexibility of state responses to the constraints imposed by central planning. A relative balance was maintained between vested interests derived from the former socialist model and emerging interests associated with market forces. By allowing the development of market relations alongside planning during the 1980s, the state ensured a minimal level of conflict over scarce resources while at the same time permitting the development of more sustainable practices for all sections of society. These practices enabled the Vietnamese economy to survive the crises of the late 1970s and the termination of Soviet aid in 1991 and created the basis for rapid growth and rising living standards in the 1990s. Nevertheless, there have been marked shifts in the balance of power which have implications for sustainability over the longer term. If the potential for conflict over scarce resources has been minimised during the period of transition, it is not yet clear that this can continue into the future. Chapter 3 by Melanie Beresford argues that growth in the 1990s was to some extent premised on an unsustainable bubble economy emerging in the South-east Asian region and was accompanied by rising inequality within Vietnam. Should a period of slower growth emerge in the coming decade, more intense competition for access to and control over resources could lead to heightened social conflicts.

A related question is whether the Vietnamese market economy, despite official pronouncements in favour of socialism, is evolving towards convergence with Western models of capitalism. Rolf Herno (1997) addressed this question directly, arguing that Western models, at least as indicated by the assumptions of neo-classical economics, are not being emulated in Vietnam. Instead he argued that Vietnamese market institutions have developed in a way which has more in common with several East Asian economies where markets are embedded in social networks. Indeed his paper was initially inspired by the work of Orrù *et al.* (1997; also Hamilton 1996) on Chinese business organisation in Taiwan, Hong Kong and South-east Asia. Elements of the Chinese experience which appear to us to apply to varying degrees in Vietnam include relations between enterprises and bureaucrats that facilitate registration procedures, acquisition of land, market access and credit; supply, marketing and financial linkages developed between large-scale SOEs and SMEs (small and medium enterprises) in both public and private sectors; the development of production linkages between SMEs such that the network can effectively act as a single firm; and the foundation of these networks in personal, clan or place of origin-based relations of trust. In the context of absent system-level trust brought about by political uncertainty, lack of a clear legal framework or unpredictable policy changes, the mutual trust developed within ongoing social relationships provides a stable basis for markets to operate. It also obviates the need for contract-based relations. In this volume, the chapters by Beresford, Tran, Abrami and Henaff, and Smith suggest that such networks are indeed an important aspect of Vietnamese market institutions. All four chapters illustrate the ways in which networks, based on connections often developed within the former centrally planned economy, can now blur the distinction between public and private sectors, while that of Tran in particular, shows how they operate within global commodity chains and capital markets.

If Vietnamese markets are not converging with Western models, does this mean that market institutions have not yet achieved a sustainable basis on which to expand further? If such networks do now form a stable institutional basis for functioning markets in Vietnam, then according to experience elsewhere in East Asia there is no reason to suppose that they are not sustainable in the long run. However, two important issues are raised by the emergence of network-based market institutions. Do these networks have the capacity to induce the kind of equitable growth pattern which the Communist Party sees as essential to regime maintenance (that is, its continuing legitimacy)? And, second, does the state possess the capacity to intervene effectively in such networks in ways that will offset any tendency to inequitable growth?

There can be no doubt that the transition from central planning has produced large increases in inequality along social class, regional and gender lines, and rural and urban divide (Beresford 2003; Desai 2000; Bui and Abrami and Henaff, this volume). Throughout most of the 1990s, however, high GDP growth rates and rapidly rising standards of living tended to blunt the social tensions which might have arisen as a result of increasing inequity.[5] There were exceptions: notably the disturbances in Thai Binh province during 1998 and in the Central Highlands in early 2001 that were reportedly at least partly due to land disputes. Bach Tan Sinh also notes in Chapter 8 the tensions which arose in Quang Ninh province when local residents felt disadvantaged by a central decision concerning the location of a new coal washing plant. Such tensions have remained local and have in no way threatened the stability of the state, but they do indicate the potential, in case living standards do not continue to increase and inequity continues to grow, for instability to become a larger problem. Moreover, from the point of view of long-term sustainability, there is broad agreement among economists that some degree of equitable growth produces superior results (see, for example, World Bank 1993, Beresford, Chapter 3).

The causes of rising inequality are much more complex and difficult to determine. The most marked divergences seem to have occurred along urban–rural lines: despite steadily rising agricultural productivity since the 1988 reform permitting household land tenure, urban-based industries and services have grown much more rapidly. It seems likely that monopsonistic practices of central and local SOEs acting as intermediaries in the purchase of farm products have turned the terms of trade against farmers and hampered surplus retention in rural areas (Ngo Thi Men 1997). Bui Van Hung in Chapter 6 also identifies a number of structural problems which have held back the development of the rural sector: lack of access to finance, poor infrastructure and inadequate development of human resources have both reduced the capacity for agricultural diversification and restricted development of non-farm employment opportunities. Established networks may also be an important element in patterns of capital accumulation, resulting in the development of a class system of winners and losers, cutting across the rural–urban divide and public–private sectors. Abrami and Henaff suggest in Chapter 4, for example, that those rural villages which have been best positioned to take advantage of market opportunities are those in which local cadres used their urban connections to find niches in urban markets. There is also abundant evidence that state enterprises, mainly those located in the urban agglomerations around Ho Chi Minh City and Hanoi–Haiphong, have also been able to use networks established during the central planning period to gain access to foreign joint-venture investment, to export quotas and to other protective measures which have given them access to higher income levels (see Chapters 3, 4, 5, 6). Individuals within SOEs and within the state apparatus have also used connections to garner a share of the available rents, whether legally or illegally acquired. Such practices would suggest that a process of class formation is underway in which social power acquired in the centrally planned economy is being translated into economic power in the market system. Abrami and Henaff also suggest, however, that these networks are by no means static and appear to be becoming more open both to competition and to state surveillance and regulation.

State intervention to offset the tendency to rising inequality has taken a number of forms. On the one hand, there have been various budgetary efforts to redress income and expenditure imbalances through poverty alleviation programmes and central subsidies to poor provinces. On the other hand, measures like the so-called Grassroots Democracy decree of 1998 are aimed at increasing the ability of ordinary people to criticise and monitor the activities of local authorities – in other words, to improve the transparency of state processes at the local level (it remains to be seen how well the general secretary, Nong Duc Manh, can mobilise internal support to initiate this process at the central level). In response to the Asian crisis, the government also shifted its spending priorities towards rural development, emphasising the importance of expanding the domestic market in order to offset vulnerability to external shocks caused by international flows of capital and trade. The extent to which such measures are successful will depend largely on the development of state capacity: the government needs to be able to mobilise domestic resources (budgets and credit), to penetrate existing market networks in order to be able to influence investment decisions and to negotiate effectively with international financial institutions and investors for long-term equitable, sustainable development in Vietnam.

The government has expended much effort in developing access to rural credit as the principal means of achieving more rapid development of the countryside, where over 70 per cent of Vietnam's population still live. To date, however, progress has been slow: according Bui Van Hung and William Smith in Chapters 6 and 7, financial deepening has been hindered by the very state policies designed to enhance it. Looking at the question from a macroeconomic perspective, Bui examines the inability of the formal financial sector to mobilise rural savings, particularly long-term deposits, which leads it to concentrate on short-term lending and, with rising levels of overdue loans, contributes to fragility of the system. In the case of semi-formal microfinance schemes operated by mass organisations (mainly the Vietnam Women's Union) uncertainty about policy and legislation, lack of clarity about accountability and institutional responsibilities are identified as causes of potential unsustainability. Underlying these factors, both Bui and Smith argue that interest rate policy is a key to the problems of the rural credit system. Very low interest-rate ceilings create excess demand for lending and force banks to ration credit, operating only in low-risk areas and reducing services in remote regions and high-risk cases. Thus regional inequality in the availability of formal financial services is reinforced. Moreover, rural households are less willing to deposit savings in the banks, while rates available in the informal sector are much higher.

In Chapter 5 Tran Ngoc Angie tackles the problem of sustainable and equitable development from a different angle. Focusing on the Vietnamese textile and garment industries (VTGI), which has been the most rapidly expanding area of manufacturing over the last decade, she examines the prospects for mitigating the more negative impacts of global influences. These negative impacts have come about principally through the growth of subcontracting arrangements with global networks that have tended to restrict Vietnamese producers and workers to low-skilled, low value-added elements of the production and distribution processes. Her chapter argues that if Vietnam is to avoid the problem of 'enclave' development in which garment production is relatively isolated from the rest of the economy through low accumulation and investment and heavy reliance on imported inputs, it must be able to develop more backward and forward linkages to both domestic and global economies. In particular, by developing the textile, accessories and machinery branches and establishing direct marketing to major foreign corporate buyers, the sector can both generate more employment within Vietnam and increase the proportion of value added accruing to the domestic economy, thereby starting a virtuous circle of growth with more equitable distribution of income. How to achieve these results in the face of intense competitive pressure within the global networks is one of the key issues confronted in Tran's chapter.

In Chapter 7 William Smith focuses on one of the least-developed areas of the country, the northern mountain region with its high concentration of ethnic minority populations. By examining consumption, saving and expenditure patterns of households he throws light on the extent to which household enterprises are integrated into the national market economy and both the opportunities and the constraints facing them in trying to develop beyond small-scale production. He shows that despite government efforts to increase the availability of both bank and semi-formal credit, there are advantages to households in continuing to rely on self-finance and informal credit. Moreover, where the multitude of microfinance schemes have entered the market, they have tended to operate in a way which raises doubts about the long-term viability of the banking system. In this case, paradoxically, state attempts to direct credit to particular types of investment have hampered rather than helped the sustainable development of village economies. His chapter again points to the lack of state capacity to anticipate and transcend unintended effects arising from policies aimed at sustainable development.

Finally, a question which cannot be ignored in any treatment of the issue of sustainability is that of environmental protection which is dealt with in Chapter 8 by Bach Tan Sinh. This chapter is the one that most explicitly addresses the question of differing rationalities and objectives of sustainability. Using a framework originally developed by Scandinavian authors he outlines the different discursive, technological and organisational approaches of the main actors in the environmental debate in Vietnam within three different domains – government, business and civil society. This is necessarily an abstract model and, as discussed above, the blurred public–private divide in Vietnam and the considerable overlap between these three domains means that such a tripartite framework does not simply suggest that government is public, business is private and civil society consists of private citizens whose interests and concerns are at odds with state interests. Through a case study of the coal mining sector, however, the framework enables Sinh to illustrate the tensions among the three overlapping domains and to discuss the institutional challenges Vietnam faces in its attempt to achieve economic growth while protecting the environment. Further, by bringing the cultural dimension to his analysis he enables us to understand the dynamics of environmental and development politics that underpin the concept of sustainable development in a transition economy such as Vietnam.

ORGANISATION OF THE BOOK

In the first part, the Chapters look at the question of sustainability from a macro perspective. Dang Phong's historical essay opens by examining the reasons for the persistence of the traditional socialist model and the ways in which this was gradually transformed during the late 1970s and into the ensuing decades. Melanie Beresford's chapter examines some of the factors underlying the very high rates of growth experienced during the 1990s and how the Asian economic crisis late in the decade calls into question the twin problems of sustaining such growth rates into the future and achieving a more equitable distribution.

The second part of the book contains five sectoral studies. These include the chapter by Regina Abrami and Nolwen Henaff on internal migration and the development of labour markets; Tran Ngoc Angie on the textile and garment industries; Bui Van Hung on rural diversification and industrialisation; William Smith on small enterprise finance in the northern mountain region; and Bach Tan Sinh on environmental sustainability in the coal mining area of Quang Ninh province.

NOTES

1 Many environmental economists appear to subscribe to these aspects of classical political economy that see the limits to growth in terms of demography and ecology. Daly (1996), for example, refers to John Stuart Mill's concept of the 'stationary state' that could be achieved without growth in population or physical capital stock but with continued human improvement, or 'improving the art of living'. Like Ricardo and Malthus, however, environmental economists have often been criticised for underestimating the capacity of capitalism for technological adaptation. Moreover, while the 'stationary state' might conceivably be appropriate for advanced industrial economies, here we are concerned with the question of sustainable growth in developing and transitional economies such as Vietnam.

2 The growth pole strategy targets three already wealthy, high-growth regions: around Ho Chi Minh City, the Hanoi-Hai Phong-Quang Ninh region and the area around Da Nang city for priority in state investment policies.

3 The SOE sector still accounted for about half of GDP at the end of the 1990s.

4 Defined as activities that seek rents, or above-normal profits, from favourable treatment by state officials and/or monopoly access to and control over state-supplied resources (land, goods, credit).

5 According to the Vietnam Living Standards Surveys carried out in 1993 and 1998, the incidence of severe poverty fell from about 50 per cent to 20 per cent in just five years (VLSS 1994 and 1999).

REFERENCES

Amsden, Alice (1989) *Asia's Next Giant: South Korea and Late Industrialization*. New York and Oxford: Oxford University Press.

Beneria, Lourdes and Martha Roldan (1987) *The Crossroads of Class and Gender: Industrial Homework, Subcontracting, and Household Dynamics in Mexico City*. Chicago and London: University of Chicago Press.

Beneria, Lourdes, Maria Floro, Caren Grown and Martha MacDonald (2000) 'Introduction: Globalization and Gender' *Feminist Economics*, vol. 6, no. 3, 7–18 November.

Beresford, Melanie and Fforde, Adam (1997) 'A methodology for analysing the process of economic reform in Vietnam: the case of domestic trade' *Journal of Communist Studies and Transition Politics*, vol. 13, no. 4, December.

Beresford, Melanie (2003) 'Economic Transition, Uneven Development and the Impact of Reform on Regional Inequality'. In Hy Van Luong (ed.), *Postwar Vietnam: the Dynamics of Transformation*. Lanham MD and Singapore: Rowman & Littlefield and ISEAS.

Daly, Herman E. (1996) *Beyond Growth: The Economics of Sustainable Development*. Boston: Beacon Press

Dang Hoang Giang (1997) 'In search of an appropriate long-term development strategy: a system dynamics approach'. Paper presented to Euroviet III Conference, Amsterdam, 2–4 July.

Desai, Jaikishan (2000) 'Vietnam through the lens of gender: five years later. Results from the second Vietnam Living Standards Survey'. FAO, United Nations Regional Office for Asia and the Pacific, November.

Hajer, Maarten and Frank Fischer (eds) (1999) *Living with Nature: Environmental Politics as Cultural Discourse*. Oxford: Oxford University Press.

Hamilton, Gary G. (ed.) (1996) *Asian Business Networks*. Berlin and New York: Walter de Gruyter.

Harcourt, Wendy (1994) *Feminist Perspectives on Sustainable Development*. London and Atlantic Highlands, NJ: Zed Books in association with The Society for International Development in Rome.

Hausler, Sabine (1994) *Women, the Environment and Sustainable Development: Towards a Theoretical Synthesis*. London and Atlantic Highlands, NJ: Zed Books in association with INSTRAW.

Herno, Rolf (1997) '"Network Capitalism" in Vietnam: some implications for understanding the "Transition"'. Paper presented to Euroviet III Conference, Amsterdam, 2–4 July.

Hirst, Paul and Grahame Thompson (1996) *Globalization in Question: the International Economy and the Possibilities of Governance*. Cambridge: Polity Press.

Ngo Thi Men (1997) 'Transition to a Market Economy: agricultural and food marketing in Vietnam: problems and challenges for reform'. Paper presented to Euroviet III Conference, Amsterdam, 2–4 July.

Norgaard, R. (1985) 'Environmental Economics: an evolutionary critique and a plea for pluralism'. *Journal of Environmental Economics and Management.*

Orrù, Marco, Nicole Woolsey Biggart and Gary G. Hamilton (eds) (1997) *The Economic Organization of East Asian Capitalism.* London: Sage.

Pearce, David (1985) 'Sustainable Futures: Economics and the Environment'. Inaugural lecture, Department of Economics, University College, London, 5 December.

Redclift, Michael (1987) *Sustainable Development: Exploring the Contradictions.* London and New York: Routledge.

Sen, Gita (1994) 'Women, Poverty and Population: Issues for the Concerned Environmentalist'. In Wendy Harcourt (ed.), *Feminist Perspectives on Sustainable Development.* London and Atlantic Highlands, NJ: Zed Books.

Shiva, Vandana (1991) *Ecology and the Politics of Survival: Conflicts over Natural Resources in India.* New Delhi: Sage/United Nations University Press.

Tran Ngoc Angie (2001) 'Global Subcontracting and Women Workers in Comparative Perspective'. In Claes Brundenius and John Weeks (eds), *Globalisation and Third World Socialism: Cuba and Vietnam.* Basingstoke: Palgrave .

—— (2002) 'Gender Expectations of Vietnamese Garment Workers: Viet Nam's Re-Integration into the World Economy'. In Jayne Werner and Daniele Belanger (eds), *Gender, Household, State: Doi Moi in Viet Nam.* Ithaca: Southeast Asia Program Publication Series, Cornell University Press.

VLSS (1994) *Vietnam Living Standards Survey*, Hanoi: State Planning Committee and General Statistical Office.

—— (1999) *Vietnam Living Standards Survey.* Hanoi: General Statistical Office.

Wade, Robert (1990) *Governing the Market: Economic Theory and the Role of Government in East Asian Industrialisation.* Princeton: Princeton University Press.

Waring, Marilyn (1999) *Counting for Nothing: What Men Value and What Women Are Worth.* Toronto and Buffalo, NY: University of Toronto Press.

World Bank (1993) *The East Asian Miracle.* Washington DC: Oxford University Press

CHAPTER 2

Stages on the Road to Renovation of the Vietnamese Economy: an Historical Perspective

Dang Phong

INTRODUCTION

In those countries that pursued a 'traditional' or 'Soviet-type' model of socialism, the path towards economic transformation has some common characteristics. First, while the degree of domination of the socialist *economic* model varied from country to country, it held at the very least a key position in all of them over a lengthy period. Second, in the *political* and *ideological* spheres, the model held an even more dominant position. Not always holding complete sway, it remained nevertheless a powerful constraint on the pace of reform, slowing it or, in the early stages especially, negating and annulling initiatives to overcome crises in the economy. While the need for reform was recognised quite early on by both economists and officials charged with implementing the model, advocacy of change was hampered by the identification, in party ideology, of this model with socialism itself. Reformers, such as E.G. Liberman in the Soviet Union, Oskar Lange and Michal Kalecki in Poland, Janos Kornai in Hungary, Ota Sik in Czechoslovakia, Sun Yefeng in China, Kim Ngoc and others in Vietnam, were often ignored, sometimes hounded and in several cases paid a heavy price.

For the above reasons, each country also suffered a prolonged stagnation or paralysis during which no solutions could be found. Faced with the defects of the model – low efficiency, high levels of waste, slow growth and even recession – people were bound to diagnose an illness, yet they dared not offer a precise diagnosis, let alone call it an 'illness'. Instead, all these defects were attributed to false causes: natural disaster, international reactionaries, poor awareness of the lower echelons, a low level of ideals among the masses and, occasionally, to the individualism of some high- and middle-ranking cadres.

Inevitably, the illness reached a crisis point where change became imperative. For each country there were different ways of resolving the crisis: in some the collapse of the old model was sudden and chaotic, in others reforms came about one step at a time, often without people realising at first the full implications of the changes. In these gradualist reforms, the initial aim was simply to patch up the old model, to overcome some of its shortcomings. However, each 'overcoming' was actually a step towards more fundamental reform and, after a series of such steps, a genuine transformation could be retrospectively recognised as something already achieved. Therefore the process could be continued.

As will become clear as we proceed, however, the process of reform was not simple and linear. There was some hesitancy to abandon the traditional socialist model, that sometimes resulted in steps backward, particularly before 1989. Commercialisation of the economy was seen by some to lead to chaotic conditions, such that legislative reforms appeared as a sort of 'tango dance' or, as the Chinese have characterised it, 'feeling the stones under one's feet when crossing the river'. For example, in 1982 Decree No. 01 from the Vietnamese Politburo regulated import and export activities, and the Resolution of the Third Central Committee Plenum called for restoration of order in goods circulation and distribution and price stabilisation. This readjustment was necessary, even if it was a step backward in order to better prepare for subsequent steps. More importantly, the reform process cannot be characterised simply as a 'top-down' one. There was a symbiotic relationship between citizens and leaders in which both played an important role.

UNDERSTANDING THE VITALITY OF THE TRADITIONAL MODEL IN VIETNAM

Beliefs and taboos

From the 1950s through the 1970s, Vietnamese leaders and intellectuals continued to put their faith in the pre-eminence of the traditional socialist model. Despite the many failures and difficulties, these were attributed to the implementation of the model rather than to the model itself. Reformists of that time never actually criticised the model but proposed different ways to implement it. Bui Cong Trung's 1963 proposal for international integration, the agricultural contract system of Kim Ngoc in 1966–68, Tran Dinh But's idea in 1972 of combining plan and market and Tran Phuong's project to reform trade in 1980 were all cases in point. Not one among them considered that Vietnam would one day become a market economy, with private property and private business, let alone domestic and international capitalism.

Why is this so? In the theoretical system of socialism some dogma were tacitly recognised as truths and it gradually became taboo to question them: public ownership of the means of production, collective labour process, a centrally planned economy, a system of fixed prices, central state monopoly of foreign trade, comprehensive leadership of the party organisation in production units, etc. Neither a worker nor a Marxist (politician, philosopher or economist) could dispute these principles. They were simply beyond discussion.

Moral authority

Although in the Soviet Union and Eastern Europe the same ideological taboos surrounded the socialist model, the legitimacy and prestige of the party appears to have been weaker. Breakaway tendencies appeared most strongly in Eastern Europe and, in some cases, played an important role in the breakdown of the whole system. In Vietnam, on the other hand, the revolution and victory in the war of national liberation gave the Communist Party and its leaders great moral authority among the people.

The power of this moral authority was manifested in two particular ways. First, any temporary alleviation of the crisis tended to discourage further discussion of reform. In fact even in the midst of crisis, and after the reform process had been set in motion, this phenomenon often played a role, as discussed further below. Second, however, the fundamental legitimacy of party rule meant that differences of opinion were treated less harshly than in other socialist countries. As Chan *et al.* correctly note: 'Ho Chi Minh and the other Vietnamese leaders did not denounce and persecute the intellectuals in the same relentless way as Mao Zedong' (Chan *et al.* 1999: 9) Within limits, therefore, discussion remained possible.

Aid

Foreign aid, mainly from the socialist countries, had the effect of an elixir of life. It was the material condition necessary to nourish a model that could not nourish itself, a kind of 'ginseng syndrome'. If not for the annual aid of around half a million tonnes of food and nearly the same amount of fertiliser, collective agriculture with its low efficiency could not have continued as it did for more than 20 years. If not for the annual aid of approximately two million tonnes of fuel, 200,000 tonnes of cotton, one million tonnes of iron, steel and essential chemicals, industry could not have stayed afloat, let alone act as the backbone of the economy generally. If not for the aid in textiles,

Figure 2.1: Structure of imports according to method of accounting 1960–80

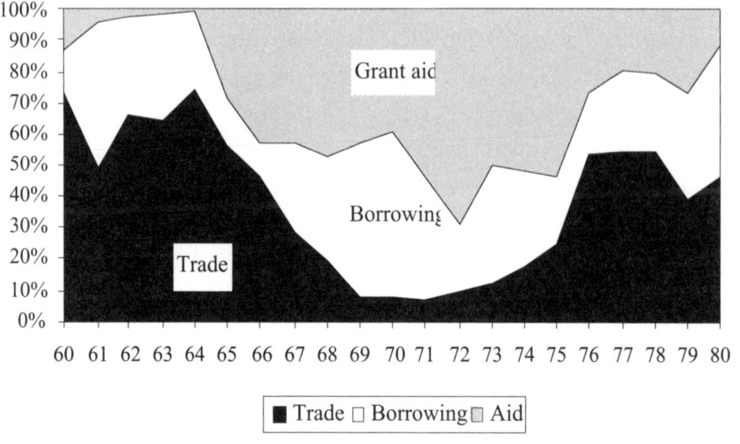

Source: GSO, *Statistical Yearbook 1981*: 274.

Figure 2.2: Aid as a share of total budget revenue (%)

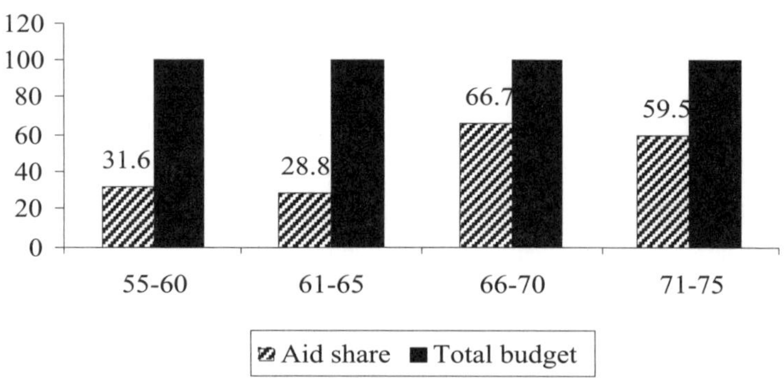

Source: GSO, *Statistical Yearbook 1976*: 76.

milk, sugar, meat, butter and plastic and aluminium goods, etc., the state trade branch would most likely have had few goods to sell to the people, despite the rationing system. Table 2.1 and Figures 2.1, 2.2 and 2.3 illustrate this 'ginseng' role of aid throughout the period in which the old model existed, while at the same time demonstrating the inevitability of a crisis when the aid dried up. Table 2.1, for example shows the declining proportion of imports

Table 2.1: Structure of import values (% of total)

Year	Trade	Loans	Aid	Year	Trade	Loans	Aid
North							
1960	72.7	14.1	13.2	1971	7.0	39.6	53.4
1961	49.4	45.7	4.9	1972	9.6	21.8	68.6
1962	65.8	31.2	3.0	1973	12.0	38.3	49.7
1963	64.0	34.6	1.4	1974	17.3	31.2	51.5
1964	74.2	25.1	0.7	1975	24.9	21.7	53.4
1965	55.7	16.2	28.1	*Whole country*			
1966	46.3	11.0	42.7	1976	53.3	20.1	26.6
1967	28.0	28.0	43.4	1977	54.1	26.3	19.6
1968	19.7	33.0	47.3	1978	54.2	25.8	20.0
1969	7.8	49.2	43.0	1979	39.6	33.7	26.7
1970	7.6	53.3	39.1	1980	47.3	44.2	11.5

Source: GSO, *Statistical Yearbook 1981*: 274.

financed from trade during the years after the introduction of the First Five-Year Plan in 1961. The decline is particularly marked after the US bombing of the north commenced in late 1965, but it also shows the inability of export income to recover sufficiently even after peace in the north was re-established in 1973–75.[1] There is a corresponding rise in foreign aid, in the form of loans at first, then grant aid during the worst years of the war and a further increase in the share of loans after the war. The data are depicted graphically in Figure 2.1. Figure 2.2 illustrates the dependence of the state budget revenues on foreign aid while Figure 2.3 shows the extent to which aid sustained domestic consumption levels. As in the case of the balance of trade, these figures demonstrate the poor recovery capacity of the socialist model even as peace was being re-established in the north.

This situation in Vietnam was very different from that in China, where Soviet aid had been cut completely in 1960. If any link existed between that aid cut and the reform process in China, then it was very indirect: it awakened the Chinese to the need to open the door to the market economies earlier and was just one among many reasons for reform in that country.

Figure 2.3: Aid as a share of the social consumption fund (%)

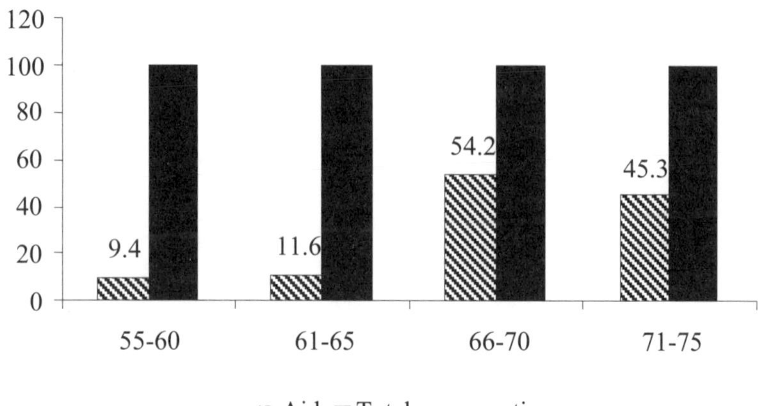

Source: GSO, *Statistical Yearbook 1976*: 74–76.

The enemy

Some factors at the opposite end of the spectrum to aid had similar significance for the vitality of the socialist model: namely, the enemies of socialism in Vietnam. Throughout two decades of building socialism, the north was faced with both the challenge and the threat to socialism of a southern region occupied by the United States. After the liberation of the south, the hostile attitude of the USA, the economic embargo, the criticism and denunciation, the activities of anti-communists, etc. unconsciously contributed to strengthening the will of the leadership to defend socialism and, by implication, the traditional economic model.

This defensiveness of the Vietnamese echoes that of several East European leaderships but differs from the case of China which, as noted above, had been able to negotiate trade and investment relations with the capitalist world after Nixon's 1972 visit without fundamentally altering the model. Vietnam would have to wait for this privilege for another two decades. Thus while China began its reforms in the context of improved relations with the West, the Vietnamese reforms were carried out under conditions of a continuing trade embargo.

THE 'WEANING' CRISIS

In Vietnam crisis began to emerge clearly during the Second Five-Year Plan (1976–80),[2] a plan which bore the marks of voluntarism and post-victory euphoria. However, it also had its material basis: aid. Aid from the more developed socialist countries was the 'mother's milk' of the infant socialist model in Vietnam.

Aid payments from the socialist countries were usually in the region of US$ 1 billion a year. In fact their true value was much higher due to the system of accounting in 'friendship prices', which were only about a third of the international prices applied within the rest of Comecon (Council for Mutual Economic Assistance). For 30 years, for example, Vietnam 'bought' from the Soviet Union about two million tonnes of fuel at the preferential price of 41.5 roubles/tonne, while the international price applied by Comecon was 151.7 roubles (one transferable rouble was valued at approximately one US$). After 1976, however, and especially after 1978, Vietnam faced some difficulties: the US embargo was in place and socialist country aid to Third World countries was reduced (either in terms of volume or value) (Dang Phong 1994: 17).

Following Vietnam's full accession to Comecon (28 June 1978), trade between Vietnam and the Comecon countries was conducted according to the Comecon system of prices: that is, according to the so-called system of staggered prices. This was a system in which the prices for each year were specified as the average world market price in the preceding five years. Thus the staggered price was a rolling average of the world market price. It was around 2.5–3 times higher than the preferential prices that the Soviet Union and other Comecon countries normally applied to poor and less developed countries like Vietnam and Angola if they were not full members. By joining Comecon, Vietnam therefore faced a 2.5–3 fold increase in import prices. In other words, the amount of aid that the Comecon countries supplied to Vietnam, while not reduced in value, was nevertheless severely reduced in terms of the quantity of goods. Previously, for example, Vietnam could import over two tonnes of oil with 100 roubles of Soviet aid, but after the application of staggered prices, this figure was reduced to half a tonne. In reality, therefore, there was a cut in aid, one that had powerful ramifications for the Vietnamese economy. Because the aid remained high in value terms, not all researchers paid attention to these development and many did not understand that in 1978–80 Vietnam was once again in a situation of severe shortage. We can comprehend this point via Table 2.2 and Figure 2.4. From Table 2.2, we see that the nominal value of imports not only did not reduce, but increased from about US$1 billion to about 1.3 billion. Vietnam had already lost its aid from China and other non-Comecon countries, but to

Figure 2.4: Imports in 1980 compared with 1976 (by volume)

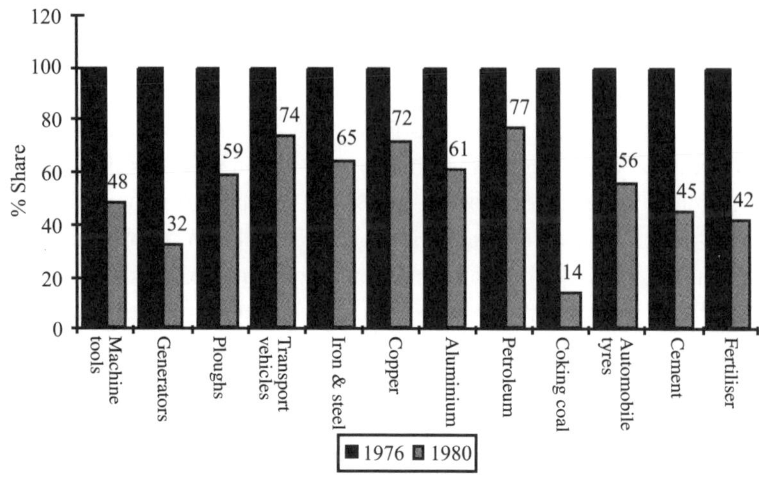

Source: GSO, *Statistical Yearbook 1986*: 267.

Table 2.2: Value of imports by category 1976–80 (m. roubles/dollars)

Year	Total value	Complete plant	Machinery	Tools and parts	Raw materials	Consumer goods
1976	1,024.1	147.5	94.0	61.8	519.2	171.6
1977	1,218.4	198.2	99.2	66.9	568.1	286.0
1978	1,303.2	291.1	130.7	69.4	500.0	312.0
1979	1,526.1	384.5	200.3	60.3	466.4	414.5
1980	1,314.2	360.4	187.4	78.5	370.6	315.4

Note: During the relevant time period, trade data were published in roubles and dollars. The two currencies were simply added together as if they were equivalent. In fact the official value of the transferable rouble was about 97 US cents.

Source: GSO, *Statistical Yearbook 1986*: 266.

compensate, the Comecon countries increased their level of aid.[3] Looking at Figure 2.4, however, we see that despite the higher aid value, the essential goods Vietnam was able to import for its production and consumption stood at around a half or two-thirds of their former volume. For a capital stock that

Figure 2.5: Paddy availability per capita 1975–81 (kg per capita)

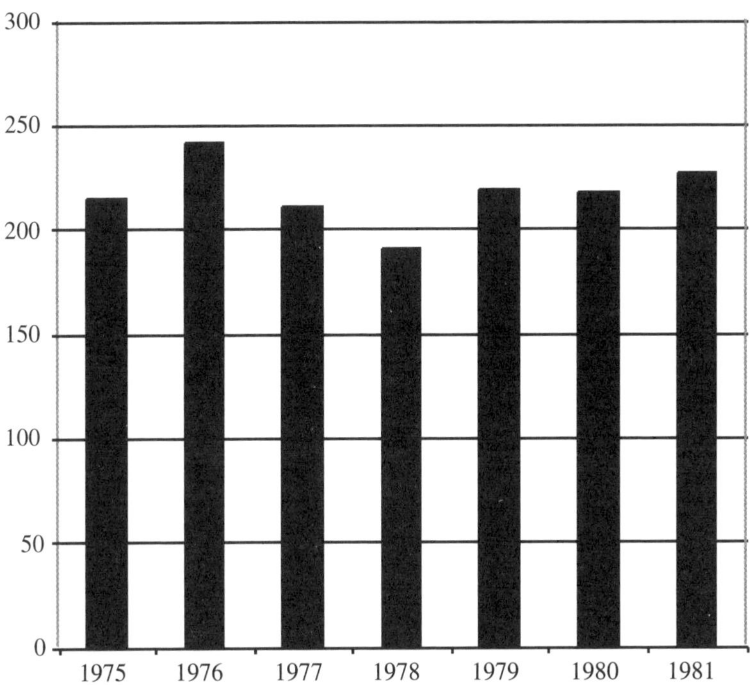

Source: GSO, *Statistical Yearbook 1981*: 52, 393.

had lived for decades on imported inputs, such a cut was a mortal blow. All the above factors converged in 1979–80 in a type of 'weaning'. By 1978–79, almost all industrial, construction and transport enterprises were operating at only 50 per cent of planned capacity and, in some cases, 30 per cent due to the shortages of materials and spare parts (State Planning Committee 1979).

In agriculture, there was a shortage of fertiliser, pesticides and fuel to run the irrigation pumps. When the state failed to supply enough of these items to the co-operatives, it could no longer pressure the farmers to sell agricultural products according to plan stipulations. Nor could the state purchase sufficient agricultural products at low official prices when the farmers had to buy most of their essential goods for production and consumption in the free market at high prices. For that reason per capita agricultural output fell and the volume of state procurement also fell sharply, as shown in Figure 2.5 and Table 2.3

Table 2.3: Cereal procurement 1976–80 (m. tonnes)

	1976	**1977**	**1978**	**1979**	**1980**
Whole country	2.06	1.69	1.60	1.42	1.98
South	1.09	0.99	0.71	0.64	1.24

Source: GSO, *Statistical Yearbook 1981*: 237–238.

(Institute of Economics 1990: 280–281). Every type of good was scarce in the market. This was a period in which coal was often used to run automobiles and tyres had to be retreaded. The state shops had insufficient amounts of everything to sell in relation to the ration coupons for cadres and soldiers. In many months coupons for meat could only buy tofu or Mongolian mutton fat.[4] The state not only lacked goods but also suffered a serious lack of funds. Since it could not pay the farmers, it also could not supply cadres and others with food. It lacked the funds to pay the salaries of bureaucrats and many offices were 'in debt' to their cadres for up to two to three months' salary. Many industrial enterprises also replaced cash salaries by payment in goods produced by the enterprise: the confectionery enterprise paid in sweets, the soap enterprise in soap, coal mines in coal, etc. Workers had to sell these goods in the free market to get money on which to live (Dang Phong 1985).

Due to the shortage of goods and money, inflation began to become an untameable horse charging around the economy (Table 2.4). Prices rose every day, something that had not happened before because of the protection provided by aid. The rapidly rising prices, falling salaries and scarce goods, caused life for all strata of society to become very difficult and social misfortune grew. People's faith in the system dwindled and the taboos began to be violated. Penalties for violations became lighter and were gradually abandoned, although the extent to which this happened varied from place to place.

FENCE BREAKING (PHÁ RÀO)

What was fence breaking and who did it? First of all, let me list in chronological order some of the most representative fence-breaking activities in the spheres of ideology and practice:

- Nguyen Duy Ky *Price Breaking,* 1961. Nguyen Duy Ky, perhaps the leading economist in Vietnam, argued that state procurement prices for agricultural products were too low. He expounded his ideas at a workshop

Table 2.4: Price index 1976–86

Year	General	Organised market	Free market	Agricultural products
1976	100.0	100.0	100.0	100.0
1977	118.6	101.1	138.0	—
1980	189.0	119.7	360.0	253.3
1984	1,400.6	1,297.8	1,540.5	1,825.9
1985	2,890.2	2,737.1	3,367.0	3,365.0
1986	1,6170.0	15,260.0	19,030.0	19,204.0

Note: The general price index is a weighted average of the organised (official) and free market price indices.
Source: GSO, *Statistical Yearbook* 1987: 255, 239.

in Hanoi on 29 November 1961 and then published them in the journal Economic Research (Nguyen Duy Ky 1962). Subsequently some articles that were severely critical of his ideas appeared in the theoretical organ of the Party, *Học Tập*.

- *Contracts in Kien An, 1962*. The contract system was the first form of practical fence breaking in agriculture and appeared in 1962 in the Kien Thuy district of Kien An province (in 1963 this province was incorporated into Haiphong), even before the oft-quoted Vinh Phuc contract system in 1966–68 (see below). It was a system of contracting to households, that is to farming families, and different from the two-way contracts applied in the co-operatives. This measure was taken secretly, but with the consent of the leaders of the district. When it came to the notice of the leadership of the province, the then secretary, Hoang Huu Nhan, not only failed to put a stop to it but organised a full on-the-spot inquiry, listening to the opinions of each farmer. He found that the programme was appropriate and, after discussion among the leaders of the provincial party, decided to allow the 'experiment' to continue. The provincial decree was issued on 19 February 1963.[5]
- *Bui Cong Trung's 'banana republic', 1963*. Bui Cong Trung was a member of the party Central Committee. In 1963, as head of the Institute of

Economics, he proposed an international division of labour ('international' in this context referred to the socialist countries) whereby Vietnam would specialise in the production of tropical agricultural products and popular consumption goods, exchanging them for imported industrial products. In this way it could achieve socialist industrialisation. The idea was most fully set out in his article in Economic Research (no. 13, 1963). At the time he was criticised for 'wanting Vietnam to become the banana republic of the socialist camp'.[6]

The novelty of Trung's open economy idea must be compared with the closed economy ideology articulated in the Third Congress Resolution of 1960. It was not until the Sixth Party Congress in 1986 that his idea saw the light of day. However, Trung's proposal contained drawbacks in that it involved specialising in low value-added products that would limit the ability to import industrial plant and equipment. From the point of view of the Party leadership, it would thus provide an unacceptably low rate of industrialisation.

- *Contracts in Vinh Phuc, 1966–68.* This programme was applied across the whole province of Vinh Phuc from September 1966 (Vinh Phuc 1966). Its real author was Kim Ngoc, the provincial Party secretary. The programme was only stopped by an order from the Party secretariat at the end of 1968 (Secretariat 1968). Contrary to widespread belief, Kim Ngoc was not disciplined but was able to continue as secretary of the province, even when the province was doubled in size and became Vinh Phu (including both Vinh Phuc and Phu Tho), on condition that he reviewed and corrected his mistakes. In fact he remained in that position for another decade, until he died in 1977.[7]
- *Tran Dinh But and the case of 'the market mechanism', 1972.* In 1972 three professors at the National Economics University in Hanoi wrote a book titled *Combining Plan with Market.* A campaign was mounted to send the three authors to prison but luckily General Secretary Le Duan – after hearing Tran Dinh But, the principal author, explain in detail their theory – showed that he agreed with many of their points. The narrow escape of these three was at least a sign that a period of change was beginning (Tran Dinh But 1996).
- *Breaking the rice price fence in An Giang, 1978.* As Figure 2.5 and Table 2.3 show, 1978 was a very difficult year for rice. The obligatory state procurement price for paddy in that year was 0.32–0.35 dong/kg for the

Mekong River delta, while the free market price was about 2.5–3 dong/kg. Naturally farmers were not prepared to sell to the state at the obligatory price. For the southern cities, most of all Ho Chi Minh City, 1978 and 1979 were also years of tragedy: the state food shops did not have enough rice and people did not have enough to eat. This was something that had never happened in the south, which for so long has been known as the granary of the whole country. The state had to take sorghum from the Soviet aid supplies normally fed to animals and sell it to cadres and others to eat instead of rice. The Ho Chi Minh City Cereal Company, directed by Nguyen Thi Thi, (aka Ba Thi) found it too painful to think that the country had liberated itself from the foreign enemy yet could not liberate itself from hunger. Going down to the countryside she found plenty of rice, but the farmers would not sell it at a price equivalent to one-fifth of production costs. Faced with an absurd situation, Ba Thi put the problem to Vo Van Kiet, then a member of the Politbureau and chairman of the Ho Chi Minh City People's Committee. She could, she said, either offer the official price of the State Price Committee and not buy anything at all, or buy at free market prices, thereby violating the central regulations but saving the people of the city from having to eat sorghum. Kiet replied, 'Go and buy rice for the people. If you end up in jail then I'll bring you rice' (Vu Quoc Tuan 1995). Ba Thi returned to An Giang to discuss with the provincial leadership the matter of purchasing rice at 2.5 dong/kg, the price at which farmers were willing to sell. Her breakthrough meant that no one any longer sold rice for 0.32–0.35 dong/kg. There was a chain reaction from An Giang all over the country, implying that the price of 2.5 dong/kg became the price which the farmers applied to the state. Looking back at Table 2.3, we see that, by 1980, as the An Giang model spread to the rest of the country, the volume of rice purchased began to increase.

By contrast with the theoretical 'uprising' of Nguyen Duy Ky 17 years earlier, this time the law of value was victorious. In 1979, the State Price Committee was compelled to raise the official price to 0.5–0.52 dong/kg, though this, of course, still left the farmers dissatisfied. This most conservative of departments was again forced to raise the price in 1981, this time to 2.5–2.75 dong/kg, but only after its leadership had been changed.[8]

- *The Sixth Central Committee Plenum, August 1979.* The official agenda for this regular meeting of the Central Committee concerned a discussion of local industry. However, as soon as the conference opened, with

Le Duan's speech on local industry, the provincial delegates pointed out a series of difficulties and bottlenecks in the whole economy, not just in local industry. During the meeting, telegrams came in from provinces about the procurement prices in An Giang setting a precedent for other provinces to 'break fences', about the scarcity of materials preventing local industry from producing, and so forth. In the end there was a 'fence breaking' of the agenda and the conference switched to discussing the economic system. Finally, some very important conclusions were reached: for the first time in the legislative history of Vietnam there appeared two phrases which were to become the bywords of the reform process – *bung ra* (burst open) and *cởi trói cho sản xuất và kinh doanh* (unbind, or free up, production and business). Of course the documents never said that anything had been tied up, so that the party must now 'unbind' them. But everyone nevertheless understood that some taboos had lost their power. Faced with the difficulties caused by the 'weaning crisis', every-one could be more economically free. If we compare Le Duan's opening and closing speeches, then we can see that after the 20-day conference, the very people who had erected the fence had secretly allowed the destruction of part of this fence (Le Duan 1979 a and 1979b; To Huu 1979). As we shall see below, the tiny break in the fence contained in this conference resolution started a wave of fence breaking in almost every area of the economy throughout the country.

- *Fence breaking in industry and transport, 1979.* In the period leading up to the Sixth Plenum nearly all industrial and transport units were in difficulties caused by the 'weaning crisis'. To save themselves, they had been furtively breaking fences by linking up with each other and, above all, with the free market. Once the party resolution, with its policies of *bung ra* and *cởi trói*, had been released, these furtive goings on built up into a movement. Fence breaking took on many shapes and forms. However, we need mention here only the three earliest and most famous cases: (1) the Vung Tau-Con Dao Fishing Enterprise; (2) the Thanh Cong Textile Enterprise in Ho Chi Minh City; and (3) the Eastern Region Bus Company also in Ho Chi Minh City (Dang Phong and Pham Thanh Giang 1996; Dang Phong 1988). All three had begun to trade at least part of their inputs and outputs in market prices during 1978.
- *Agricultural contracts in Do Son district, 1980.* Given the 'bung ra' policy of the Sixth Plenum, the city of Haiphong decided to regularise the con-

tracting model that had been applied in one of its districts since 1962. Doan Duy Thanh, then chairman and later party secretary of the province, was the principal author of this innovation. By contrast with Kim Ngoc's earlier experience in Vinh Phuc, his fence breaking was a success, partly because the situation was different and partly because his way of working was subtler. He organised a pilot contract system in Do Son, a seaside district where Politburo members were in the habit of spending their weekends, because he wanted them to see with their own eyes the efficacy of the system. Before putting it into effect, however, he also took care to explain his plan to the general secretary, who gave his agreement. He then went on to persuade Truong Chinh who, at their fifth meeting, not only agreed but gave enthusiastic support and encouragement.[9]

- Not long afterwards, in October of that year, Thanh was appointed to a subcommittee charged with drawing up a plan to implement contracts nation-wide. The result was Order No.100 of the Party Secretariat in January 1981, permitting the application of the contract system across the country (Do Son 1980; Doan Duy Thanh interview, 14 May 1996; Huu Tho 1996: 159–169; Tran Duc 1994: 100–110; Dang Phong 1995).
- *The one-price system in Long An, 1980.* According to some veteran cadres of Long An, it was actually from 1977 that the leaders of the province, finding the existing two-price system absurd and tiresome, had sought permission from the centre to buy and sell at market prices. However, they chose the wrong person and the wrong time to put forward their proposal. Nguyen Van Chinh (alias Chin Can) secretary of the province met Pham Hung, who was then the member of the Politburo responsible for the south and deputy prime minister responsible for trade and finance. He was not in accord with Chinh's suggestion and the province had to drop the idea. After the Sixth Plenum, however, Long An cadres saw that they had the chance to break fences. Drawing on their experience of 1977, they chose their lobby itinerary very carefully, starting with Le Duc Tho, number two in the hierarchy, a Politburo member and chairman of the Party Organisation Committee. Having secured Tho's agreement, the province leaders then sought out Nguyen Van Linh, the Politburo member who had replaced Hung in charge of the southern provinces. Once he knew that Le Duc Tho had agreed, Linh also gave his consent and, with two very important 'tickets' in their pocket, the Long An leaders approached Le Duan who also gave his permission to 'try it out'. Nearly all goods

> could be sold at market prices: that is, in practice the system of state prices was abolished. The results were very good. Other provinces sought permission to visit Long An to study their experiences, thus proving that the market price mechanism had become the wish and imperative of the whole country. Even the unhappy conservatives had to keep silent and 'wait and see' in the face of such a groundswell. Ultimately, every province and branch in the country one by one turned to the one-price system following the lead of Long An in using market prices (Dang Phong 1987; Tu Giao 1996).

Surveying this series of fence breakings we can see some characteristic features of the transformation process in Vietnam. First, fence breaking was not simply a conflict between those who erected the fences and those destroying them. Perhaps initially it was like that, but later on it was often those who had built the fences who began to clear them away. Moreover, once the need for reform was sensed by middle-level leaders like Doan Duy Thanh and Nguyen Van Chinh, or directors of key enterprises like Ba Thi, they could use their connections with higher-level leaders who likewise had become open to such ideas, to push reforms through.

Second, many non-Vietnamese researchers think that fence breaking was done by the people, while raising the fences and protecting them was done by the state, meaning that the people were more dynamic and progressive and the state sluggish and conservative. Explanations like this are more like the script of a play than the real history of Vietnam. Bui Cong Trung, Kim Ngoc, Doan Duy Thanh, Chin Can and Ba Thi were all members of the Vietnamese state apparatus. And what of the top leaders of the party and state like Le Duan, Truong Chinh, Le Duc Tho, Nguyen Van Linh and Vo Van Kiet? Were they the representatives of the fence raisers and against the fence breakers? In my opinion, fence breaking was a pressing need of the whole society, that ripened gradually in perception, in needs and in the capacity of the economy, arriving earlier in some places, and later in others.[10]

Third, I mentioned above the problem of moral authority. Here I would like to add that this authority had the power to contribute to the rapid awakening and to creating the conditions for fence breaking to take place. In Vietnam there was in fact a 'super-taboo' which was the interest and aspiration of the people. When it became apparent that a change was necessary to rescue the economy and livelihoods of the people from crisis, then sooner or later all the Vietnamese politicians changed too. In particular, those who failed to change in time were removed,[11] and this certainly did not happen to the fence breakers. We should take note of the fact that in Vietnam the conditions do not exist for those in power to ignore the people for too long. Therefore, we should not put too much emphasis on the contradictions in fence breaking, because in those contradictions there was also accord.

REFORM

Fence breaking and reform are not two mutually exclusive things. Each incident of fence breaking was also a small reform, not yet written into law. Each reform measure was also a case of fence breaking, or legalisation of fence breaking. In most cases, but not always, the fence breaking came first and the reform later or, as the Vietnamese put it: 'the first knee is followed by the other'.

In relation to the reform measures, I mention here only the most important:

- *Resolution of the Sixth Central Committee Plenum, August 1979* which, as already noted above, permitted an explosion and freeing up of business. This document also approved for the first time the idea of 'three interests' (the interests of the state, the collective and the individual). It was the opening of economic reform in Vietnam and simultaneously a case of fence breaking in both thought and economic legislation.
- *Order of the President No. 20–LCT, 7 February 1980* on appointment and dismissal of certain members of government, from deputy prime minister to ministers. The effect of this order was to replace several leaders with some representatives of the reform tendency (Cong Bao 1980: 58).
- *Decision No. 40–CP of the Government Council, 7 February 1980*, permitting certain localities to engage directly in foreign trade within narrow limits. This was the first step in breaking down one of the most important taboos surrounding the central monopoly of foreign trade (Cong Bao 1980:73).
- *Circular No. 22 of the Party Secretariat, 21 October 1980*, permitting provinces to experiment with implementation of the contract system in agriculture, but only in paddy cultivation. It was the precursor to Order No. 100 three months later.
- *Order No. 100 of the Party Secretariat, 13 January 1981*, allowing the contract system to be applied in agriculture across the country.

- *Decree No. 25–CP of the Government Council, 21 January 1981* on the application of the '3 plan' system in industry. Plan A was that determined by the centre; Plan B was left up to enterprises and their local authorities to arrange among themselves; Plan C, the so-called subsidiary plan, comprised production for the market. Earlier, there had only been one plan decided by the central government for the whole country as laid down in the classical theory of the socialist economy. With Decree 25–CP that principle was violated: the state accepted the reality that had already been in existence for some years. Since the state no longer had the capacity to guarantee the material and financial conditions of production units, it had to allow them to establish relations with each other and with the free market.
- *The proposal for trade reform.* In January 1981 Tran Phuong, an economist and reformer who was close to Le Duan, was appointed minister for domestic trade and given the opportunity to implement his ideas for reform. After a month, he produced a plan for reform of the domestic trade branch, the main content of which was to abolish the subsidy system in buying and selling and rescue the state budget from the large deficits caused by overuse of the rationing system. His proposal was not fully accepted by the Politburo, which permitted only partial implementation: people not directly employed by the state were removed from the rationing list, the special subsidies directed towards high-ranking cadres (from vice-minister up) were reduced and prices for non-essential consumer goods were increased to the level of market prices in order to raise budget revenues. In addition the number of goods subject to rationing was reduced from 40 to nine (including rice, meat, sugar, soap, cloth and fuel).
- *Order No. 109 of the Politbureau* and, following that, *Decree No. 220–CP of the Government* on the reform of the entire pricing system. Prices were increased to the level of market prices, that is, by ten to 15 times their previous levels.
- *Resolution of the Eighth Central Committee Plenum, August 1985*, on the implementation of a general adjustment of prices and salaries. This was the second price reform, raising official prices once again to the level of market prices and abolishing nearly all rationing. Almost all goods could now be bought and sold at prices equivalent to market prices.[12]
- *Resolution of the Sixth Party Congress, December 1986.* This congress can be seen as the most important milestone in the Vietnamese renova-

tion, and is usually regarded as the official starting point of economic reform. Arising from this congress a number of key programmes were developed and written into law. First, the 'multi-sectoral' character of the Vietnamese economy was accepted, particularly two sectors which until then had been banned – the private and foreign capitalist sectors. Second, it was accepted that Vietnam would have a 'commodity economy' or, in other words, a market economy. Third, in contrast to the Third Congress Resolution of 1960 which had decreed the construction of a largely closed economy with 'relative integration', the Sixth Congress moved towards an open economy. Fourth, it was decided to concentrate on three 'spearhead' branches – production of export goods, consumer goods and foodstuffs. The last of these meant that the priority to heavy industry decreed by the Third Congress was abandoned. These plans created the space for a series of reform measures to take place in the following years.

- *Decree No. 217–HDBT of the Council of Ministers, 14 November 1987* gave state enterprises the right to manage their own production and business, that is, it unbound them from the constraints of the central plan. Whereas before enterprises had to meet nearly ten targets set by the State Planning Committee, they now were responsible only for contributing to the state budget. In other words, they were subject to taxation as in other market economies.

- *The Foreign Investment Law, 29 December 1987*, permitted foreign capitalists to do business in Vietnam. Hereby one of the biggest taboos was broken.

- *Decision No. 27–ND on private business* and *Decision No. 29–ND on family business* were published on 9 March 1988. These two documents accepted the legal right of private individuals to set up businesses in production, domestic and foreign trade, banking and services, etc. The two measures thus reinstated the rights of a sector that had been suppressed during the reforms of 1958 in the north and 1978 in the south.

- *Resolution No. 10 of the Politbureau, April 1988* on improving the contract system in agriculture went a step further than Order No. 100 of 1981. It allowed farmers to manage their entire production process, decide what to produce, what to invest and to sell all their output at market prices. Obligatory sales to the state were abolished, greatly reducing their real tax burden, the burden of having to sell to the state at below market prices.

From then on, the state could procure agricultural products only at market prices in competition with other buyers.

- After the Sixth Party Congress the government *continued to adjust prices of inputs sold to enterprises and co-operatives.* Drawing on the experience of the two earlier price reforms, this time, to soften the blow to enterprises accustomed to receiving subsidies, the state raised prices gradually and in many stages. Over a two year period beginning in 1987 there were six or seven price adjustments, until finally in 1989 the wholesale prices of enterprise inputs had reached world market prices and the official price system was abolished. By that time, having weathered a two-year process of adjustment, enterprises were able to operate at market prices. The leadership had learned from its earlier reform errors, the partial and largely unsuccessful price reforms of 1981 and 1985 and, as well, most of the economy was now operating at market prices, enabling a relatively smooth transition to take place.
- The most important adjustment of all during this period was that of the *exchange rate.* Under the old system there had been multiple exchange rates – for exports, for counter trade, for overseas visitors, etc. – all of which were well below the actual market rate. A large piece of earth-moving equipment, for example, with a market value of US$200,000–250,000, would be priced the same under the official exchange rate regime as a small motorcycle on the free market. The exchange rates therefore gave enterprises a very low rate of depreciation and contributed to high budget deficits.[13]
- From 1987 until 1989, however, rouble and dollar exchange rates were adjusted in the same way as other prices.
- In March 1989, the Central Committee passed a *Resolution against capital subsidies,* while on the 10th of the same month, Prime Minister Do Muoi issued *Decree no. 55–TT raising interest rates on credit* above the rate of inflation. A month later, on 10 April, the prime minister issued a further decree increasing the savings rate to 13 per cent per month. These bold measures produced a fierce reaction from enterprises that had been used to preferential interest rates on capital supplied from the state budget, usually at rates well below the inflation rate. They also produced two 'miraculous' effects: (1) they eliminated the state budget deficit by means of 'weaning' thousands of 'infants', namely the state enterprises; (2) the

increase in the savings rate above the rate of inflation attracted a large amount of money into the hands of the state banking system. The inflationary fever was brought to a halt (Table 2.5).

Table 2.5: Savings rate

	Interest rate (% per month)		**Price index** (previous month = 100)
	Long term	3 months	
March 1989	9	12	105.4
June 1989	7	9	97.1
July 1989	5	7	98.5
February 1990	4	6	103.8
March 1990	2.4	4	101.9
July 1991	2.1	3.5	102.5
June 1992	1.8	3.0	100.1
August 1992	1.2	3.0	100.3
October 1992	1.0	2.0	99.8
April 1993	0.8	1.7	99.8
October 1993	0.7	1.4	99.7

Source: Le Xuan Nghia, 1993: 10.

Once inflation was brought under control, the interest rate could be brought down again, but as soon as the savings rate fell too far, inflation re-emerged, as in 1991 (82.7 per cent) (World Bank 1994: 131). Such a stop–start policy was due to the fact that in socialist ideology raising the interest rate had been something of a taboo because it was tantamount to admitting the existence of inflation. Nevertheless, the government decrees of early 1989, in which Do Muoi played the decisive role, raised the savings rate and had an impact on several fronts:

- They reduced the volume of money in circulation, thereby reducing demand;
- As demand fell, the balance between supply and demand improved;
- As equilibrium between supply and demand improved, the rise in prices halted and then reversed for the first time in the history of Vietnamese socialism.
- A further desirable effect was that goods became plentiful on the market. During the inflation, while demand outstripped supply, enterprises and households alike kept hoards. Enterprises would try to increase their input norms in order to hoard any surplus to production requirements. Likewise, households battled to buy anything they could lay their hands on in order to hoard consumer goods such as soap, rice, sugar, fish sauce, salt or cloth. The fear of shortage and of price increases created a spurious demand. Once prices had stopped rising and the savings rate was increased, a new kind of fear arose. Enterprises that had hoarded a lot of raw materials now had to pay high interest to the state on this capital, and to reduce the interest bill they began to dump goods on the open market. During the three months from April to June 1989 they sold petroleum, iron and steel, cement, coal, plastic, textiles, cotton and yarn at prices even below the old official state prices. At the same time, householders saw that putting money in the bank would now produce a higher return than buying goods to hoard. This phenomenon well illustrates the growing effectiveness of state monetary policy in regulating the economy.
- The above two responses produced a more general social response: money from the market was drawn into the state coffers, reducing the purchasing power of society, while there was excess supply of goods on the market. The relations between supply and demand had gone into reverse and inflation stopped.

HISTORICAL FEATURES OF THE REFORM

Through examining the developments above we can see that before 1986 a series of reform measures was implemented, demonstrating that the Vietnamese reform was a prolonged and rather *ad hoc* process and certainly not a campaign which precisely defined the moment to open fire.

In Vietnam, even during the most thorough period of socialist transformation, the free market and private economy were never fully eliminated.

Figures 2.6 and 2.7 show that they not only existed but also accounted for no small part of economic life. The Vietnamese reforms therefore did not just create something new but to a large extent accepted that hitherto illegal phenomena continued to exist. Private production still had a share in the manufacture of everyday goods such as garments, building materials and household utensils, and in services such as repairs, restaurants (Figure 2.7) and light transport (using bicycles, pedicabs and carts). Petty commerce, in particular, was never eliminated. Although collectivism was in principle applied to agriculture, it never gained a complete hold. In the southern region the co-operatives never became an important element of agricultural life, while in the north from the outset of collectivisation, the so-called subsidiary economy, on the 5 per cent of land retained by households, accounted for 30–50 per cent or even 60 per cent of farmers' incomes.[14]

If we compare the situation in Vietnam with that in Eastern Europe, the differences are large. In certain parts of Eastern Europe the share of the state

Figure 2.6: Value of industrial production by sector (1985–95)

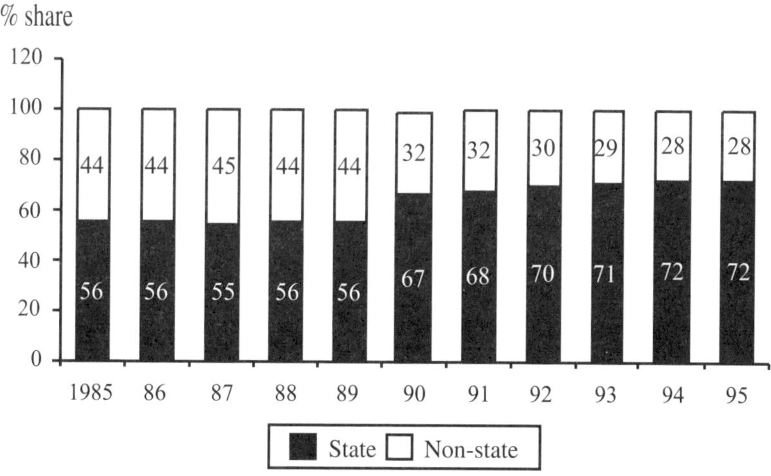

Note: The non-state sector includes a small and declining proportion of co-operatives. The decline in the number of co-operatives explains the apparent paradox of a rising share in state output after the price and interest rate reforms.

Sources: GSO, *Statistical Yearbook 1990*: 30, *Statistical Yearbook 1996*: 115.

Figure 2.7: Share of retail sales in the restaurant sector (1960–82)

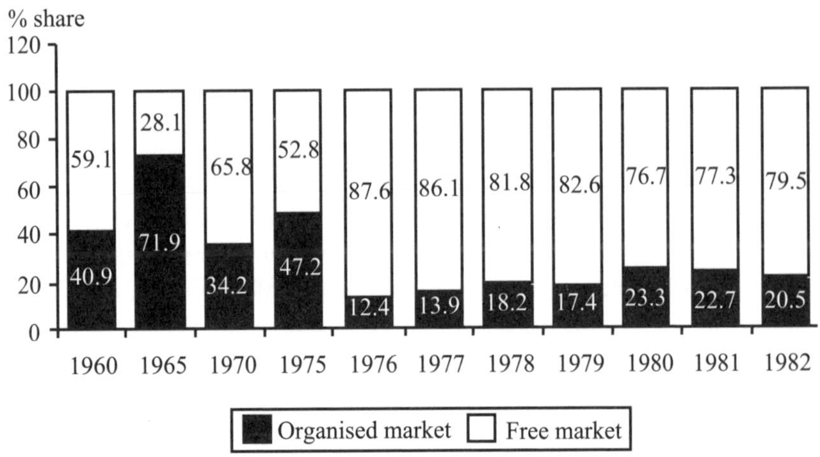

% share

	1960	1965	1970	1975	1976	1977	1978	1979	1980	1981	1982
Free market	59.1	28.1	65.8	52.8	87.6	86.1	81.8	82.6	76.7	77.3	79.5
Organised market	40.9	71.9	34.2	47.2	12.4	13.9	18.2	17.4	23.3	22.7	20.5

Note: Figures for 1960–75 are for the north only. Figures for 1976–82 are for the re-unified country. In 1976, the northern figure for the organised sector (state and co-operative) remained high, at 41.9 per cent and fell only slowly thereafter. The graph thus indicates the much stronger prevalence of the private sector in the southern part of the country throughout the socialist period.

Source: *Statistical Yearbook 1981*: 255; *Statistical Yearbook 1987*: 281

sector was very high, as shown in Table 2.6 (most shares were over 65 per cent compared to about 55 per cent in Vietnam before 1990). Such differences can contribute to an explanation of why, when the traditional economic model was in crisis, affecting above all the state sector, then the entire economy and social life of those countries fell into deep crisis. In Vietnam, on the other hand, the crisis was less profound due to the ever-present private sector even at the height of the socialist transformation period. Moreover, in China, where the state sector also held a less dominant position in economic life, the capacity of the economy to ride out the crisis in the state sector was probably not very different from that in Vietnam (Vu Quang Viet 1993: 13).

We should also note that in Vietnam, even after 1975, one-half of the country remained under the sway of the market economy, in which elements of capitalism also persisted. In Saigon, Da Nang, Hue and Can Tho and almost all the rural areas of the south, the market and private sectors were not merely remnants of the US occupation but continued to grow in strength via their relations with overseas Vietnamese (Beresford and Phong 2000: 97–101). The latter proved to be a fermenting agent that was not easy to eradicate

Table 2.6: State sector production in some East European countries

	Share of SOEs in social production (%)	Rate of growth during the crisis period (% p.a.)	
Czechoslovakia	97.0 (1986)	-3.1	-14.0
German Dem. Rep.	96.5 (1982)		
Poland	81.7 (1985)	-12.0	-10.0
Hungary	65.2 (1984)	-5.0	-7.0
Romania	n.a.	-7.9	-18.0
Bulgaria	n.a.	-13.6	-23.0

Sources: B. Lipton and J. Sachs, *Reforming Central and Eastern European Economies: Initial Results and Challenges*, World Bank, Washington DC, September 1991.

and their role might be compared with that of the Hong Kong Chinese in China. This point can also help explain why the transformation in Vietnam unfolded more favourably, with fewer hitches and, despite some shocks, did not lead to the chaos and collapse experienced in Eastern Europe.

Once the reform process was under way, in many instances it was the state that took the lead, pushing the production units to reform. Raw material prices were raised, forcing enterprises to accept inputs at world market prices, exchange rates for machinery and equipment became market rates, fixed asset depreciation was set at realistic rates, and interest rates were raised in 1989. These measures showed that the provincial SOEs were manifestly more backward and sluggish than those of the centre, although they had previously provided some of the strongest support for the reform process while complaining that it was the centre which was conservative and stagnant.

As in China, where it would have been difficult to promote the reform without Deng Xiaoping, in Vietnam it was often the architects of the old model who became the key supporters of reform. Without their moral authority, the reform would not have been so easy. Notably, Truong Chinh (who during 1966–68 had been the chief critic of Kim Ngoc's contract system) in 1981 gave positive encouragement to the contract system in Haiphong's Do Son district. Over the next few years, after a hesitant start, he was to become one of the leaders of the reform movement.

An interesting feature of the Vietnamese reform is that its leaders aimed to repair the old model; they certainly did not intend to move towards a market economy. But each attempt at repair took them a step further away from that which was to be repaired. Only when one foot was already on the new shore could it be seen that there was nothing dangerous, in fact many things were better, and the new model could be affirmed. Such a method of change explains why the reform had no general plan and no single leader but was the fruit of many plans and many leaders.

In the Vietnamese economic transformation, specifically in the strengthening of the free market and the private economy, we must mention the key role played by Vietnamese residing abroad. Here, there are some similarities as well as differences with the other socialist countries. There are about 25 million overseas Chinese, a good part of whom are well established in business and they have contributed directly to capital formation both of the Chinese state and subsequently of private companies. In the case of Eastern Europe, on the other hand, the expatriate Poles, Czechs, Romanians and Albanians played a more important role in destabilising the political system than in aiding the economy. While many overseas Vietnamese were opposed to the socialist system and some attempted to destabilise it, they in fact had little political impact inside the country. But when it came to economic matters, those who went to live and work abroad made their contribution by sending money and goods back home. The money could create capital for business or increase the purchasing power of society, while the greater part of the goods were sold on the free market and strengthened the development of that market (Beresford and Phong 2000: 97–101).

An even more important contribution was made by the Vietnamese guest workers and students in the socialist countries, especially in the Soviet Union, East Germany, Czechoslovakia, Poland, Bulgaria, as well as a few Third World countries such as Iraq and Algeria (Beresford and Phong 2000: 72–96). Numerically, this category was far smaller than the overseas Vietnamese (200,000 as against two million), but it had a much larger impact on the development of the market in Vietnam, particularly in the markets for housing, unofficial exports (such as clothing, cosmetics, etc.) and imported consumer goods. This was true, even when Vietnam suffered from severe shortages, in a way that did not apply to countries such as China, Cuba or North Korea in periods of hardship. Consumer goods of various types – bicycles, motorcycles, clothing, butter, milk, sugar, small electrical appliances, shoes, water pumps – and even small items of production inputs such as metals, ball points, flints, and buttons could still be bought and sold on the free market at prices that were not too high.

Besides these historical influences on the economic transformation process, we should mention in addition the geographical or, more correctly, geopolitical factor. In this regard it is worth remarking on two points. First, the stature of a nation state has a decisive influence on the path it takes. Vietnam is a nation of average stature with respect to its area, population and the significance of its economy and politics in both the region and the world as a whole. It is not very large like China and has neither the strength nor the difficulties of such a colossus. With such a stature as China's, every Western country has to pay due respect to its interests: its purchasing power, its selling power and its investment market. Faced with this problem in relation to China, the attitudes of the United States, Japan or the European Union hardly ever differ. Vietnam, on the other hand, does not have such great weight that it can compel the governments of these countries to pay attention to it. Therefore the relations between Vietnam and the Western world are less clear and often not very favourable to Vietnam. An example is the continuation of the US embargo on Vietnam long after normal trade relations had been established with China. Relations with the United States, in particular, were complicated by a somewhat vengeful attitude over the loss of the war as well as energetic political lobbying by relatives of those missing in action.

However, Vietnam is not so small as to have as little significance in global economic relations as countries such as Cuba and North Korea. Thus, although there were difficulties in the relations with the United States, in the end the United States still had to end its embargo. Japan, the European Union, India and even China as well as other countries in the region acknowledged Vietnam as a country worth paying attention to. Once the market-orientation of the economy had been established and the Soviet prop removed, a potential market of over 70 million and offering cheap, yet skilled, labour could scarcely be ignored.

Second, Vietnam lies in the middle of a rather busy and free region. Unlike Cuba which is isolated from all sides and North Korea which is surrounded by big powers such as Russia, China and Japan, Vietnam lies in Southeast Asia and has long-established relations with China, Hong Kong, Thailand, Indonesia, India, the Philippines, etc. This means that Vietnam has never been completely isolated, even while the United States maintained its embargo. It was able to poke holes in the net established by the embargo in order to buy and sell what it needed. During the early stages of its market transformation, Vietnam was in a position to increase its trade with several regional countries (Beresford 1989: 412–416; Beresford and Phong 2000: 45–46). Thus, despite the US embargo and the reduction in socialist country aid, Vietnam was not as isolated as Cuba and North Korea. In reality, Vietnam had already cleared a path towards the capitalist world even before the socialist bloc disappeared. By 1989, that is while Eastern Europe and the Soviet Union continued to support Vietnam, the share of Comecon imports had fallen to only 59 per cent of the total (World Bank 1992: 27). This factor also explains why the transformation in Vietnam was not so sudden as in other countries.

In conclusion, historical features of the transformation process in Vietnam illuminate the confluence of both domestic and external factors which assisted the reform process. Domestically, the persistence of the private sector throughout the socialist period demonstrates the important role of the symbiotic relationship between citizens and leaders, the maturity of societal needs pressing for change as well as the learning and adjustment processes of the top leadership. External factors such as the diminishing aid from socialist countries, the sustaining trade with other Asian countries even during the US economic embargo and the incoming money and goods from overseas Vietnamese have assisted and at times softened the sharp edges of the reform process in Vietnam.

AUTHOR'S NOTE

The author wishes to thank the editors of this volume for their helpful suggestions for the improvement of this chapter. He alone, however, remains responsible for any remaining errors.

NOTES

1 Of course, during those years the war effort continued in the south, so it is unlikely that such a recovery could have been very great.

2 No planning was possible during the war years from 1965 to 1975.

3 Aid was increased after the Le Duan–Brezhnev negotiations in 1975 and 1977.

4 All these issues were reported in the newspapers at the time. More recently, they were reiterated by Tran Phuong (1995) and Vu Trong Nam (1995).

5 The full contents of the measure can be found in the Haiphong party decision (Haiphong 1963), signed by Hoang Huu Nhan. I am grateful to Ngo Kim Chung for this document.

6 Related by Phan Van Tiem (1987). Bui Cong Trung family archive.
7 I am grateful to Ngo Kim Chung, who interviewed Kim Ngoc's former private secretary, for this information.
8 Doan Trong Truyen replaced To Duy as head of the SPrC. See Doan Trong Truyen (1983) and Dang Phong (1983: 12).
9 Truong Chinh had previously been the most forthright opponent of the Vinh Phuc experiment.
10 While I have focused here on higher-level fence breakers, Chapter 4 in this volume by Abrami and Henaff provides details of fence breaking by state officials at the commune and district levels.
11 As, for example, happened in the case of the chair of the central party Agricultural Committee and the head of the state Price Committee in 1981.
12 See Beresford and Fforde 1997, for a more detailed discussion of this reform and the reasons for its unworkability
13 Under the system of state ownership, depreciation funds were transferred to the state budget rather than being retained by the enterprise. Since the politicians preferred new construction to renewal of existing equipment, enterprises rarely upgraded their production lines with the result that, by the early 1990s, most machinery dated from the establishment of the enterprise, or even earlier in the case of machinery purchased second hand.
14 These data are based on various interviews.

REFERENCES

Beresford, Melanie (1989) 'Vietnam's trade with the non-communist world' in Peter Limqueco (ed.), *Partisan Scholarship: Essays in Honour of Renato Constantino.* Manila: JCA Publishers.

Beresford, Melanie and Dang Phong (2000) *Economic Transition in Vietnam: Trade and Aid in the Demise of a Centrally Planned Economy.* Cheltenham UK and Northampton MA: Edward Elgar.

Beresford, Melanie and Adam Fforde (1997) 'A methodology for analysing the process of economic reform in Vietnam: the case of domestic trade'. *Journal of Communist Studies and Transition Politics*, vol. 13 no. 4, December.

Chan, Anita, Benedict J. Tria Kerkvliet, and Jonathan Unger (eds) (1999) *Transforming Asian Socialism: China and Vietnam Compared.* Lanham MD, Boulder CO and New York: Rowman and Littlefield.

Cong Bao (1980*) Cong Bao nuoc CHXHCNVN* [Official gazette of the SRV]. Hanoi: n.p.

Dang Phong (1983) 'Nhin lai cong tac gia ca nhung nam qua' [Reviewing recent work & prices]. *Tap chi Vat Gia* [Price review], no. 1.

—— (1985) 'Khao sat doi song cong nhan va can bo tai tinh Quang Ninh' [An inquiry into the life of workers and cadres in Quang Ninh province], *Tap chi Vat Gia* [Price review], August.

—— (1987) 'Long An sau 7 nam thuc hien co che gia moi' [Long An after 7 years of implementing the new price regime]. *Nhan Dan* [The people], 6 August.

—— (1988) 'Nhung cach phan phoi lai qua mot ve xe khach' [Redistribution via a bus ticket]. *Dai doan ket* [Great solidarity], July.

—— (1994) 'Viewing the decade 1976–1986 in Vietnam vertically and horizontally'. *Australian Vietnam Research Project Working Papers*, no. 1, July.

—— (1995) 'Aspects of agricultural economy and rural life in 1993'. In J. Benedict Tria Kerkvliet and Doug J. Porter (eds), *Vietnam's Rural Transformation*. Boulder CO: Westview Press.

Dang Phong and Pham Thanh Giang (1996) 'Qua trinh chuyen doi o Cong ty xe khach Mien Dong thanh pho Ho Chi Minh 1976–1996' [The process of transforming the Eastern Region Bus Company of Ho Chi Minh City 1976–96]. Australian Vietnam Research Project, unpublished, April.

Do Son (1980) Nghi Quyet so 05/NQ–HU 'Ve cong tac thu hoach vu chiem va buoc vao lam vu mua 1980' [On the work of the fifth-month harvest and the coming autumn harvest in 1980]. Do Son District People's Committee, 4 June.

Doan Duy Thanh (1996) former party secretary of Haiphong, interview with Dang Phong, Hanoi, 14 May.

Doan Trong Truyen (1983) 'Bao cao tai hoi nghi toan quoc nganh vat gia' [Report to a national conference of the price branch]. Hanoi: State Price Committee, 7 January.

General Statistical Office (GSO), *Nien Giam Thong Ke* [Statistical yearbook]. Hanoi: Statistical Publishing House, various years.

Haiphong (1963) 'Bao cao tong ket phong trao hop tac hoa nong nghiep ngoai thanh Hai Phong' [Report summing up the collectivisation movement in agriculture in the Haiphong suburbs]. Document No. 4/BC–TU of the Communist Party of Vietnam, Haiphong branch, 19 February.

Huu Tho (1996) 'Nho Hoi Nghi Con Son' [Remembering the Con Son Conference] in his *Nho mot thoi lam bao Nhan Dan* [Memories of working at the Nhan Dan newspaper]. Hanoi: National Political Publishers.

Institute of Economics (1990) *45 Nam Kinh Te Viet Nam* [45 years of the Vietnamese economy]. Hanoi: Social Science Publishers.

Le Duan (1979a) 'Address of comrade Le Duan at the 6th Central Committee Plenum, 7 August 1979', unpublished.

Le Duan (1979b) 'Address of Comrade Le Duan concluding the 6th Plenum of the Central Committee, 27 August 1979', unpublished.

Le Xuan Nghia (1993) 'Nhin lai lam phat nam 1993 va trien vong' [Review of inflation in 1993 and outlook]. *Kinh Te* [Economy], no. 93.

Lipton, B. and Sachs, J. (1991) *Reforming Central and Eastern European Economies: Iinitial Results and Challenges*, Washington DC: World Bank, September.

Nguyen Duy Ky (1962) 'Mot so y kien ve gia mua nong san' [Some opinions on agricultural procurement prices] *Nghien Cuu Kinh Te* [Economic research], no. 9.

Bui Cong Trung family archive.

Phan Van Tiem (1987) former chair of the State Price Committee, interview with Dang Phong, Hanoi, 16 February.

Secretariat (1968) 'On correcting the work of three contracts and land management in agricultural co-operatives of some localities', Circular 224 TT–TW of the Communist Party of Vietnam Secretariat, signed by Le Van Luong, 12 December.

State Planning Committee (1979) 'Report to the Politbureau', Hanoi: State Planning Committee.

To Huu (1979) 'De cuong gioi thieu Nghi Quyet Hoi Nghi Trung Uong lan thu 6 ve tinh hinh va nhiem vu cap bach' [Introducing the Resolution of the 6th Central Committte Plenum on the situation and urgent tasks]. Speech to a conference of cadres convened by the central party organisation, 3 October.

Tran Dinh But (1996) interview with Dang Phong, Ho Chi Minh City, 12 August.

Tran Duc (1994) *Hop tac trong nong thon xua va nay* [Co-operation in the rural areas, past and present]. Hanoi: Agricultural Publishers.

Tran Phuong (1995) former minister of domestic trade, interview with Dang Phong at the Vietnam Economics Association, Hanoi, 9 June.

Tu Giao (1996) former deputy president of Long An province (1979–86) and secretary of Nguyen Van Linh (1986–90), together with Dang Van Sang, deputy director of Long An Department of Finance and Prices, interview with Dang Phong and Melanie Beresford, 12 April.

Vinh Phuc (1966) 'Ve mot so van de quan ly lao dong nong nghiep trong hop tac xa hien nay' [Some problems of agricultural labour management in today's co-operatives]. Nghi Quyet so 68 NQ–TW, signed by Tran Quoc Phi, deputy party secretary of the province, 10 September.

Vu Quang Viet (1993) 'So sanh tinh hinh phat trien kinh te Trung Quoc va Viet Nam' [Comparing the economic development of China and Vietnam]. *Dien Dan* [Forum], no. 21, July–August.

Vu Quoc Tuan (1995) assistant to Prime Minister Vo Van Kiet, interview with Dang Phong, Hanoi, 13 July.

Vu Trong Nam (1995) vice-minister of domestic trade, interview with Dang Phong at the Vietnam Economics Association, Hanoi, 9 June.

World Bank (1992) *Vietnam: Restructuring Public Finance and Public Enterprises*. Hanoi: World Bank, 15 April.

—— (1994) *Vietnam: Public Sector Management and Private Sector Incentives*. Hanoi: World Bank, 20 September.

CHAPTER 3

Lessons from the Asian Crisis for the Sustainability of Vietnamese Economic Development

Melanie Beresford

INTRODUCTION

Following the disappointments of the Soviet-style socialist development project, the major economic reforms of the 1980s and the termination of Soviet aid, the Vietnamese Communist Party leadership set its sights in the early 1990s on 'catching up' to its neighbours in Southeast Asia. The first part of the slogan which encapsulated its vision for the future – 'rich people, strong country, civilised and equitable society' – indicated the need for sustained high growth rates over the next few decades, while the final part expressed the party's desire to continue to develop in a socialist direction. In reality during the decade of the 1990s, however, the explosion of growth which occurred was accompanied by rapidly widening income inequality, between social classes, regions and genders, leaving many people wondering exactly how the 'socialist' part of the vision would be implemented. Moreover, the impact of the Asian economic crisis at the end of the decade slowed the economy and raised new questions concerning the long-term sustainability of the ways in which the vision has been implemented to date.

Vietnam experienced a marked, though relatively mild reaction to the Asian crisis. The GDP growth rate fell from 8.9 per cent in 1997 to 4.0 per cent in 1998, while other regional countries experienced large and catastrophic falls (in 1998 Indonesia's GDP fell by 13.2 per cent, Thailand's by 10.4 per cent, Malaysia's by 7.5 per cent, South Korea's by 5.8 per cent).[1] For comparative data see Table 3.1. In this table three countries stand out. Japan's poor performance in recent years has been prolonged and can be seen as one of the factors triggering the crisis elsewhere in the region. As such, it

Table 3.1: Dimensions of the crisis – a comparative overview (annual percentage GDP growth rates)

	1995	**1996**	**1997**	**1998**	**1999**	**2000**
China	9.9	9.7	8.8	7.8	7.1	7.9
Hong Kong	4.0	5.0	5.0	–5.1	3.1	10.5
Indonesia	7.2	8.0	4.7	–13.2	0.8	4.8
Japan	1.0	3.8	–0.7	–2.1	0.2	1.9
Malaysia	9.2	8.6	7.5	–7.5	6.1	8.3
Philippines	5.6	5.7	5.2	–0.5	3.4	4.0
Singapore	8.3	6.9	8.9	0.2	5.9	9.9
S. Korea	9.2	7.1	5.0	–5.8	10.9	8.8
Taiwan	6.6	5.7	6.8	4.7	5.6	5.8*
Thailand	8.6	5.5	–1.8	–10.4	4.2	4.3
Vietnam†	9.5	9.3	8.9	4.0	4.8	5.5

Notes: (*) Estimated.

(†) Official Vietnamese data are more optimistic than the World Bank estimates shown here: according to official data, growth rates for 1998 and 2000 were 5.8 per cent and 6.2 per cent respectively.

Sources: World Bank 2000a, 2000b, 2002b; *Far Eastern Economic Review*, various issues.

is not of immediate concern here. China and Taiwan experienced hardly any impact at all. The Vietnamese pattern lies somewhere in between: it suffered more than China, the other transition economy in the region, but much less than most of its other neighbours. This Vietnamese response to the crisis raises some interesting questions. First of all, are the delayed reaction and recovery a result of the external shock of the Asian crisis itself or are there domestic factors, pertaining to the course of Vietnam's transition from plan to market, at the root of the problem? Second, what can be done to revive the prospects for high and sustained growth?

One explanation commonly put forward for the comparatively small drop in growth during 1998 is Vietnam's relative isolation from the global economy. In particular, because it is a latecomer in terms of integration into global markets, it has not undergone the rapid financial liberalisation which so greatly increased the vulnerability of other economies in the region and led to massive capital outflows. The major impact on Vietnam has been via foreign direct investment, inflows of which have nevertheless remained positive throughout the crisis, and to a lesser extent exports. Vietnam has thus suffered a slowdown, but not a crisis. Moreover, as other regional economies slowed again in 2001, under the impact of global recession, the Vietnamese economy appeared again to be rather insulated.

An alternative view is that the slowdown in Vietnam is only partly related to the Asian crisis but reflects problems that have built up over a number of years within the domestic economy. Most notable, according to this explanation, has been the slowdown in the reform process itself. Foreign investors and aid agencies in particular have complained about the continued excessive red tape, lack of transparency in regulations, over-protection of the state-owned enterprises and lack of incentives for development of private sector activity (*The Economist* 8 Jan. 2000: 65). Proponents of this view can point to the fact that foreign direct investment (FDI) in fact began to drop as early as 1996, at least a year before the crisis hit Thailand. Moreover, despite signs of recovery, foreign investor caution remains high (World Bank 2000b). Thus the Asian crisis may have acted as a signal to increase investor caution about Vietnam, but it is not in itself the major cause of that caution.

This chapter argues that the truth lies somewhere between these two alternative explanations. On the domestic side, it is true that the Vietnamese government has applied a stop–go approach to economic reform and, after a slower pace of reform in the mid-1990s when things were going well, the noticeable effects of the crisis prompted a new round of reforms in 1998–99. Indeed, there are few governments in the world which are free from guilt in that regard. However, this chapter is critical of the view of most Western economists that it is the 'partially reformed' nature of the Vietnamese economy that lies at the root of the problem. The notion of 'partial reform' implies that the destination, the 'complete reform', is known in advance (and is modelled on advanced Western economies). It is argued here that the problems facing the Vietnamese economy are better understood, not through measuring its alleged inadequacies against some unattainable ideal model, but via an examination of the real development of the institutions and structure of Vietnamese market relations over the past decade, including their historical foundations within the old centrally planned economy.

On the other hand, Vietnam has also been subject to external developments largely beyond its control, and in the 1990s a major influence was the development of an unsustainable bubble economy elsewhere in the region. If we use the analogy of a fever, which has a lot in common with the language of speculative booms and crashes, the crisis can be seen as the turning point at which the body either gives up and dies or wins the battle (since an economy does not die, the recovery is brought about by a process of forced restructuring). The crisis is not the fever itself. In order to understand the fever, we need to examine the causes of infection, the weaknesses in the body that permit the infection to gain a hold and the strengths which enable it to fight. In the case of the Asian crisis, the financial disaster of 1997–98 was the turning point, but the causes lay in the deeper economic and institutional structures which had developed over the previous decade or more. This chapter argues that the boom in the Vietnamese economy during the 1990s was at least partly a result of the fever developing in the rest of the region and that its slowdown during 1998 and subsequently can also be attributed to the crisis which ended the fever.

The above arguments are set out as follows. The next section surveys the underlying causes of the regional fever, while that following examines the principal means FDI by which the fever and subsequent crisis affected Vietnam. We then turn to domestic factors in the Vietnamese slowdown, focusing on the question of the public sector, still the largest contributor to GDP, its relation to emerging forms of ownership and control of assets (including FDI) and some of the current obstacles in the way of developing a sustainable state-led pattern of growth. The final section we review the main sources of economic growth for the economy as a whole over the 1990s and, drawing on the arguments of the previous sections, point to ways in which the economy could shift towards a more sustainable growth path in the coming decade.

Some characteristics of Vietnam need to be kept in mind before we proceed. While the Vietnamese escaped the worst ravages of the crisis, they nevertheless remain more vulnerable than their neighbours on two counts. First, Vietnam is one of the poorest economies in the region, with per capita GDP only about 10–20 per cent that of Thailand and Malaysia and around half that of Indonesia. Three decades of war combined with two or more decades of central planning left it with an unsustainable economic system. The 1980s decade of reform, although it improved the vitality of the economy, also created considerable turmoil and suffering for significant sections of the population – notably as a result of the very high inflation rates prevailing in the latter half of the decade. It has only been since the early

1990s that the country has experienced the sort of growth rates enjoyed by its neighbours for nearly four decades since 1960. While living standards have undoubtedly risen during those half dozen years, they have done so very unevenly. The populations of urban centres like Ho Chi Minh City and Hanoi have benefited disproportionately while incomes of the rural population have grown much more slowly. The majority of Vietnamese people thus lack a cushion of safety between their current standards of living and the earlier widespread privation.

Second, Vietnam is vulnerable because many aspects of its economic system are still transitional in nature. The last remnants of central planning were finally abolished in 1989 and, since then, resource allocations have essentially been based on the market mechanism. While these market mechanisms by no means conform to the 'Western' ideal favoured by neoclassical economists, they are nevertheless rather well-established and exhibit many characteristics in common with other regional countries. In a nutshell, market relations are based on personal connections with large elements of clientelism as opposed to the 'rule of law' prevalent in Western markets (Herno 1997). At the same time, a number of other aspects of the old socialist model remain relatively intact. In particular, for the Communist Party the principle of public ownership of major means of production remains a defining characteristic of a socialist economy: state domination of the 'commanding heights' will continue to give it the capacity to propel society in that direction. The vulnerability arises, in my view, because in the process of dismantling the central planning regime, the state apparatus has lost a considerable amount of its former coherence and thereby its ability to influence the direction of development. Instead, state institutions have become more open to a variety of political pressures, a fact which is most visible in the gap that has opened between party ideology and the way in which policies are implemented (or not implemented) in practice.[2] The state not only lacks resources and administrative capacity, but, beyond the generalities mentioned above, it also lacks a clear and cohesive definition of its socialist goal.

In spite of these areas of vulnerability, the Vietnamese state has shown considerable adaptability in the past. When faced with severe economic crisis at the end of the 1970s, it embarked on a process of reform which despite, or perhaps because of, the lack of a 'road map' succeeded in restoring the vitality of the economy without any major political upheaval and without the prolonged misery experienced in many parts of Eastern Europe. Vietnamese politicians do not come from the mould of banana republic dictators, or even of regimes closer to home (Thailand, Burma and the Philippines, for example) which for substantial portions of the post-War period, imposed their developmental priorities on the population by force of arms. The present confusion, therefore, can also be seen in a positive light. In the past, the capacity and coherence of the Vietnamese state has derived from its broad based legitimacy among the population and, during the transition, it has largely been able to manoeuvre to maintain this legitimacy. The relative loss of coherence during the transition process reflects the emergence of new societal interests and the adaptation of state institutions to reflect shifting power alignments. Whether such changes will enable the state to continue to maintain its broad-based legitimacy in the future will depend on how well it can manage the ramifications of the Asian crisis in the interests of different sections of the population.

SOME LESSONS FROM THE REGION

When we look at the other countries in the region, the ultimate causes of the financial crisis, which first of all hit Thailand and then spread in a panic reaction to other countries, lay not in the financial system itself but in the economic structures which had developed during previous decades. To say this is not to underestimate the importance of global finance in triggering the crisis but, paradoxically, to emphasise it. In the decade prior to the crisis most regional countries had not only massively increased their exposure to volatile international capital flows but had in the process reduced the capacity of their governments to pursue a coherent development strategy. Over-concentration by governments and their economic advisers on fiscal rectitude and monetary stability, at the expense of sectoral planning to deepen the industrialisation process, during the decade prior to the crisis had allowed structural problems to emerge which were scarcely noticed by the economic experts. In previously interventionist countries, financial deregulation exposed structural weaknesses and led to disaster. As Singh and Weisse (1999: 212) put it: ‘It was precisely by abandoning the main tenets of the Asian model [of co-ordinated investment activity] through financial liberalisation that the present imbalances were allowed to occur.’

Even now, the focus of economic advice to the stricken economies tends to be on extending the financial liberalisation process in order to create a more competitive environment in which the international capital can operate unhampered by what are seen as corruption, red tape and privileges meted out to political cronies.[3] Little attention is paid to where the private sector invests its money and whether this is to the long term benefit of economic development – whether from the point of view of the industrialisation process or from the point of view of social equity and the participation of the majority of the population. The oversimplifications of neo-classical economics, based on Adam Smith's 'invisible hand' and the assumption of the essential harmony of economic interests, continue to underpin economic advice. Governments should intervene to 'facilitate' market processes; they should not intervene to attempt to reconcile conflicting interests by pushing the market in directions it would not otherwise go. At the same time, the extensive literature on structural adjustment programmes applied in other developing countries since the 1980s shows that liberalisation and deregulation neither automatically produce renewed growth nor necessarily have the social benefits assumed in the theoretical models upon which they are based (Elson 1995).

Technology, structural bottlenecks and over-investment

In the case of the Southeast Asian economies, the crisis in the financial system expressed, in a quite disastrous way, a number of underlying bottlenecks in the real economy which had been foreseen or partially foreseen by some economists, even while the majority ignored their significance. A view popularised by Paul Krugman in the mid-1990s was that much of Asia's high economic growth of the previous decades had been based on extensive rather than intensive development. In other words, growth had been based on increased inputs – capital, labour and raw materials – rather than on technological change and rising productivity (Krugman 1994).[4] As an early and, at the time, rather lonely Cassandra had noted, Southeast Asian development was 'technology-less' development (Yoshihara 1988). Extensive development inevitably leads to slowing growth when input shortages raise costs and reduce returns. Supporters of this view were thus among the few economists who predicted the end of the 'Asian miracle'.[5]

Their claims were, however, rather exaggerated due to faulty methodology.[6] Expansion of the stock of capital and labour itself embodies significant technological change over time, a point which is especially true of late industrialising countries where great leaps forward can be attained by copying existing technologies from more advanced industrial countries. Indeed differences in income between developed and less developed countries can largely be accounted for by the levels of technology embodied in capital and labour (human development) themselves. High rates of capital investment have undoubtedly been the major factor in Southeast Asian growth over the past few decades and labour-force skills have certainly improved. A better, though not ideal, measure of productivity growth is therefore the growth in productivity of labour, or output per worker. This measure, which captures the increases in productivity which are the result of both more intense labour and more skilled labour working with more technologically advanced machinery and equipment, is shown in Table 3.2. Note, however, that the results might be affected by changes in working time (longer or shorter hours, changes in the proportions of full-time and part-time work). Data to obtain a more accurate measure, real output per worker hour, are not available.

Table 3.2: Growth in labour productivity 1965–98 (% p.a.)

	Indonesia	Malaysia	Philippines	Thailand	Singapore	Vietnam
1965–73	6.2	3.8	3.3	5.4	9.6	n.a.
1970–80	5.1	4.2	3.6	4.3	4.0	n.a.
1980–90	3.2	2.4	–1.9	5.0	4.3	1.9
1990–97	5.0	6.0	0.6	6.0	6.8	6.6

Sources: Calculated from World Bank, *World Development Report*, various issues.

Nevertheless, the Krugman argument does point to a significant problem for newly industrialising countries which is that extensive development in one sector, using existing technologies copied from more advanced countries, does eventually lead to diminishing returns, *unless* new processes embodying new, more productive technologies are continually introduced. The fluctuations in productivity growth shown in the table are indicative of the boom and slump cycle that this may induce, as growth based on extensive development in one area comes to an end and new products and technologies are introduced. (In the Vietnamese case, as we shall see later, the upsurge in the 1990s was due to a combination of labour shedding and higher capacity utilisation as well as the introduction of more productive technologies.)

In the Southeast Asian case, for nearly three decades there was a heavy reliance on growth of labour-intensive exports, chiefly garments, shoes and electronic components, to fuel the development process.[7] The boom in such manufactured exports was largely the result of changes in the West, where declining profitability in the late-1960s had prompted a redistribution of certain components of manufacturing to low-wage countries, usually under subcontracting arrangements (the so-called New International Division of Labour). Western industrialists took advantage of post-war developments in international transport and communications infrastructure to relocate labour-intensive manufacturing to those countries which combined a comparative advantage in cheap labour with a relatively advanced infrastructure and apparent social and political stability. Given the Western quotas on imports of manufactures from less developed countries (LDCs) (notably in garments), the Southeast Asians entered a market in which they competed fiercely with each other to gain foreign investment in these areas through tax concessions and other subsidies, cheap infrastructure and cheap labour. Production expanded rapidly and manufactured exports soon outstripped more traditional primary commodity exports. Manufactured exports of Malaysia, for example, rose from 12 per cent of total exports in 1970 to 22 per cent in 1980 and 48.5 per cent in 1988 (Jomo 1990: 56). For the Philippines the growth was from 8 per cent in 1970 to 58 per cent in 1993 (Hutchison 1997: 70). In Thailand labour-intensive manufactures grew from 20 per cent of exports in 1981 to 57 per cent in 1993 (Jomo *et al.* 1997: 69). In Indonesia they rose from just over 1 per cent in 1980 to 30 per cent in 1992 (Hill 1996: 163). Few would disagree that the economic 'miracle' was very largely based on the rapid growth of such exports.

Just as over-reliance on primary commodity exports in the colonial period was perceived to be an obstacle to modernisation in the post-Independence era, over-reliance on a handful of labour-intensive manufactures emerged as a problem in the 1990s. By that decade, the more developed ASEAN countries were facing increased competition from China, Vietnam, Bangladesh and other countries with even lower wages. The effect of rising domestic incomes was exacerbated by policy-induced stability of exchange rates (loosely pegged to an appreciating US dollar). Cumulative export growth in Malaysia, Indonesia and Thailand during the first half of the 1990s was only a third or a half of what it had been in the second half of the 1980s (BIS 1998: 36). Large and persistent current account deficits emerged in these countries (BIS 1997: 41), though they were concealed by capital inflows (of an increasingly short-term nature)[8]. Some early indicators of difficulties were the slowdown in growth of Thai textile exports early in the 1990s and a large slump, due to global oversupply, in semiconductor exports in 1996. In the latter case, US dollar prices crashed by 80 per cent and created a flow-on effect in the prices of other electronic goods (BIS 1997: 40).[9]

It would be wrong to end the story simply by pointing to the closure of opportunities for labour-intensive export expansion, however. One of the major obstacles has been the sheer difficulty of making the transition to higher value-added sectors. Among the reasons for this phenomenon were the entrapment of market-orientated exporters in subcontracting arrangements and the lack of linkages developed between export sectors and the domestic economy. Only in Singapore, where labour shortages had developed by the late 1970s, and in Malaysia, where they had also emerged in the late 1980s, was any real attention paid by government to upgrading human resources and technology and to deepening the industrialisation process by developing backward and forward linkages to the domestic economy. For other ASEAN countries, where unskilled labour remained plentiful, there was little incentive for either business or the rather conservative government technocrats to promote research and development, skills training and investment in more capital-intensive production.

One indication of the effort being put into development of human resources is the proportionof the relevant age cohort in secondary school shown in Table 3.3. Given the significant time lags involved in creating an educated labour force, it can be seen that in several cases efforts to upgrade educational attainment came rather late. Wade points out that Thailand's gross enrolment ratio in 1992, at 32 per cent, was less than half of Taiwan's in 1978 at a time when Taiwan had the same per capita income as Thailand in 1992 (Wade 1998: 1537). Relative to its income and level of industrialisation, Vietnamese educational attainment compares very favourably to that of its higher-income

Table 3.3: Age cohort in secondary education (%)

	1982	**1990**	**1997**
Indonesia	33	48	56
Malaysia	49	56	64
Philippines	64	73	78
Singapore	66	72	76
Thailand	29	26	48
Vietnam	48	38	55

Note: For Thailand and Vietnam, data in the first column are for a different year.
Sources: World Bank 1985, 1999b, 2000a.

neighbours. While the data show a (short-lived) fall off in secondary school attendance during the transition years, the long-term educational legacy of the traditional socialist system gives Vietnam the advantage of a reasonably well-educated workforce which should not be frittered away by over-emphasis on development of industries using predominantly unskilled labour. However, in both Vietnam and most other countries shown in the table, improvements in general education have not been matched by upgrading of professional and technical training.

Given that labour-intensive exports had provided the engine of growth over the previous two decades, the slowdown of external demand left its mark elsewhere in the Southeast Asian economies. Domestic market growth was already constrained by its fairly narrow concentration in urban areas. Yet in its 1998 *Annual Report* the Bank for International Settlements identified a tendency to keep on increasing capacity in existing sectors, not only in the labour-intensive export industries, notably electronics, but in import-substituting industries and non-trade areas like automobiles, electricity generation and property development, leading to reduced rates of return as one of the major causes of the crisis (BIS 1998: 35–36).

Such over-investment is indicated in the Thai case by low-capacity utilisation rates in industry (averaging 72.4 per cent in 1996) and a 59.6 per cent occupancy rate of new housing built between 1992 and 1996 (Leightner 2000: 387). As global demand for Southeast Asian export goods slowed, competitive pressures increased and both foreign and domestic capitalists responded by redoubling their saving and investment efforts.[10] The rate of investment in Thailand rose from 30 per cent of GDP in 1985–89 to between 40 and 44 per cent in 1990–96 (Lauridsen 1998: 1575), further restraining domestic consumption and necessarily increasing the speculative nature of investments such that 'the paper they left in the hands of investors was wastepaper instead of representing sound liens upon future production' (Mummery and Hobson [1889] cited in Leightner 2000: 388).

Diminishing opportunities for further labour-intensive manufactured export growth and rising levels of foreign debt after the mid-1980s[11] initiated a debate about how to make the transition to more high-tech, high-value-added exports. As Yoshihara put it,

> What is important is a country's ability to generate new exports one after another … in a flying-geese pattern. This enables the country to move on to a new product which fetches

> a better price when the old product ceases to be an attractive export (and eventually cannot be exported) either because of increased costs (due to increased wages) or new competition (from new entry or new products). (Yoshihara 1988: 102)

Such considerations are what prompted Malaysia's technology deepening strategy (Rasiah 1997) and the programmes of deregulation and privatisation of state assets in Malaysia, the Philippines, Thailand and Indonesia. However, while Malaysia may have attempted at least partially to emulate the successful state-led strategies of South Korea and Taiwan, the widespread recession of the mid-1980s had produced pressure from multilateral institutions to deregulate the economy, particularly the financial sector. Across the region, lack of transparency and the existence of cronyism meant that liberalisation led to significant losses of state technocrats' ability to even perceive what was going on. While most economists, particularly the World Bank and IMF advisers, maintained their focus on major macroeconomic 'fundamentals', their faith in market forces meant that neither the emerging meso-level structural problems nor the micro-level processes leading to massive over-investment were paid sufficient attention.

Meanwhile, capital searched for new, more profitable avenues of investment of an increasingly speculative and short-term nature. The long property boom which began in 1990–91 in all the crisis countries was one manifestation of this speculative tendency which resulted in inflation of property values and of the value of loan collateral (Lauridsen 1998: 1577; Grabel 1999: 9). Further, the long-term stability of currencies encouraged investors to take large unhedged exposures in foreign currencies (BIS 1998: 37–38). Fuelled by increasing global financial flows, themselves responding to developments elsewhere,[12] the bubble economies of Southeast Asia began to emerge.

The contribution of inequality

High levels of income inequality were another factor contributing to the development of bottlenecks in the economic system in Southeast Asia.[13] Economists differ on the impact of inequality on sustainability of growth. On the one hand, most Keynesian-type theories, for example, argue that inequality between capitalists (whose behaviour is characterised by saving) and workers (who mainly consume their income) is a necessary condition for growth, while Seguino (2000) shows that gender inequality has been important in sustaining manufactured export growth in 20 semi-industrialised countries.[14]

On the other hand, inequality can also place limits on expansion of domestic demand, lead to excessive congestion of infrastructure and environmental destruction, contribute to low quality of human resources and provoke social and political conflicts which may reduce investor confidence and slow growth. All of these negative consequences were present in Southeast Asia before the crisis and, in light of subsequent developments, their contribution must be taken seriously. Moreover, while some degree of inequality seems inevitable, the ultimate goal of human development[15] is certainly compromised by disparities which restrict people's capability to take advantage of new economic opportunities.

In Southeast Asia inequality, especially urban–rural disparities, added further to the difficulties of many countries in obtaining a more skilled workforce. The labouring poor had few incentives to keep their children in school, while inadequate provision of secondary education outside the major cities and a bloated, elite-orientated tertiary education system rendered their opportunities equally poor. Despite the relatively widespread adoption of Green Revolution technologies, agricultural production systems continued to require relatively low levels of technology and management skills. Large numbers of rural–urban migrants thus arrived in the cities with few prospects for moving into higher productivity sectors. In the prosperous urban enclaves, the more high-tech industries which did develop had to rely on foreign technicians and managers. A combination of (unskilled) labour surplus and (skilled) labour shortage thus contributed to the closing down of long-term investment opportunities and to development of the bubble economy.

Predatory, rent-seeking behaviour by the urban elites is another factor which must be mentioned in this context. In a number of countries, nationalist economic policies favouring indigenous capitalists over the ethnic Chinese had created accumulations of capital in the state sector (for example, the public assets held 'in trust' for *bumiputera* Malaysians, the use of state enterprises as 'proxy capitalists' in Indonesia) which were increasingly privatised after the mid-1980s. Regulations requiring firms to include indigenous capitalists in the ownership structure (as well as the labour force) of local firms led to arrangements whereby the indigenous owners became rentiers while their ethnic Chinese partners also benefited from political protection. Even where ethnic bias was not evident (as in Thailand), management of state enterprises by military personnel, state bureaucrats and those with personal connections to the political leadership was characterised by corruption and cronyism. Vested political interests had grown up demanding continued protection of inefficient and sometimes technically bankrupt enterprises which nevertheless continued to provide a source of private capital accumulation for those in charge of them. Other private-sector activities tended to be 'crowded out' by these politically privileged firms – a factor which contributed to the narrow base of economic development and, in the 1990s, forced firms both to concentrate on short-term profits at home and to look abroad for longer-term investment.

This kind of inequality is, of course, not unique to Southeast Asia. Rent-seeking was also encouraged among the Korean *chaebol* and provided an important source of primary capital accumulation. As Amsden (1989) emphasises, however, the ability of the Korean government to impose discipline on these large oligopolies, at least prior to the mid-1980s, was an important factor in their success. This factor has been absent from most of Southeast Asia. Moreover, among those excluded from the wealth-creation process, social tensions emerged which could be subdued while growth remained high or else by sheer repression. In the wake of the crisis, however, the vulnerability of everyone from the poor to the middle classes has been fully exposed. In the worst affected country, Indonesia, just two years was sufficient not only to undo three decades of poverty reduction but to threaten the very survival of the nation. However, anti-foreign and anti-globalisation sentiments, anti-government demonstrations, labour disputes, ethnic riots and separatist movements have appeared or revived in most of the crisis countries and put the prospects for a stable recovery under a cloud.

FOREIGN DIRECT INVESTMENT IN VIETNAM: A SIDE-EFFECT OF THE BUBBLE ECONOMY

Since openness to foreign direct investment (FDI) is one of the few areas in which Vietnam has been relatively exposed to the forces of globalisation and heightened international financial flows, an examination of FDI is the obvious place to begin a study of the impacts of the Asian crisis on the country.

Incentives and disincentives facing foreign investors

Vietnam's Foreign Investment Law, passed in December 1987, was at the time one of the most liberal in Southeast Asia, permitting 100 per cent foreign ownership, tax holidays and full profit repatriation. In 1988 it began to attract a trickle of FDI, but it was not until after the reforms of 1989, and most notably the upsurge of Western development assistance in 1992, that FDI levels began to grow very rapidly.[16] Soviet aid terminated from the beginning of 1991, causing total aid disbursements to halve in that year compared with 1990. In 1992 aid disbursements rose again, to $540 m. or more than double their 1990 level, while FDI inflows increased from $165 m. to $333 m. and reached $2,236 m. in 1995 (World Bank 1999a). These figures represent an annual average growth rate of 92 per cent in FDI. By 1995 foreign investment represented 32 per cent of all annual investment (GSO 2000: 226).

In the late 1980s when the FDI law was passed, few commentators expected the bonanza that would emerge a few years later. Vietnam was acknowledged to be a 'difficult' country for foreign investors. Even after the major reforms of 1989, the country suffered from poor infrastructure, a legacy of Soviet- and East European-trained managers and bureaucrats who lacked experience of market economies, a bureaucracy in which avenues of responsibility were unclear and a regulatory system which lacked transparency. Prospective investors were often tied up for years in red tape. Moreover, the rules did not allow foreign investors to raise capital locally.

The Vietnamese, on their part, bent over backwards to encourage investment. Whereas under central planning, generous Soviet aid had greatly enhanced the state's power over resource allocation, the sheer shortage of investible capital in the new situation correspondingly reduced this power. Much of the former coherence of the development strategy had been lost in the process of transformation. Targeted areas of export income, technology transfer, processing of local raw materials were therefore put on hold, while the investors who did come before 1992 concentrated their efforts in hotel and office block construction: only later did they turn to industry.[17] The State Committee for Co-operation and Investment (SCCI) was established, effectively bypassing the more conservative State Planning Committee which, up to that time, had been responsible for dealing with foreign aid and investment projects. Over the years, new regulations were introduced in an attempt to speed up the rate of project approval and to simplify the bureaucratic process by providing a 'one-stop shop' within the SCCI.[18]

Nevertheless, problems continued to occur. Investors with approval from the central authorities might have difficulty getting it from provincial authorities or vice versa. Many early investors disliked the system of state ownership of land which they felt provided insecure tenure. Joint venture with state-owned enterprises became the preferred option of the overwhelming majority of investors, largely because well-connected SOE directors could open doors while SOEs benefited more than the Vietnamese private sector from access to land, credit and protection from international competition. Moreover, the Vietnamese state also favoured joint ventures as one of the principal means of achieving technology transfer to SOEs and improving their capital base. For foreigners, there were disadvantages to the joint-venture model: while SOEs generally could provide a capital contribution only in the form of land (usually deemed to be equivalent to 30 per cent of the total capital), they were given a veto over major decisions of the enterprise. By the mid-1990s, many joint ventures were starting to break up because the two parties could not get along with each other, often due to differences in management style and objectives. The numbers of wholly foreign-owned enterprises began to increase rapidly. A by-product of the uncertain investment climate was that projects remained small: at the end of 1995, the average value of capital commitments was only US$12 million (GSO 1998: 242). Moreover, projects were very heavily concentrated in the two relatively 'safe' urban agglomerations around Ho Chi Minh City and Hanoi-Haiphong.[19] There is little doubt that such a high concentration contributed substantially to the sharp widening of urban–rural income differentials during the 1990s (Beresford: 2003).

The boom and its end

Despite all these difficulties, FDI increased at a dramatic rate after 1992 and, as noted above, accounted for 32 per cent of gross capital formation by 1995. If we compare Vietnam with other countries in the region (Table 3.4), it becomes clear that, despite its difficulties, FDI represented an extraordinarily high proportion of capital formation by Asian standards. In the region, only Singapore and Malaysia have come anywhere near this figure in recent years and not one country has relied to such an extent on foreign investment in the early stage of its development. The very high share of FDI in Vietnam during the mid-1990s is therefore quite surprising.

Moreover, in comparison with countries at a similar level of development, the level of foreign investment in Vietnam was also unusually high (Table 3.5). During these years, much to the surprise of those with a more sober assessment of realities, the newspapers (especially the English-language *Vietnam Investment Review*) were full of reports of enthusiastic Asian investors describing Vietnam as 'the last frontier' and 'a mountain of treasures waiting to be exploited'. The language of these reports itself hints that investment in Vietnam was indeed a side-effect of the developing Asian bubble economy. Over-investment in other regional economies shifted attention to 'green field' sites such as Vietnam and, in the face of greater competitive pressures, investors were prepared to cast aside rational evaluation in

Table 3.4: FDI as a share of gross capital formation (%)

	1971–75	**1991–93**
East Asia		
S Korea	1.9	0.6
Taiwan	1.4	2.6
Hong Kong	5.9	5.7
China	0.0	10.4
Southeast Asia		
Singapore	15.0	37.4
Malaysia	15.2	24.6
Thailand	3.0	4.7
Indonesia	4.6	4.5
Philippines	1.0	4.6

Source: Jomo K.S. *et al.* 1997: 14

Table 3.5: FDI per capita in some low-income countries (1996)

	GDP per capita (PPP $)	**FDI per capita ($)**
Pakistan	1590	5.0
Ivory Coast	1640	1.4
India	1650	2.7
Vietnam	1670	19.5
Senegal	1670	5.0
Ghana	1790	6.7
Guinea	1850	3.4

Source: World Bank 1999c.

order to climb on the bandwagon. The more important thing was to be in on the boom, to grab market share before one's competitors could. The parallels with the speculative booms which have characterised bubble economies since capitalism began could not be more evident.

For Vietnam, the crash certainly came in 1998. FDI inflows fell in that year by more than half from their levels of the previous year (from just over US$2 billion to US$800 million) and fell further in 1999. For the year 2000, despite renewed growth in the economy, the inflow was still only US$800 million (World Bank 2002a: Table 3.1) and, compared with the figure in Table 3.5, per capita FDI had fallen to US$10.3. This sharp decline reduced overall investment from 29 per cent of GDP in 1997 to just 19 per cent in 1999 (World Bank 1999a) and accounts for a large part of the falling GDP growth rate in those two years. However, this fall was not simply a result of the meltdown in the rest of Asia. After the initial bandwagon effect of the early 1990s, a slowdown in new FDI commitments had become apparent as early as 1996,[20] a year or more before the July 1997 events in Thailand. As new commitments continued to fall throughout the second half of the 1990s, disbursements were also bound to fall. By 1999, project commitments had fallen well below their 1992 level and were only 18 per cent of their 1996 level (GSO 2000: 246).

Thus while the difficulties building up within the regional economy were more than likely the major cause for the extraordinarily high levels of FDI entering Vietnam between 1992 and 1995, the rather slow deflation of the bubble came sooner in Vietnam than elsewhere. We therefore have an indication that the Asian crisis itself is not the only cause of the slowdown Vietnam has experienced since 1998. Moreover, although it is still too early to say whether the recent recovery of the other regional economies is based on more solid foundations than before, we would not expect the levels of FDI in Vietnam to recover their previous levels in the near future. We need to look further afield, not only to the external factors influencing commitments of foreign investment but at the economic and institutional structure of the Vietnamese market economy. What are those domestic factors which both led to the early deflation of the bubble and, in the absence of the bubble, would probably have kept Vietnamese growth rates at less exciting levels than those experienced in the 1990s? To answer this question we need to examine the influences on development of the transitional character of the Vietnamese economy.

A STATE-LED MARKET ECONOMY?

Institutional change in the enterprise sector: policy and reality

The Communist Party leadership decided at the Sixth Party Congress that Vietnam would pursue the path of a socialist market-orientated economy under state guidance. Since the former system of central planning had largely disappeared, if not by that time then certainly by 1989, the state-owned enterprise (SOE) sector became the principal means by which state guidance was to be achieved. Indeed, SOEs now represent the only actually remaining plank of the traditional socialist model – public ownership of the major means of production. Holding the 'commanding heights' of the economy is seen as the principal means by which the state, as representative of the whole society, can exercise its leading role. Through the SOE system, the state can develop productive capacity in industries which it considers crucial to the long-term development of the national economy – electronics, metallurgy, fuel and power, machinery and petrochemicals – and in less developed regions of the country (Phan Van Tiem and Nguyen Van Thanh 1996: 4–5; Hoang Cong Thi 1992: 3). Telecommunications is another industry which has been added to the list more recently. The sector also remains to this day the largest contributor to GDP. Relations between the state sector and the emerging private sector are therefore a key element in the development of the domestic economy.

The attitude of the regime towards the state sector is conditioned by the goal of creating a public sector which is a primary locus of accumulation. While private sector activity is encouraged in order to tap its potential, it has in practice had to take the back seat. Moreover, the transition process created a blurring of the distinction between public and private property, in which individuals and groups have increasingly gained 'use rights' over state and collective assets, and this has so far assisted the state to keep the non-state sector in a subordinate position. Not only has much capital accumulation in the non-state sector been in some way dependent upon access to resources available in the state sector[21] but large parts of the non-state sector have grown up in leasing, supply or subcontracting arrangements with state enterprises and are therefore vulnerable to fluctuations in activity within the state sector. These kind of relations between dominant firms and small suppliers and subcontractors are quite normal in the global market economy (Borrus *et al.* 2000; Gereffi and Korzeniewicz 1994). The major difference here is that the dominant firms tend to be in the state sector. This point is something that tends to be overlooked in the discourse of Western transition economics with its largely ideological focus on a state–private dichotomy.

In principle, the main advantage of shifting to a market economy is the benefit that can be derived from competition, specifically the impetus that competition imparts to technological progress and productivity growth. By producing more efficiently, firms can increase their profitability and thereby the pace of accumulation. Transition to a market economy increases the ability of firms to adjust input and output to meet changes in demand, to reduce waste of inputs and labour, and to make competitively driven decisions to invest in new plant and equipment, raising the potential of both SOEs and others to create a more dynamic economy.

For the Vietnamese SOEs, however, it has proven difficult to take advantage of the more competitive environment brought about by marketisation. It has been especially difficult for them to compete against imports from East Asia (including goods smuggled from China) which flooded into the country following liberalisation of the trade regime at the end of the 1980s. The reasons for these difficulties lie largely in the legacies of the socialist model of earlier years, and it is recognition of this legacy that has led to the ongoing protectiveness towards SOEs which is the butt of so much Western criticism.

SOEs have been faced with some formidable obstacles on the road to international competitiveness – particularly in upgrading of technology to raise productivity. At the beginning of the 1990s, the majority of enterprises were small in size and had much obsolescent and incompatible equipment. Some 92 per cent had 'self-financed capital' of less than US$1 million, 46 per cent had less than 100 workers and 89 per cent less than 500 (Nguyen Ngoc Tuan *et al.* 1996: 23). Most equipment remained obsolete: only 18 per cent having been able to invest in any new technology between 1986 and 1995. A study of 48 northern region SOEs carried out by the present author in 1992 indicated a strong relationship between the date of establishment of the SOE and the age of machinery and equipment. In fact much of the equipment had been purchased *second-hand* at the time of establishment (Beresford 1992). Only 25 per cent of SOEs could be described as having integrated plant and equipment (not necessarily modern), while others suffered from incompatibility of machinery purchased from a variety of suppliers in the Soviet Union and Eastern Europe (Nguyen Ngoc Tuan *et al.* 1996: 24–25).

Moreover, at the beginning of the 1990s, SOEs were caught in a vice: on the one hand the legacy of the planning system and underdevelopment had left them with insufficient capital to operate effectively, let alone modernise their equipment, while on the other hand, the progressive hardening of budget constraints after 1989 made it increasingly difficult to raise this much needed capital. As increasing enterprise autonomy widened the range of use rights over state assets, many SOEs therefore resorted to activities outside those for which they were registered, particularly activities offering quick returns in trade, renting out land or constructing hotels. In many cases, it is these businesses which have enabled the enterprises to remain afloat and to bolster the incomes of employees (both managers and workers). However, the process has also often involved neglect of their official business, so that quite a few SOEs are in effect 'shell' companies while the incomes from their 'sideline' activities effectively go into private hands. One indication of the extent of private capital accumulation inside SOEs is the fact that in 56 per cent of equitised firms, employees were able to buy a majority of shares (World Bank 1999a).[22]

Patterns of investment and capital accumulation

Despite these activities and their nominally large share in the economy (over 40 per cent of GDP) (GSO 2001: 23), investment by SOEs has been relatively small. Table 3.6 shows that compared with domestic capitalist and foreign-invested firms, SOEs have undertaken a rather low rate of investment. Moreover, only a small proportion of government investment was capital invested in SOEs, mainly via credit (which is also largely of a short-term nature).[23]

Table 3.6: Investment shares 1991–99 (%)

	1991	1992	1993	1994	1995	1996	1997	1998	1999
(1) Share of GDP									
Gross Capital Formation	15.0	17.6	24.9	25.5	27.1	27.9	29.2	27.0	18.7
State investment	5.9	6.8	12.2	10.8	10.3	13.2	14.8	14.6	11.0
(2) Share of total investment									
Government investment					24.4	31.2	36.3	33.3	47.0
State budget					19.9	20.8	22.6	22.8	30.5
Credit					4.5	10.4	13.7	10.5	16.6
SOE investment					13.8	13.9	14.4	20.7	11.8
Domestic private investment					29.4	26.2	21.9	21.1	29.4
Foreign investment					32.3	28.6	28.4	25.0	11.8

Note: State, domestic private and foreign investment do not add to 100 per cent. The residual is mainly investment by household enterprises.

Sources: GSO 1997, 1998, 2000; World Bank 2000a.

Before the crisis therefore, total investment in SOEs amounted to probably not more than a fifth of all investment. Some of this took the form of creating new enterprises rather than modernising older ones. The capitalist sector, both domestic and foreign, undertook half of all investment in 1997, though it accounted for only 17 per cent of GDP.

Government policy was to merge small and medium-sized SOEs into larger groupings, known as general corporations (*tổng công ty*), suggesting an attempt to follow a South Korean-type strategy of building up a handful of large corporations having significant concentrations of capital to carry out the investment necessary for modernisation.[24] According to one source, the corporations should receive government support for about a decade, during which time they would be expected to become internationally competitive, followed by partial privatisation in order to enable them to expand their capital base.[25] Partial privatisation of some non-core operations could also occur earlier, as has already happened in a number of cases. However, the formation of the corporations also meant that they would have to subsidise loss-making member enterprises, effectively diluting rather than concentrating capital. The most spectacular case of bailing out a loss-making enterprise to date was the rescue launched by the textile corporation (Vinatex) of the Nam Dinh textile mill which, by 1996, had accumulated debts of around $50 million, largely arising from its attempts to modernise its huge and rather ancient workshops.[26] The economy of Nam Dinh is heavily dependent on the mill, and its closure would have been a disaster for the whole town. Thus while some of the dynamism of the more effective member units may have been lost in the bail-out process, this case also reveals the determination of the government to soften the blow in order to maintain the support of its popular constituency.

In practice, joint ventures with foreign companies have been the principal means by which SOEs have been able to raise sufficient capital to achieve the sort of modernisation which would enable them to become competitive. Nevertheless, the total number of FDI industrial projects, including 100 per cent foreign-owned, in 1998 was only 881, leaving over 1,800 SOEs to manage on their own. Joint ventures have been most common in lower value-added areas such as production and assembly of consumer goods for the domestic market, labour-intensive exports as well as primary resource extraction (mainly oil) but have had relatively little impact on the more sophisticated, high value-added industries like engineering and petrochemicals which the government would like to develop.[27]

While official development assistance (ODA) under bilateral agreements with advanced industrial country governments has flowed into the country since 1993, it has been primarily to finance infrastructure and provide institutional support for market-orientated activities. Western aid donors are not interested in providing capital to modernise the state-owned industrial sector. Moreover, unlike South Korea, during its rapid industrialisation phase, the Vietnamese government is not in a strong position to use the domestic banking system to finance the sort of large-scale industrial corporations it envisages (cf Amsden 1989). The effect of heavy reliance on joint ventures with foreigners has therefore been at least partly to tie the fortunes of the SOE sector to flows of private international capital.[28]

A further strategy adopted by the government for raising capital for the SOE sector is 'equitisation'. Rather than wholesale privatisation, the government opted in 1992 for partial privatisation, selling shares in SOEs to managers, workers and other Vietnamese nationals, but retaining a controlling share itself in many enterprises. At first, equitisation proceeded very slowly and, while the rate increased towards the end of the 1990s, only a small proportion of the total number of SOEs had been equitised by the end of the decade.[29] Of these only 14 per cent had majority shareholdings by outside investors, while in 56 per cent of cases the majority of shares were held by employees.[30] However, in over a third of all cases, the state retained a sufficiently large shareholding (more than 35 per cent) that it would be likely to have a controlling interest in the equitised firm (World Bank 1999a; 2000c). In relation to the 'insider' equitised firms, an area needing further research is the influence of hitherto close relations between enterprise managers and their 'owning' authorities on future state–business relations. It is not yet clear if or how state influence will continue to be felt in these enterprises.

Access to the state banking system was the major means by which SOEs were able, after 1989, to avoid the full consequences of hardening budget constraints. Although in principle banks were supposed to lend on the basis of commercial criteria, there were few possibilities in practice for them to do this. Not only were standardised accounting practices absent, leading to a prevalent view among the banks that SOEs were less risky because more likely to be bailed out by the government, but banks were pressured into lending on favourable terms to politically supported enterprises. There were, however, both a reluctance of banks to give long-term loans, due to low, government-imposed interest rates, and an inability by SOEs to consider long-term investments because of a shortage of working capital. Strong demand from SOEs for short-term loans to cover working capital resulted in the build up of high levels of indebtedness and, despite increases in bank deposits, low levels of bank liquidity. In late 1996 the government made an attempt to restrict debt levels of SOEs by preventing them from borrowing an amount higher than their legal capital. Pressure from both the enterprises, which claimed they would need to severely limit production, and the banks, which were threatened with widespread defaults, led to a suspension of the decision (*TBKT* 22.1.97). As at the end of 1997, 1,989 'poorly performing' SOEs, employing 583,000 workers had debt levels reaching 42.5 trillion dong, equivalent to 82 per cent of their invested capital (World Bank 1999a).

SOE performance and its implications for the state-led development strategy

Despite these difficulties, there were some indicators that state enterprises were becoming more efficient. Real gross output per worker more than doubled between 1990 and 1995, the sharpest increases (26 per cent p.a.) occurring during 1990–92, as the sector underwent labour shedding and increased its rate of capacity utilisation. After that the increase was more sedate, averaging 11 per cent p.a. in 1993–95 and 6 per cent p.a. in 1996–97 (Beresford 2000).[31] Incremental capital–output ratios of industrial SOEs also showed a marked improvement during the shakeout of 1991–92, when the net increase in capacity fell and sharp increases in output were recorded, although they have risen again since 1993. Nevertheless for every 100 dong worth of new capacity created, output rose by 117 dong in 1995–96 compared with 83 dong in 1990 (Beresford 2000).

Few data are available on the export performance of the SOE sector that might serve as indicators of competitiveness. One source suggested that 'a mere 15 per cent of the output from Vietnam's SOEs is suitable for export' (Nguyen Ngoc Tuan *et al.* 1996: 27). By contrast, a survey of domestic capitalist firms reported that 82 per cent of them had exports as their main source of revenue (MPDF 1999: 38), although they accounted for only 10 per cent of manufacturing output (compared with 54 per cent for the SOE sector). Yet during 1999 the state sector accounted for 57 per cent of the total number of exporting firms (World Bank 1999a). A proportion of these, however, are engaged in proxy trading on behalf of other firms or in subcontracting production to the non-state sector. Others are involved in primary production (e.g., Petrovietnam, Vinacafe) and since such goods form a high proportion of total exports, a reasonable presumption is that industrial SOEs are not very export-orientated. There are some exceptions however. Garment exports are dominated by SOEs and joint ventures between foreign investors and state enterprises (Tran, Chapter 5 this volume).[32] The high export volume of this sector can possibly be accounted for by the low technology transfer requirements and high labour intensity, as well as learning by doing, enabling more rapid improvements in quality and productivity than in other SOEs.

Given that the state sector companies, including trading companies, still dominate international trade, subcontracting by SOEs to private concerns is one of the means by which the export income of the state sector is boosted. From the SOE point of view, subcontracting can have the advantage that, where enterprises are faced with hardening budget constraints, as happened for example during the fiscal squeeze in China during 1989, small companies can be peremptorily dropped and production activities and workforces consolidated within the enterprise itself (Hannan 1995: 97). Even if the state enterprises themselves are not highly profitable, the relations of dependency thus established ensure that they are in a stronger position to survive than the private sector.

The protective attitude of the government towards state enterprises shows up in several areas in which there are significant policy-induced barriers to entry for privately owned firms: registration procedures,[33] export–import quotas (Tran, Chapter 5 this volume) and deferment of debt payments. The creation of general corporations, in which loss-making enterprises were incorporated together with more profitable ones, was another means by which the state avoided a wholesale weeding out of the SOE sector. Enterprises are also able to rent out those areas of their generally extensive and often prime inner-city factory sites. Indeed in some cases access to this rent may be the only thing keeping them solvent. Protectionism in trade policy does not explicitly discriminate in favour of the state-owned sector, but since most Vietnamese industrial capacity remains within that sector, it has the effect of permitting inefficient state-sector producers to remain in business.

However, despite the protection currently afforded to SOEs, there are strong indications that, in some areas of policy, the government also takes very seriously the goal of maintaining the liberalisation process. Vietnam, by joining ASEAN in 1995, signalled its commitment to the creation of an ASEAN Free Trade Area, in 1999 it joined APEC and has expressed its desire to join the WTO, both organisations committed to liberalisation of international trade. Post-crisis, moreover, a July 1998 reform freed up trading rights for non-state companies, resulting in a large drop in the share of SOEs in the total number of exporting firms, from 70 per cent to 57 per cent (World

Bank 1999a). Thus it seems that over the medium term liberalisation measures are likely to intensify the pressure on SOEs.

Subsidisation and protection of firms can be justified on socio-economic development grounds and has been extensively and successfully used elsewhere in East and Southeast Asia. However, while an accelerated pace of equitisation of smaller SOEs and foreign-invested joint ventures have given some of them much needed capital injections, the prospects for modernisation of the majority through investment in new technologies remain weak. A danger attending this gradual process of restructuring is therefore that international competitiveness will not arrive soon enough to counter the impacts of increasing liberalisation of the foreign trade regime. There has already been large-scale import penetration of the domestic market for both consumer goods and means of production such that in 1996 the trade deficit rose to 17 per cent of GDP (World Bank 1999a),[34] though the gap was reined in again by 1998 (5.6 per cent) as growth and imports slowed. If Vietnamese firms continue to require subsidies in the longer run, there is, therefore, a high risk of incurring external debt to finance both the internal and external deficits, the servicing of which may slow growth significantly in future. Given the party and government's commitment to promoting SOE-led growth, it is important that measures to increase cost effectiveness and genuine profitability within the sector are maintained. However, the liberalisation measures will not aid this process without a substantially larger commitment of investment.

Further, while enterprise restructuring proceeds at a slow pace, the rest of the population suffer. It is well known that corruption and other rent-seeking activities increased as a result of the marketisation of the economy, and there is some evidence that a significant part of the benefits of state protection of SOEs is going straight into the pockets of managers, state bureaucrats and party officials. Such rents have often been used to provide additional income to state employees, thus saving the state budget from the trouble of paying higher wages, unemployment or redundancy monies. However, in other cases, the rents have been used for private capital accumulation and indeed to undermine the employment and working conditions of state workers. Some glaring instances of this kind of behaviour in the coal mines were discussed in the pages of *Lao Dong* newspaper (Greenfield 1999). A contradiction has thus emerged between the desire of the party and government to use state enterprises as a means to economic development and the siphoning off of rents for essentially private purposes.

The weak situation of SOEs at the start of the transition process can therefore be seen to have had important effects on the development of the market economy in Vietnam during the 1990s. Government has attempted to nurture the sector as a means of achieving its goals of 'state guidance' and there have certainly been some achievements in terms of improved performance. However, lack of investible capital has forced many SOEs into dependence on FDI as the main means of modernising their production processes. This reliance in turn rendered the state sector vulnerable to the development of the bubble economy in the rest of Asia.

The impact of vested interests inside the SOEs has also shown up in the patterns of accumulation within the sector and in its relations with the emerging private sector, much of which has grown up under the 'umbrella' of SOEs. While a considerable portion of the domestic private sector remains dependent on rents and contracts from the SOE sector, a question arising for the government is whether the patterns which have been observed amount to a case of the FDI and private sector 'tail' wagging the SOE 'dog'. In other words, has the Party's intention to use the state sector to achieve its development goals been undermined by the way in which this symbiosis between state and private sectors has emerged? Further, have the combined effects of 'bubble-driven' foreign investment, low rates of investment in SOEs and the resulting patterns of private sector accumulation not only limited the capacity for state-led development but also pushed the economy on to an unsustainable growth path?

SOURCES OF GROWTH IN THE 1990S AND BEYOND

Using the same method previously used to look at growth in the other Southeast Asian economies, it is possible to provide an approximate breakdown of the respective contributions of employment and productivity growth to growth of output in Vietnam during the 1990s (Table 3.7). The data in Table 3.7 show that for GDP as a whole, the contribution of expanding employment was quite large. This was particularly the case in agriculture and, later on, in services, whereas for the industrial sector (including mining, manufacturing and public utilities) employment grew slowly and unevenly and the impact of productivity growth was much greater.

Employment and the productivity of labour

As noted above, in relation to SOEs, a major source of productivity growth in the early 1990s was improvements in efficiency brought about by the

Table 3.7: Sources of growth 1991–97 (% p.a.)

	1991	**1992**	**1993**	**1994**	**1995**	**1996**	**1997**
Total							
GDP	6.0	8.6	8.1	8.8	9.5	9.3	8.2
Labour force	2.3	2.7	2.8	2.9	2.7	3.5	3.6
Productivity	3.7	5.9	5.3	5.9	6.8	5.8	4.6
Industry and construction							
GDP	9.0	14.0	13.1	14.0	13.6	14.5	12.6
Labour force	0.1	1.4	2.2	4.7	0.2	1.0	0.9
Productivity	8.9	12.6	10.9	9.3	13.4	13.5	11.7
Agriculture							
GDP	2.2	7.1	3.8	3.9	4.4	4.4	4.7
Labour force	2.7	3.2	3.0	2.6	–1.6	2.7	2.7
Productivity	–0.5	3.9	0.8	1.3	6.0	1.6	2.0
Services							
GDP	8.3	7.0	9.2	10.2	10.2	8.8	7.1
Labour force	2.2	1.3	2.7	2.9	6.1	8.5	8.3
Productivity	6.1	5.7	6.5	7.3	4.1	0.3	–1.2

Sources: World Bank 1999a, GSO 1995, 1997.

shedding of labour, reorganisation of production and better incentives in the wake of the 1989 price reform. The numbers employed in the state sector as a whole fell by nearly a third, from 3.8 million in 1989 to 2.9 million in 1993, while numbers in state industry fell from 905,000 to 687,000 over the same period.[35] Labour shedding in the co-operative industrial sector was even greater. At the same time official unemployment data rose to around 13 per cent, though by 1995 it had fallen again to 6 per cent. A majority of the unemployed are now school leavers who, in the old system, would have been absorbed into the state and co-operative sectors. Large numbers of former state and co-operative sector workers eventually found work in the household economy, setting up micro-enterprises or working in the so-called informal sector (ILO 1994; Abrami and Henaff, Chapter 4 this volume).

The growth of this type of employment was phenomenal: the official data record that in the industrial sector alone, the number of non-state enterprises rose from 374,837 in 1992 (including 5,723 co-operatives and 1,114 capitalist companies) to 623,710 in 1996 (GSO 1994, 1997). As of mid-1995, these enterprises employed 2.5 million people (MOLISA 1998: 102). An ILO survey in 1994 indicated that workers in the micro-enterprises had often gained both skills and capital through working in SOEs (ILO 1994).

After the initial shake-out of the state and co-operative sector, employment growth has occurred mainly in the household sector. While employment growth in SOEs has resumed since 1992, and that in private domestic and foreign-invested firms has also increased, these three together still employed only a small percentage of the workforce. The state sector, the largest of these, employed only 9 per cent of the total workforce (3.4 million) in 1998, of whom 842,500 were in industry (GSO 1999). Domestic capitalist companies employed around 320,000 in manufacturing and nearly one million in total.[36] Foreign-invested companies also reportedly employed 300,000 (World Bank 1999a). Yet the state sector accounted for 49 per cent of GDP (54 per cent in manufacturing), while the foreign-invested and domestic capitalist sectors together accounted for 17 per cent of GDP (28 per cent in manufacturing). The numerically large household sector, including farmers, accounted for 34 per cent of total GDP and 18 per cent in manufacturing.

It is not hard to work out from the above figures that, at least in manufacturing, labour productivity is much higher in the SOE and foreign and domestic capitalist sectors than it is in the household sector.[37] From the point of view of sustaining rapid long-term growth, this is a highly unsatisfactory situation as it shows that the growth rates of the pre-crisis period depended very largely on precisely those sectors which are now most severely affected.

Micro-enterprises, while clearly providing the majority of employment growth are seriously constrained when it comes to productivity growth. First, they have low capital inputs, a situation which is exacerbated in the Vietnamese situation by the collateral-dependence of the banking system and their consequent lack of access to credit. Second, Vietnamese agriculture, which employs around 70 per cent of the workforce, suffers from widespread under-employment which both reduces average labour productivity and limits income growth for farmers. In a situation where both further expansion of the cultivated area and raising productivity are difficult, increasing off-farm employment will need to be found for large numbers. Third, public expenditure cuts during the reform period have also increased the workload of households, especially women and children, in unpaid reproductive work such as health care and child care.[38] Very long hours of work in the household sector may also contribute to low productivity in income-earning activities.

It comes as no surprise then that in the 1990s economic growth has been concentrated in the urban agglomerations around Ho Chi Minh City, Hanoi, Haiphong-Quang Ninh and Da Nang, where most SOEs and foreign-invested enterprises are located. The eight provinces which contain these agglomerations have all grown at above average rates and have above average per capita GDP. With some notable exceptions, the majority of poor rural provinces have grown much more slowly and are therefore being steadily left behind. While there has been some attempt at fiscal redistribution to the poorest provinces, the rich high-growth provinces have also been able to maintain higher per capita levels of government expenditure (Beresford: 2003). The danger here is of creating urban enclave economies with few linkages to the hinterland and exposing future economic growth to the constraints of a narrow domestic market and low capacity for dynamic human resource development, as happened in several other Southeast Asian economies.

The contribution of investment

Based on the analysis so far, we can say that the principal sources of growth in the years prior to the Asian crisis were as follows:

- a once-off effect of labour shedding and improved organisation and management in SOEs;
- rapid growth of foreign investment, together with expanding investment by SOEs and the domestic capitalist sector, leading to rather high productivity growth in those sectors;
- rapid employment growth in the household sector, combined with low productivity growth.

Putting these three together, it is probably safe to conclude that the largest impact, accounting for the very high rates of growth from 1992–97, was from foreign investment, both in its direct impact on manufacturing productivity and indirectly through supplying new technology to the SOE sector. Falling employment growth in industry and construction is noticeable in Table 3.7 during 1996–97 as foreign investment began to decline and the construction boom ended. Slowing FDI fed through to industrial productivity growth by 1997, while a sharp decline in growth of productivity in the service sector (where a large amount of foreign investment was concentrated) is also noticeable. Because of the large share of industry and services in total output, the effects flowed through to GDP as a whole. The 'tail' did indeed 'wag the dog'.

Looking back at the data on investment rates in Table 3.6 we can see that whereas total investment had fallen from nearly 30 per cent of GDP in 1997 to just 19 per cent in 1999, the fall was largely due to the sharp decline in FDI and, to a lesser extent, SOE investment. A shift to domestic sources of investment, in both SOEs and the private sector companies, will thus be needed if lower GDP growth rates are to be avoided in the future.[39] Moreover, increased public investment is likely to have beneficial effects: not only infrastructure investment (including social infrastructure such as education and health for human development) but investment in SOEs, given their position in the public–private networks, is also likely to have 'crowding in' effects on the growth of investment overall.

If, as argued earlier, FDI is fairly unlikely to recover to its former levels, what will be the sources of growth in future? How can Vietnam resume high rates of growth and rising living standards if it is forced to rely more on domestic investment, particularly in manufacturing with its capacity to generate productivity increases?

Building a more diversified export economy

One way of achieving this result is greater export orientation of industry. Export income is important because it enables higher levels of imports of capital equipment embodying new technologies and involves less reliance on capital inflows to generate such imports. It must be said that a major impact of the Vietnamese economic reforms was a dramatic improvement in export performance. From 1990 to 1996 exports grew at an average annual rate of 27 per cent, tending to accelerate towards the end of the period. Having accounted for 26.4 per cent of GDP in 1990 exports had risen to 43.6 per cent in 1997. In 1998 export growth fell to only 2 per cent as the Asian crisis bit (World Bank 1999a). However, the recovery was rapid – exports rose by 23 per cent in 1999 and, in the first eight months of 2000 had increased by 27 per cent over the same period in the previous year, partly due to rising world oil prices (World Bank 2000b: 3). Garment and footwear exports also recovered particularly fast, mainly due to an increase in footwear orders from Europe during 1999 that, however, did not recur in 2000.

On the less encouraging side, just four categories of goods – crude oil, seafood, garments and footwear – now account for no less than 53 per cent of total exports (World Bank 1999a), demonstrating Vietnam's continued vulnerability to fluctuations in demand for just a handful of commodities. Indeed wearing apparel is the only significant category of manufactured exports for

Vietnam (see Tran, Chapter 5 this volume). In the mid-1990s, 57 per cent of exports comprised unprocessed and semi-processed primary products (Beresford and Dang 2000: 60–61), leaving Vietnam very exposed to commodity price fluctuations. With such an open economy as Vietnam now is, such fluctuations can bring large shocks as happened in 1998. Indeed in 2001 exports were estimated to have grown at only 7 per cent, with a further slowdown in 2002. All the growth was accounted for by large increases in volume (particularly of coffee and pepper) to offset falling commodity prices (World Bank 2002a: 25, 34).

The limited diversification of exports to date also raises issues of environmental damage and social tensions which threaten long-term sustainability. In the central highlands, especially, where coffee production has undergone a massive expansion since Doi Moi, there has been extensive degradation of forest and soil as well as at times acute social disturbances over land distribution (see Bui Van Hung, Chapter 6 this volume). Not only has growth of Vietnamese coffee production been a major contributor to falling world prices,[40] but there also seems to be little room for further expansion without exacerbating these problems.

Diversification of exports, particularly diversification of manufactured exports, would therefore seem to be an important priority for the medium-term future. This becomes especially apparent in light of the experience of Vietnam's neighbours, both those who have remained reliant on the export of a few labour-intensive manufactures during the past three decades and those who succeeded in making the transition to higher value-added industries to gain dynamic comparative advantage. A strategy is needed to help create the flying geese pattern of export diversification referred to above. Liberalisation of the regulatory regime is insufficient to achieve this by itself. Indeed given the recent experience of private capital inflows and poor state capacity to influence their direction, further liberalisation seems unlikely to be the most helpful approach. The state needs to play a more active role in coordinating investment activities.

In the past FDI has not contributed a great deal to the increase of manufactured exports, largely because of the incentives to hook up with domestic market-orientated SOEs. Moreover, the difference between exports and imports by this sector accounted for a large and rising share of the trade deficit in the 1990s (Beresford and Dang 2000: 55).[41] However, if SOEs are encouraged to become more export-orientated, then foreign investors are also likely to become more export-inclined. Until now, however, it has been the domestic capitalist sector which has shown greater inclination to produce exportable goods. The vast majority of these firms had foreign markets as their main source of revenue, although a very high proportion (41 per cent) were producing garments, and the median percentage of imported inputs was as high as 70 per cent (MPDF 1999: 38, 40), showing a low level of linkages to the domestic economy. The authors of the study cited were also surprised to find a very low level of domestic market penetration by these domestic capitalist firms and suggested the possible causes were 'crowding out' by SOEs and competition from cheaper Chinese imports (MPDF 1999: 39).

As noted above, however, many of these firms are in subcontracting arrangements with SOEs. Improved health of the SOE sector is likely not only to increase opportunities for export diversification among private firms but to increase the ability of exporting firms to establish backward linkages to domestic suppliers. Moreover, Tran (Chapter 5 this volume) has shown that, after the initial influx of cheap Chinese imports, domestic market penetration by textile and garment firms has in fact increased in recent years. SOEs and private firms need not be seen as in competition with each other (as in the neo-classical transition economics framework). Instead the emerging pattern is one in which private and state firms are linked by production and investment networks. Investing in better performing SOEs is therefore likely to expand these networks and create more, not fewer, opportunities for private sector SME employment. Experience elsewhere in Asia, notably in Taiwan, has shown that a combination of SOE dominance of upstream industries supplying inputs to small, highly flexible export-orientated private producers is a model that works well from a development perspective.[42] It can encourage the development of more domestic linkages, including the all-important rural diversification which will lead to a more equitable and sustainable development process (Bui Van Hung, Chapter 6 this volume). Additionally, instead of relying on powerful global networks to supply inputs and contracts, the development of domestic networks involving both state and private firms can increase the value added accruing to domestic producers, give them more flexibility in responding to new export demands and enable them to create the 'flying geese' pattern of industrial deepening.

CONCLUSION

During the course of the Asian economic crisis, Vietnam has benefited from its relative insulation from global capital flows. As so often happens, however, the external shock has exposed some inherent weaknesses in the country's economic structure and institutions, many of which can be seen as legacies of the old centrally planned system. In particular, I have argued in this chapter that the very high growth rates experienced during the first part of the 1990s were mainly the result of the developing bubble economy in the region. Despite its large size, the state enterprise sector was saddled with mostly obsolete equipment and has shown relatively low rates of investment, meaning that it was incapable of imparting a dynamic impetus to the economy as a whole. After 1992 that impetus came primarily from foreign investment so that, in the absence of the bubble, the rate of growth of employment would have been the principal determinant of the rate of growth of GDP (growth would have been 'extensive' rather than 'intensive). In other words, growth would have been much slower and the party's commitment to catch up to its more prosperous neighbours would have been a hollow one.

Moreover, over-dependence on FDI has, in terms of the party's stated objective of creating a market economy under state guidance, led to a situation of the 'FDI tail wagging the SOE dog'. Not only has it rendered the whole economy more vulnerable to the volatility of international capital flows but indiscriminate acceptance of FDI has helped to create an economic structure which is unsustainable in the long term – a combination of high rural–urban inequality, lack of investment in export diversification projects, over-emphasis on hotel and property development.

This rise in vulnerability is related to and reinforces the loss of coherence within the state apparatus. As centres of capital accumulation outside the state have expanded (whether foreign, private-domestic or quasi-private) there have also arisen vested interests capable of influencing state actions on their behalf and affecting both the cohesion of the party's vision of 'socialism' and its ability to influence the direction of development. As noted in the introductory section, however, confusion is not necessarily a bad thing. Dang Phong argued in Chapter 2 that the Vietnamese state has a long history of flexibly adapting to changing circumstances. In many cases, this adaptation has been forced by external shocks bringing to maturity the contradictions inherent in the existing set of state-society relations. In the past, the capacity and coherence of the Vietnamese state has derived from its broad-based legitimacy among the population. During the transition, it has largely been able to manoeuvre to maintain this legitimacy, and it has again begun to do so in light of the reduction in FDI inflows since 1998.

In the wake of the crisis, it seems unlikely that foreign investment will recover to its previous levels. Particularly if the restructuring of the other Asian economies leads to expansion of more profitable investment opportunities at home, the attraction of Vietnam will be less. Thus if Vietnam is to resume the sorts of growth rates that it experienced earlier, it is imperative that it gets its own house in order. That means raising the rate of domestic investment and, in particular, increasing investment in the SOE sector, a process which will itself remove many of the current obstacles to development of the non-state sector.

Under pressure from Western aid donors, the continuing reform of the SOE sector is in some ways misguided. Instead of focusing on pushing more investment funds and new technology into a very cash-strapped sector, the state has largely left the SOEs to their own devices and equitisation has proceeded too slowly to be able to make much difference. Reform has concentrated on removing institutional obstacles to private sector growth (creating a 'level playing field'). However, because they are based on the false assumption that state and private sectors are always in competition with each other, such reforms can work against development in two ways.

First, SOEs are hampered, despite their obviously improving performance, in becoming the 'leaders' of the development process that the party-state wants them to become. Managers, faced with limited opportunities to expand their legitimate business, have diverted capital to 'sideline' businesses independently of government priorities. While such quasi-private initiatives are not necessarily detrimental to long-term income growth and could be encouraged in so far as they help to develop productive linkages and employment, many have been of a primarily rent-seeking nature. Promotion of state-sector investment needs, therefore, to be accompanied by financial discipline, greater transparency and continuing pressure to become export competitive. South Korea and Singapore have both provided good examples of state capacity to combine both nurture and discipline of firms in ways that promote their long-term development, not only technologically but also in generating employment and enhancement of skills.

Second, in the absence of new technologies supplied by FDI, the relatively slow development of SOEs limits the expansion of the production and investment networks which have so far been one of the mainstays of growth. The continued existence of rent-seeking behaviour in the state (and its joint ventures) also creates massive inequalities, especially along the urban–rural divide, which slow the rate of growth of the rural economy, constrain rural diversification and prevent the continuous upgrading of human capabilities that are essential to maintain the dynamism of economic development.

I have suggested that one way out of the difficulty that the state sector currently finds itself in is to pursue a strategy of export diversification. Without the high capital inflows of the past, increased export income is vital for Vietnam's ability to invest in upgraded technology. But the sources of export income need to become much more diversified than they now are if the country is to create dynamic competitive advantage and avoid the South-east Asian problem of over-investment in low value-added, low-skilled industries. Creating the institutional bases for export diversification will involve a deliberate, interventionist strategy to develop more linkages between firms currently producing for the domestic market and those producing for export, particularly by extending production and investment networks into the rural hinterland. An expanding and healthy domestic market can render domestic export-oriented firms less vulnerable to external shocks like recession and/or protection in other countries. It can afford firms the benefits of learning by doing, economies of scale and upgrading of workforce skills which ultimately enable them to become internationally competitive. And it can provide the possibility of sustainable and *equitable* development which the Vietnamese Communist Party avowedly pursues.

NOTES

1 The renewed growth shown for 2000 in Table 3.1 in fact stalled again in 2001 under the impact of the spread of recession to the rest of the globe and is predicted to be only moderately improved in 2002 (World Bank 2002a: 22). In the context of global recession, however, these rates remain rather high.

2 The gap has always existed. Even in the heyday of central planning in Vietnam, considerable areas of economic life remained relatively immune from its influence (see Dang Phong, Chapter 2, this volume). However, since the early 1980s, this gap has widened considerably and, for many, evasion of state regulations has become a way of life.

3 These of course are scarcely unique to Asia.

4 See Felipe (1999) for a critical review of Krugman and other studies of total factor productivity in Asia such as those by Alwyn Young and Kim and Lau.

5 Note, however, that this type of analysis predicted a slowdown in growth rather than the meltdown which actually occurred.

6 Actually the Krugman-type argument based on growth of total factor productivity has little credibility. In this type of neo-classical analysis, productivity growth is a residual which miraculously appears from nowhere after the contributions of labour and capital to output have been deducted. What this factor in neo-classical theory most probably measures in the case of late industrialisers is something akin to Kalecki's 'u' factor in which increases in output occur due to less tangible improvements in organisation, elimination of waste, etc. (Kalecki 1972: 11). Under these circumstances a better measure of productivity growth is derived from Kalecki's own equation $1 + r = (1 + a)(1 + n) = 1 + a + n + an$ (where r is the rate of growth of output, n is the rate of growth of employment and a is the rate of growth in productivity of labour). Disregarding the product an in the equation, since it is likely to be insignificant, we have the approximate equation $r = a + n$ or $a = r - n$ (Kalecki 1972: 24).

7 The major exceptions were Singapore – which had early in the 1980s attempted to trigger a 'Second Industrial Revolution' and make the shift to more high-tech, high-value-added goods – and Indonesia which had waited until the mid-1980s and the end of its oil boom to begin its labour-intensive export-oriented manufacturing.

8 By the end of 1995 bank claims maturing within one year made up 70 per cent of the total for Korea, 69.4 per cent for Thailand, 61.9 per cent for Indonesia and 47.2 per cent for Malaysia (Singh and Weisse 1999: 211)

9 Electronic products accounted for a quarter of Thai exports and half of Singaporean exports. Semiconductors alone accounted for 10 per cent of exports in Singapore and Malaysia (BIS 1997: 40).

10 Net capital flows to developing countries in the East Asia and Pacific region rose from US$13.1 bn in 1980 to US$27.8 bn in 1990 and US$95.9 bn in 1995 (Singh and Zammit 2000: 1251). Thus, while they doubled in the decade 1980–90, they more than trebled in the next five years (while the total for all developing countries rose by 135 per cent). According to IMF data (Singh and Weisse 1999: 210), no less than $80.9 bn, or 84 per cent of the 1995 total, went to just five countries: Malaysia, Indonesia, Thailand, South Korea and the Philippines. Moreover, many of these inflows were subject to what Lauridsen terms 'currency mismatch' and 'term mismatch': the former refers to investments in sectors with no foreign exchange receipts, the latter to the application of short-term loans to long-term projects (1998: 1576).

11 Indonesia's debt service ratio rose from 14 per cent of exports in 1980 to over 30 per cent by the 1990s (due largely to the collapse of oil prices in the mid-1980s) (Hill 1996: 72). While other countries suffered less dangerous debt service levels, the increasingly short-term character of

the debt was the main worry. In Thailand, for example, the ratio of short-term debt to foreign reserves rose from 0.6 in 1990 to 1.0 by 1995 (Lauridsen 1998: 1576).

12 One can point, for example, to the rising value of the Yen and trade measures in major markets against Japan and the East Asian NICs (Rasiah 1997: 130) as reasons for increased interest in Southeast Asia during the early 1990s. The same period also saw a cyclical decline in short-term interest rates in the industrial economies which facilitated borrowing by less developed countries (BIS 1997: 101). See Wade (1998: 1538–1539) for a lucid summary of developing excess liquidity in the global financial system.

13 Inter-household income inequality was higher in Southeast Asian crisis countries than in Korea. Data for Thailand also show that inequality had increased over the high growth decades (Hewison 1997: 111).

14 By increasing the profitability of export industries, together with state policies designed to ensure that profits were parlayed into investment in new technologies, she concluded, for example, that the higher gender wage differential in South Korea accounted for nearly half the difference in average growth rates over the period 1975–95 between that country and Chile (Seguino 2000: 1218).

15 Or, in Vietnamese parlance, a 'civilised and equitable society'.

16 The restoration of Western aid is commonly linked to Vietnam's withdrawal from Cambodia (which happened in 1989). However, a much more important event was the collapse of the Soviet Union and the end of the cold war in 1991.

17 As at the end of 1994, 29 per cent of all investments were in hotels and real estate development and a further 18 per cent in construction activities. Over 60 per cent of investment came from Asian countries (*Vietnam Investment Review*, Vietnam Investment Projects database on CD-ROM).

18 SCCI was reintegrated with the State Planning Committee in 1995 to form the Ministry of Planning and Investment.

19 In 1993 and 1997 these two areas contained 87 and 80 per cent respectively of all foreign-invested capital. During the three years 1995–97 they accounted for over 90 per cent of foreign-invested industrial output. (Beresford: 2003)

20 Official data recorded a rise in commitments for 1996, but this was only achieved by the approval of a single very large project on 31 December of that year which then made the decline in 1997 look larger. Average annual commitments for 1996–97 were US$6,479.9 m., or 99 per cent of the 1995 level (GSO 1999: 246).

21 Fforde and de Vylder (1996) provide a discussion of the way in which capital accumulation 'in the periphery' arose in the 1980s through rents available within the state sector.

22 'Equitisation' is the term the Vietnamese use instead of privatisation to describe the process of selling off shares in SOEs which, however, usually remain at least partly under state ownership.

23 The proportion of credit allocated by the state banks to SOEs declined steadily from around 90 per cent at the beginning of the 1990s to 50 per cent in 1997 and only 40 per cent in 2001. This decline was the result of government policy of promoting credit allocation to agriculture (World Bank 2002a: 31).

24 Corporations were established in, for example, electric power generation, coal, cement, steel, oil, the national airline, rubber, textiles, leather and shoes, post and telecommunications and railways.

25 Examples cited were POSCO, the South Korean steel company which began as a 100 per cent state-owned enterprise, but is now 65 per cent privately owned, and Singapore Airlines, state equity in which has been reduced from 100 per cent to 54 per cent since 1985 (Phan Van Tiem, then minister in charge of the Commission on State Enterprise Reform, 3 January 1995).

26 *TBKT* various issues. The mill had been one of the flagships of Vietnamese industry but suffered from loss of CMEA markets after 1991 and allegedly corrupt management. Most of its machinery was more than 30 years old, while a large proportion of the spinning mill comprised English equipment from the 1930s. A rescue operation was mounted by Vinatex and involved some successful southern companies in providing capital to renovate production facilities as well as subcontracting garment orders to maintain employment at the plant. One thousand of the nearly 20,000 employees were laid off (*VNN* 13 January 1997).

27 Telecommunications, a priority sector in which foreign investment has been prominent, are an exception here.

28 That foreign joint ventures have sometimes thrived at the expense of other SOEs in the same sector is illustrated by Bach Tan Sinh (this volume) in the case of coal mining.

29 224 enterprises in total by the end of 1998 (World Bank 1999a) rising to 451 as of August 2000 (World Bank 2000c).

30 The data refer to 1998 (World Bank 1999a). State policy appears to favour such insider equitisations, presumably because one of the major factors accounting for the slow rate of progress has been concern

expressed by managers and workers about the possible loss of benefits such as welfare and bonus payments if outsiders gain a controlling interest (Nguyen Ngoc Tuan *et al.* 1996: 29).

31 Data on GDP per worker are available only from 1990–94 (NGTK various issues; World Bank 1999) but show the same pattern.

32 Garment exports alone grew at an annual average rate of 29 per cent in 1990–95 (GSO 1998: 210). There were 107 SOEs in the sector at the end of this period (Nguyen Ngoc Tuan et al. 1996: 27).

33 Recent reforms have aimed at removing restrictions and thereby increasing the transparency of the private economy.

34 Again the official Vietnamese data show a more positive picture than the World Bank, putting the deficit at only 11 per cent (GSO 2000: 29).

35 An estimated 70 per cent of the employees laid off were women (Beresford 1997: 17).

36 Recent figures for domestic capitalist firms are not available. However, it is possible to make an estimate. At the end of 1994, 7,619 enterprises employed 286,159 persons, while in manufacturing, 2,466 firms employed 139,697 (MOLISA 1998: 94–95). By 1999, the World Bank noted the existence of 5,600 manufacturing firms, so assuming similar average firm size we can arrive at an approximate employment figure of 320,000. Further if the ratio of manufacturing firms to total firms has remained the same, the total workforce in private companies would be 980,000.

37 About 1.3 million workers in the SOE, FDI and domestic capitalist sectors produced 82 per cent of manufacturing GDP, while something over 600,000 household enterprises (and 2.5 million workers) produced a mere 18 per cent. See also Beresford (2000) for estimates of industrial productivity in SOE and non-state enterprises.

38 According to data provided by the National Council for the Advancement of Women, the average working day for rural women is now 15 hours, while that for men is 9 hours (women's hours in paid work are also slightly longer than men's).

39 Domestic investment did rise in 2000, but not sufficiently to offset the stagnation in foreign investment (World Bank 2000b: 3).

40 According to Food and Agriculture Organisation data, Vietnam accounted for 62 per cent of the growth in world coffee exports during 1998–2000 and 58 per cent of the growth in output (http://www.fao.org/waicent/faoinfo/economic/ESC/esce/cmr/cmrnotes/CMRcofe.htm).

41 The current account deficit rose to 9 per cent of GDP in 1995 and 11 per cent in 1996 (17 per cent according to the World Bank) but fell to 2 per cent in 1999 (GSO 2000: 29) as the government imposed import restrictions.

42 In the 1950s, SOEs accounted for nearly 50 per cent of manufacturing value added in Taiwan. After that, the SOE contribution declined until 1971 when it levelled out at an average of 14 per cent over the next 15 years. In other words, from 1971 until 1986, the SOE sector grew at about the same rate as the rest of the economy (Hamilton 1997: 243). Together with large private business groups, the SOE sector continues to supply inputs to export producers.

REFERENCES

Amsden, Alice H. (1989) *Asia's Next Giant: South Korea and Late Industrialization*, New York and Oxford: Oxford University Press.

Beresford, Melanie (1992) 'Notable Features of Vietnamese Industrial Development since 1986'. Northwest Regional Consortium on Southeast Asian Studies Conference, University of British Columbia, 16–18 October.

—— (1997) *Impact of Macroeconomic Reform on Women in Vietnam.* Bangkok and New York: United Nations Development Fund for Women.

—— (2000) 'The role of the state in the Vietnamese transition: the process of state enterprise reform', *Business and Society*, vol.1, no. 1.

—— (2003). 'Economic Transition, Uneven Development and the Impact of Reform on Regional Inequality'. In Hy Van Luong (ed.), Postwar Vietnam: *the Dynamics of Transformation.* Lanham MD and Singapore: Rowman & Littlefield and ISEAS.

Beresford, Melanie and Dang Phong (2000) Economic Transition in Vietnam: Aid and Trade in the Demise of a Centrally-Planned Economy. Cheltenham UK and Northampton, MA, Edward Elgar.

Borrus, Michael, Dieter Ernst and Stephan Haggard, (eds) (2000) *International Production Networks in Asia: Rivalry or riches?* London and New York: Routledge.

BIS (Bank for International Settlements) (1997) *67th Annual Report*, Basle, June.

—— (1998) 68th Annual Report, Basle, June.

Elson, Diane (1995) 'Gender Awareness in Modeling Structural Adjustment', *World Development*, vol. 23, no. 11, pp. 1851–1868.

Felipe, Jesus (1999) 'Total Factor Productivity Growth in East Asia: A Critical Survey'. *Journal of Development Studies*, vol. 35, no. 4, pp. 1–41.

Fforde, Adam and de Stephan Vylder (1996) *From Plan to Market: the Vietnamese Economy in Transition*. Boulder CO: Westview Press.

Gereffi, Gary and Miguel Korzeniewicz (1994) *Commodity Chains and Global Capitalism*. Westport CT: Greenwood Press.

Grabel, Ilene (1999) 'Rejecting exceptionalism: Reinterpreting the Asian financial crisis'. *Working Paper Series*, Centre for Japanese Economic Studies, Macquarie University, Sydney, February.

Greenfield, Gerard (1999) 'Vietnam: The Collapse of Nationalised Coal Production. Mass Lay-offs of Miners in the Face of "Temporary" Pit Closures'. *International Viewpoint*, September.

General Statistical Office (GSO) (1994) *Statistical Yearbook 1993,* Hanoi: Statistical Publishers.

—— (1997) *Statistical Yearbook 1996,* Hanoi: Statistical Publishers.

—— (1998) *Statistical Yearbook 1997.* Hanoi: Statistical Publishers.

—— (2000) *Statistical Yearbook 1999.* Hanoi: Statistical Publishers.

—— (2001) *Statistical Yearbook 2000.* Hanoi: Statistical Publishers.

Hamilton, Gary G. (1997) 'Organization and market processes in Taiwan's capitalist economy'. In Marco Orrù, Nicole Woolsey Biggart and Gary G. Hamilton (eds), *The Economic Organization of East Asian Capitalism*. London: Sage.

Hannan, Kate (1995) 'Building socialism with Chinese characteristics'. In Hans Hendrischke (ed.), Market Reform in the Changing Socialist World. Sydney: Macquarie University, Centre for Chinese Political Economy.

Herno, Rolf (1997) '"Network Capitalism" in Vietnam: some implications for understanding the "Transition"', paper presented to Euroviet III Conference, Amsterdam, 2-4 July.

Hill, Hal (1996) *The Indonesian Economy since 1966*. Cambridge: Cambridge Univesity Press.

Hewison, Kevin (1997) 'Thailand: Capitalist Development and the State'. In G. Rodan, K. Hewison and R. Robison (eds), *The Political Economy of South-East Asia*. Melbourne: Oxford University Press.

Hoang Cong Thi (1992) 'Capital for State Enterprises', *Economic Problems*, Hanoi, January–March, pp. 3–8.

Hutchison, Jane (1997) 'Pressure on Policy in the Philippines'. In G. Rodan, K. Hewison and R. Robison (eds), *The Political Economy of South-East Asia*. Melbourne: Oxford University Press.

ILO (1994) International Labour Organisation, *Home-based Workers in Vietnam: An Exploratory Survey in Selected Areas*. Hanoi (unpublished).

Jomo K.S. (1990) *Growth and Structural Change in the Malaysian Economy*. London: Macmillan.

Jomo K.S *et al.* (1997) *Southeast Asia's Misunderstood Miracle*. Boulder CO: Westview Press.

Kalecki, Michal (1972) *Selected Essays on the Economic Growth of the Socialist and Mixed Economy*. Cambridge: Cambridge University Press.

Krugman, Paul (1994) 'The Myth of Asia's Miracle'. *Foreign Affairs* (at http://web.mit.edu/krugman/www/myth.html).

Lauridsen, Laurids S. (1998) 'The Financial Crisis in Thailand: Causes, Conduct and Consequences?', *World Development*, vol. 26. no. 8, pp. 1575–1591.

Leightner, Jonathan E. (2000) 'Asia's Financial Crisis, Speculative Bubbles, and Under-Consumption Theory'. *Journal of Economic Issues*, vol. XXXIV, no. 2, June, pp. 385–392.

MPDF (1999) Mekong Project Development Facility, *Vietnam's Undersized Engine: a Survey of 95 Larger Private Manufacturers*. Hanoi: MPDF, 12 June.

MOLISA (1998) Ministry of Labour, Invalids and Social Affairs, *Statistical Yearbook of Labour, Invalids and Social Affairs 1997*. Hanoi: Statistical Publishing House.

Nguyen Ngoc Tuan, Ngo Tri Long and Ho Phuong (1996) 'Restructuring of State-Owned Enterprises towards Industrialization and Modernization in Vietnam'. In Ng Chee Yuen, Nick J. Freeman and Frank Hiep Huynh (eds), *State-Owned Enterprise Reform in Vietnam: Lessons from Asia.* Singapore: Institute of Southeast Asian Studies.

Phan Van Tiem and Nguyen Van Thanh (1996). 'Problems and Prospects of State Enterprise Reform,1996–2000'. In Ng Chee Yuen, Nick J. Freeman and Frank Hiep Huynh (eds), State-Owned Enterprise Reform in Vietnam: *Lessons from Asia*. Singapore: Institute of Southeast Asian Studies.

Rasiah, Rajah (1997) 'Class, Ethnicity and Economic Development in Malaysia'. In G. Rodan, K. Hewison and R. Robison (eds), *The Political Economy of South-East Asia*. Melbourne: Oxford University Press.

Seguino, Stephanie (2000) 'Gender Inequality and Economic Growth: A Cross-Country Analysis', *World Development*, vol. 28, no. 7, pp. 1211–1230.

Singh, Ajit (2000) 'International Capital Flows: Identifying the Gender Dimension'. *World Development*, vol. 28, no. 7, pp. 1249-1268.

Singh, Ajit and Bruce A. Weisse (1999) 'The Asian model: a crisis foretold?'. *International Social Science Journal*, no. 160, pp. 203–215.

Singh, Ajit and Ann Zammit (2000) 'International Capital Flows: Identifying the Gender Dimension', *World Development*, vol. 28, no.7, pp. 1249–1268.

SRV (1995) *Law on State Enterprises* (English translation by UNDP), Hanoi, April.

TBKT *Thoi Bao Kinh Te* (Economic Times), Hanoi, various issues.

Tran Tien Cuong (1996) 'Restructuring of State Owned Enterprises and the Relation Between the State and State Owned Enterprises in Vietnam'. Paper presented to the AIELEC Conference, Hanoi, August.

UNDP/UNICEF (1996) 'Catching Up: Capacity Development for Poverty Elimination in Vietnam', Hanoi, October.

VET 2000. *Vietnam Economic Times* at http://www.vneconomy.org.vn

VNN *Vietnam News*, Hanoi.

Yoshihara, Kunio (1988) *The Rise of Ersatz Capitalism in South-East Asia*. Singapore: Oxford University Press.

Wade, Robert (1998) 'The Asian Debt-and-development Crisis of 1997–?: Causes and Consequences', *World Development*, vol. 26, no. 8, pp. 1535-1553.

World Bank (1985) *World Development Report 1985*. New York: Oxford University Press.

—— (1995) *World Development Report 1995*. New York: Oxford University Press.

—— (1999a) *Vietnam: Preparing for Take-Off.* Report for the Consultative Group Meeting, Hanoi, December 14–15.

—— (1999b) Country data at http://wbln0018.worldbank.org/eap.nsf September 1999.

—— (1999c) *World Development Report 1998–99*. New York: Oxford University Press.

—— (2000a) www.worldbank.org.vn/econdev, 20 March

—— (2000b) 'Vietnam: Macroeconomic Update'. www.worldbank.org.vn September.

—— (2000c) 'Vietnam: Corporate Update', www.worldbank.org.vn, September.

—— (2002a) 'Vietnam Development Report 2002', at www.worldbank.org.vn/data_pub/reports/Bank1/rep34/vdr2000.htm

—— (2002b) www.worldbank.org/data/countrydata/countrydata.html

CHAPTER 4

The City and the Countryside: Economy, State and Socialist Legacies in the Vietnamese Labour Market

Regina Abrami and Nolwen Henaff

INTRODUCTION

This chapter examines the impact of economic reform on labour market development in Vietnam, focusing especially on the increasing number of farmers who now earn their livelihood away from their places of origin.[1] Beginning prior to economic reform and experiencing a dramatic rise after 1988, population mobility has once again emerged as a key policy concern of the Vietnamese government.[2] As Vietnam remains a largely agrarian economy, the bulk of the mobile population hails from the countryside with much of the mobility that we see underway being rural-to-rural migration. For the state, the departure of farmers to other areas where they engage in a wide range of economic activities is viewed simultaneously as a harbinger of development and disorder. Interestingly, the migrants themselves often see their own mobility in quite similar terms. Such shared sentiments suggest that non-economic factors have played a role in the development of labour market institutions in ways that perhaps neither state nor migrants comfortably accept.

In what follows, we examine the origins of the Vietnamese labour market and the nature of its segmentation. For much of the literature on labour market dynamics, market segmentation, variously conceptualised as 'dual' or 'split' markets, signals the intervention of overt discrimination between different segments of the labour force in the market realm (Bonacich 1972; Reich, *et al.* 1973; Buraway 1976 and others).[3] Segmentation, consequently, is by definition a negative outcome, a signal of market failure and a demonstration that those in power, whether defined as state policymakers, big business or dominant social groups, are able to structure market opportunities in ways exclusively to their advantage.[4] Such is not the case for Vietnam, where it appears that labour market segmentation worked to the mutual benefit of all market participants until the mid-1990s. To account for this, we examine how the confluence of international and domestic factors facilitated the development of differently segmented but basically non-competitive networks of labour distribution.

In making this argument, we do not ignore how formal state institutions and informal networks impose barriers to market entry. Nor are we denying the role of gender and age in shaping labour market outcomes. But, taken alone, these factors conceal more than they reveal about how segmented networks in Vietnam tempered conflict between urban residents and in-migrants, aided in the development of forward and backward linkages between the city and the countryside, and isolated the impact of the Asian financial crisis to specific and often better-skilled segments of the Vietnamese labour force. As such, segmentation should not in itself be assumed to be a negative outcome. More important in the context of Vietnam have been the constraints against own account and private sector activities. They pressed against rural households and narrowed the terms of their participation in off-farm activities in the 1990s.[5] Only in the past two years have we begun to see a significant upward trend in the number of *officially* registered private businesses, largely because of a dramatic decline in the number of licences required for business registration and thus more expedient turnaround of Enterprise Law compliance.[6]

The development of labour market institutions, in other words, cannot be understood apart from an in-depth understanding of the political, social and cultural mechanisms shaping market formation in Vietnam. In this chapter, we discuss these mechanisms in detail, drawing on our extensive case studies of migrants found in the construction and petty trade sectors. Through our case materials, we show that migrants who early on pursued strategies of self-employment were by the mid-1990s being forced into virtual employee status by other network participants. This shift in the distribution of power is attributable both to changes in the regulatory environment and the relative entrenchment of some migrants, more than others, within narrow networks of employment and commerce.

Our research contributes to a large and diverse body of literature on the institutional legacies of state socialism (Bunce 1999; Oi and Walder 1999;

Elster, *et al.* 1998; Stark and Bruszt 1998; Verdery 1996; Lampland 1995; Jowitt 1992; Nee and Stark 1989 and others). This literature, arising in response to easy assumptions about the proper formula of 'transition' and ahistorical accounts of market-building, has increasingly emphasised the role of non-economic factors in shaping post-economic reform trajectories. These include elite political interests, the on-going legacy of socialist era institutions that give form to networks of market-based exchange and access to resources, and socio-cultural norms that shape the normative rules of economic behaviour and social inclusion and exclusion. Our findings suggest that these factors do not operate in a zero-sum fashion and, more importantly, that their impact changes over time. We therefore need to specify their articulation in the economy in order to address more concretely questions of equity, economic growth and sustainability. Our concept of 'segmented networks' allows us to do so by highlighting the inter-linked nature of economic activity in Vietnam. Specifically, we show how unequal opportunities and power vested in social networks have shaped labour's capacity to respond to state policy and economic change.

To examine the development of labour market institutions both before and after the Asian financial crisis of 1997, we draw on surveys conducted jointly by the Institute of Research for Development (Paris) and the Ministry of Labour, Invalids and Social Affairs (MOLISA) (Hanoi), along with available data found in various government statistical reports and other secondary sources.[7] Each of these materials speaks to the relationship between labour mobility and population mobility. These data were complemented by historical and field research in several villages in the Red River Delta, northern Vietnam and field research in Hanoi in key sectors where the number of rural migrants is particularly high.[8] Taken together, they allow us to provide a fuller account of how social networks define the scope of both state policy efficacy and micro-level response to broad macro-level economic change.

POPULATION MOBILITY AND LABOUR MOBILITY IN VIETNAM: AN OVERVIEW

In the earliest days of socialist transformation, the Vietnamese government justified its attack against feudalism and capitalism as part of the broader effort to end the exploitation of labour. In subsequent years, any sign of spontaneous labour market development, while perhaps tolerated at the local level, was subject to harsh sanction by the central leadership. It is, consequently, odd that the Vietnamese Communist Party remained silent about the potential for labour market development in the early years of reform. Instead, farmers were encouraged to commercialise their agricultural surplus, to engage in non-agricultural activities, such as handicraft production and animal husbandry, and to continue their participation in state organised migration programmes to New Economic Zones located in highland areas throughout Vietnam.[9] No doubt Vietnam's largely agrarian economy fostered such Chayanovian images of economic development, but as this section elaborates, it came at the price of a clear policy stance towards a key source of economic opportunity and prosperity – out-migration.

Part of the reason is the government's own internal contradictions. For example, successive Vietnamese constitutions declared a citizen's right to freedom of movement, but at the same time population mobility and, consequently, national labour market formation were controlled prior to economic reforms. Two key institutions, the state rationing system and the household registration system, were central to the efficacy of mobility controls. They linked access to housing, welfare benefits and subsidised food to an individual's place of permanent registration.[10] Each system reinforced the other to the degree that Vietnam, like China, sustained remarkably low urbanisation rates despite urban industrial development. To 'rationally' allocate labour, the state relied instead on organised migration campaigns, most notably the movement to build New Economic Zones in upland areas, and recruiters within state organisations and labour bureaux. Spontaneous migration (*di cu tu phat*) was an illegal act in Vietnam. Even today, individuals are expected to register with local police for temporary residence status when residing more than five days in locales other than their place of permanent household registration. The Vietnamese-American War and a substantial underground economy meant, however, that prior to 1979 state control of population mobility was never as strictly maintained as had been the case for China.

Beginning in the early 1980s, spontaneous migration began to increase for several reasons, including reunification, failures in the state's development programme such as the collectivisation of the south, and the return of peace, refugees and overseas contract workers. The end of the American War in 1975 and the Vietnam–China conflict in 1978 made part of the army redundant and prompted large-scale demobilisation. A second influx of demobilised soldiers followed in 1990, after Vietnam withdrew from Cambodia. Shortly thereafter, the collapse of East European socialism brought overseas workers back to Vietnam. In addition, Vietnam was required to take back refugees that in many cases had spent years living in camps throughout Southeast Asia and Hong Kong.

Throughout the 1980s, individuals transferred to upland areas under state organised migration programmes also began to return to their places of origin, especially in the north.[11] In the case of Hanoi, they resettled with family members who remained behind or built shacks along the urban periphery.[12] In the southern province of Dong Nai, one of the main destinations of organised migration, it is estimated that 92 per cent of the people who moved there between 1981 and 1989 were spontaneous migrants (Doan Mau Diep 1997: 2). In other new economic zones, as many as 20 per cent of the organised migrants left for other areas, such as Hanoi and Ho Chi Minh City (Doan Mau Diep *et al.* 1997: 2). The final challenges to state control over population mobility were the agricultural reforms of 1988 and the formal elimination of the state subsidy system in 1989. These policy changes weakened the efficacy of the household registration system, making it easier for households to pursue both long- and short-term employment opportunities elsewhere.

Changes in the distribution of the labour force, including urban and rural employment, as well as agricultural and non-agricultural activities, were consequently due to increases in *both* population mobility and labour mobility. The share of employment in agriculture increased until 1985, stabilising at about 72–73 per cent. This increase in agricultural employment, largely fuelled by demobilised soldiers and migration (organised and spontaneous) from rural and urban areas to new economic zones, offset an increasing flow of illegal migrants leaving rural areas and agriculture to settle down in urban areas to pursue non-agricultural activities (Henaff and Martin 1999: 78–85).[13] As a result, during the period 1986–90, the relative share of agriculture in employment creation increased. But Vietnamese households, including rural households, had begun to diversify their income base during these years, and by the 1991–95 period the share of trade in total employment had increased dramatically, with petty trade representing as much as 95 per cent of total employment in commerce.

Not until 1994–95 do we actually see a drop in the share of agriculture in total employment. But, this change is matched with a parallel decline of employment within the industrial and construction sectors. Consequently, it should not be read as a trend toward greater employment in higher value-added sectors (see Figure 4.1). The changes that occurred in employment since the mid-1980s more accurately reflect the responses of the labour force to the

Figure 4.1: Trends in sectoral employment of the labour force

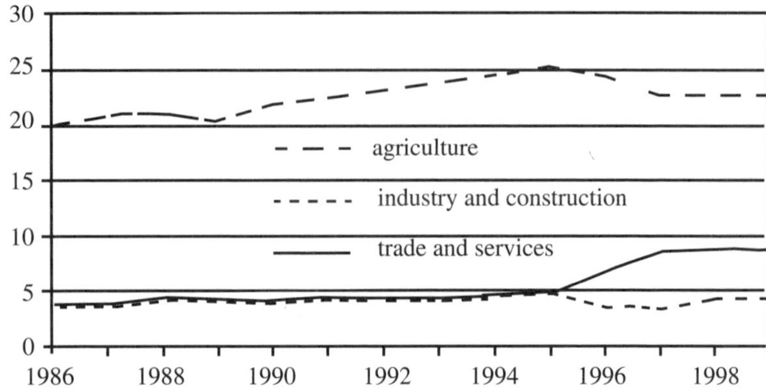

Sources: GSO, Statistical Yearbooks and MOLISA, Status of Labour–Employment in Vietnam (1997–1998).

changes perceived or endured in the frequently changing economic and regulatory environment.

These responses took a variety of forms depending on the region, location, abilities, capital, networks, and the attitude of local cadres. For example, important differences in behaviour toward labour mobility can be observed between the southern part of the country, where capitalism prevailed until reunification, and the northern part of the country, where central planning was the norm until 1986. In southern Vietnam, 78 per cent of the population never changed employment, while in the north the figure was as high as 86 per cent as of 1997. Further, the share of voluntary employment changes after 1986 comprised 64 per cent of total employment changes in the north and 82 per cent in the south (MOLISA/ORSTOM household survey 1997). In other words, southern Vietnam is characterised by a more dynamic labour market, including higher levels of voluntary labour mobility, than northern Vietnam, where the restructuring of the state sector, including layoffs within state enterprises, accounts for a somewhat lower rate of voluntary employment change. Differences in the patterns of migration to their respective main urban centres, Hanoi and Ho Chi Minh City, support this conclusion.

Migration to Ho Chi Minh City is about five times more important than migration to Hanoi (Doan *et al.* 1997: 2).[14] In Hanoi, 23.5 per cent of the population within the urban core was born in another province, nearly two-thirds of the migrants coming from the surrounding Red River Delta provinces (IRD/MOLISA household survey 1997). In Ho Chi Minh City, the proportion of migrants reaches 38.4 per cent, and their origin is far more diversified, with approximately one-third of in-migrants hailing from the north, mostly the Red River Delta area and Hanoi, the rest from central and southern regions. This can be explained by the number of people from the north sent to Ho Chi Minh City to work as civil servants, by the people who migrated to the new economic zones and later proceeded to Ho Chi Minh City and by the number of rural-to-urban migrants who came to Ho Chi Minh City and surrounding areas in search of work.

Nevertheless, the geographical mobility of the labour force has remained limited despite the increasing mobility of the population (see Table 4.1). Indeed, the labour market in Vietnam appears so highly segmented geographically that it makes little sense to speak of a national labour market. There is, instead, a multiplicity of localised labour markets, the functioning of which varies across Vietnam. The labour markets in the south appear to be more open and competitive than in the north, where, throughout the second half of the 1980s and the first half of the 1990s, labour has shifted but largely within narrower geographic areas than has been the case in southern Vietnam.

Table 4.1: Geographical extension of the search for employment, 1997

Geographical Extension	Urban	Rural	Total
Same sub-district, commune	8.9	27.5	22.0
Same district	14.4	20.3	18.5
Same province	46.7	16.5	25.5
Other province	16.3	13.0	14.0
Indifferent	13.6	22.7	20.0
Total	100.0	100.0	100.0

Source: IRD/MOLISA household survey (1997).

THE ROLE OF THE PRIVATE SECTOR IN LABOUR MARKET ALLOCATION

The private sector has played an important role in solving problems of employment generation for newcomers to the labour market and for retrenched workers, such as laid-off state sector employees and demobilised soldiers. More than 80 per cent of individuals who changed employment during the height of these major changes, the mid-to-late 1980s, pursued work in either household-based or individual own-account activities (Henaff and Martin 1999: 55–56). Migrants have also benefited from the legal sanctioning of private sector activities through self-employment and work in private enterprises. As of 1996, 75.8 per cent of migrants in Hanoi and 71.2 per cent of migrants in Ho Chi Minh City were employed in the private sector (Doan *et al.* 1997: Appendix IV.6: 18; Vien kinh te TPHCM 1997).[15]

Many of them, however, are engaged in own-account activities as independent contractors, casual labourers, petty traders, marketplace vendors and service-sector providers. In this respect, the Vietnamese pattern of internal migration is somewhat different from what occurred in China. Vietnamese labour mobility and labour market structure is defined more by processes of commercialisation than by industrial development, as has been the case in China. Put simply, the explosive growth of village- and township-owned enterprises in China fuelled a transition from farmer to factory worker that to this day remains less prominent, and at this stage less likely, in rural Vietnam.

Vietnam is not unique, however, in having a large segment of its population engaged in self-employment activities. Such a pattern is common to other developing economies as well, often serving as the bridge from agricultural to urban-based livelihoods. But, in the broader context of economic reforms, the preponderance of self-employment signals some of the important institutional barriers forestalling further private industrial development, even in the wake of the new Enterprise Law passed in 2000. Some of the most commonly cited factors include limited access to formal bank credit, costly business licensing fees and narrow supply markets.[16] These factors are important, but so too is political bargaining between state and private sector actors. It would be a mistake to assume that businesses tend to be small simply because they lack the capital to expand. Enterprise owners also make choices to avoid the costs of tax collection and bureaucratic interference, especially in the countryside, by claiming to limit their entrepreneurial activities to the household level as a 'sideline production' (Abrami 2002a). As Woodside's (1997:63–64) account of state–business relations in Vietnam attests, distrust of government intentions has historically played a role in the calculations of private sector participants in Vietnam.

Problems of labour market development in Vietnam consequently are not simply a matter of creating a private sector. After all, if we factor in household and small-scale enterprises, peddlers and other independent workers, then the 'private sector' is the first employer in Vietnam, comprising 82.4 per cent of the total labour force in 1997 (Henaff and Martin 1999: 56). The problem, more appropriately, is how the private sector has developed and the extent to which it is a resource for sustainable economic growth and employment. The shifts that have occurred in the structure of employment since the Renovation (*Doi Moi*) programme began, whether measured in terms of new forms of property ownership or economic activities, were possible largely through the unplanned mobility of the labour force. But, as Vietnam does not enjoy the dramatic growth in rural-based industry found in China, it is nevertheless hard to imagine how existing small-scale entrepreneurial activity will sufficiently absorb what the state openly acknowledges as a redundant rural labour force. Some indication of the state's thinking can be found in its push for a revival of traditional handicraft specialisations and the revised Law on Co-operatives that now encourages co-operative development between private sector actors.

There are other signs as well supporting the view that the Vietnamese state will not encourage 'free migration' or 'freer markets' in the near future. For this reason, it is important to hold enthusiasm in check. It is true that non-state economic actors have responded enthusiastically to the new Enterprise Law. But, at the same time, the government's tendency has remained one of increasing efforts to gain control over private sector economic activities. In addition to laws related to administrative reform and anti-corruption, there have been the 1997 revision of household registration laws, the Labour Code and the party's decision not to invite private sector actors into the Communist Party (while *at the same time* claiming that existing party members could engage in private economic activities).[17] These suggest a long-term goal of limiting unregulated private sector development. Thus far, it appears to be doing so by defining the terms of political power of the non-state sector and cultivating and controlling population mobility in ways believed conducive to state economic goals.

Changes that have occurred in the Vietnamese economy over the past ten years mean, however, that the state is no longer working with a relatively blank slate in so far as private sector activities are concerned. And, as we will show in our case studies, the state's effort to impose economic order and regulation is leaving rural labour, in many cases, with a narrower field of choices and quite different distributions of power in the networks in which they historically operated.

THE JOB SEARCH, EMPLOYMENT SECURITY AND MIGRANT LABOUR DISTRIBUTION

As in other countries, informal networks are central to understanding the mechanisms of labour market segmentation. But, in Vietnam, there is the additional layer of a household registration system that works to differentiate access to employment in terms of an individual's status as either a permanent or temporary resident. The market allows that individuals without permanent registration may continue to make a living away from their places of origin. Still, the lack of permanent resident status often denies migrants easy relations with the local state bureaucracy. For example, registering a vehicle, building a house, admitting children to school or opening a business all require permanent resident status.

Migrants with the right connections or sufficient capital can work around these restrictions. They do so in two ways. First, their social networks provide access to long-term employment within the public sector, a factor that allows an individual to change their household registration status on the basis of official sponsorship. Second, it allows some individuals to bend the rules further than others. In some cases, bending the rules includes a change in residence status or household registration. In other cases, it allows a migrant to register as a long-term temporary migrant.[18] Others are relegated to the most marginalised status of 'seasonal' migrant.[19] As our field research in Hanoi discovered, however, seasonal migrants are keenly tuned into the political climate – knowing when they can violate rules and when it will be costly. For example, during the 1997 Francophone Conference, urban police cleared the streets of street vendors, warning them that the penalties would be severe. Local authorities in the migrant-dense wards of Phuc Xa and Phuc Tan, reiterated this message by encouraging the temporary migrants to return to the their places of origin. Many did, not returning until two weeks after the conference.

The 1997 reform of the household registration system worked to reinforce the distinction between migrants with urban-based connections and those lacking them, by allowing a one-time transfer of residence status to long-term migrants. In both Hanoi and Ho Chi Minh City, long-term migrants who owned a house in these cities and could demonstrate active employment within the city were granted permanent resident status. In the case of Hanoi, many of the newly urbanised areas where houses were illegally constructed, such as Phuc Tan, Ho Tay and Phuc Xa, largely remained villages of migrants, except for those who could, once again through connections, secure the necessary paperwork to prove a legal right to the property and land where they had built houses. Similarly, viable employment could be easily demonstrated through letters provided by friends and family with legitimate urban-based businesses or affiliation with the state and civil sectors.

This difference in the nature of their migrant social networks, urban-based versus rural-based in origin, finds expression in the distribution of migrants in the urban economy. We found that 50 per cent of temporary migrants created their own business after arrival in Hanoi, 25 per cent relied on a private contractor to aid the job search and 24 per cent participated in day labour markets found along the streets of Hanoi.[20] In the case of Ho Chi Minh City, 25 per cent of temporary migrants seek employment through day labour markets, suggesting that quite similar dynamics are underway. Despite other regional differences between northern and southern Vietnam, as measured in the cases of Hanoi and Ho Chi Minh cities, the experience of temporary migrants is quite similar.

There is consequently little competition between migrants with connections and those who lack them or between long-term permanent migrants and short-term or seasonal migrants. For long-term migrants, their status as migrants is a formality tempered by the right kind of social ties. Temporary migrants, in contrast, bear the brunt of the local state bureaucracy. Comprising mostly unskilled labour from rural areas, they do so, not because they are migrants, but because the majority of them claim to have little interest in long-term migration and this factor at least partially affects how they invest in social relations. For these migrants, their social connections lie at their places of origin and are often used to secure a place in the urban economy.

Not surprisingly, family, relatives and friends remain the most frequent channel to employment.[21] But, as elaborated above, the network of family, relatives and friends matters. Indeed, employers most frequently rely on their employees for the further recruitment of workers. In the 1996 surveys, half of the migrants interviewed in Ho Chi Minh City and 60 per cent of those interviewed in Hanoi searched for employment through family and friends. In 1999, Henaff and Martin found that 49 per cent of unskilled labour, 63 per cent of skilled labour, and 33 per cent of cadres were recruited through family and friends of individuals either responsible for recruitment within public and private sector firms or employed by them. Moreover, half of the enterprises using temporary labour recruited these workers through family and friends, with 65 per cent of them using no other channel of recruitment. Social networks, in other words, are a defining feature of the Vietnamese labour market.

EXPLAINING SEGMENTATION OF THE LABOUR MARKET

The above discussion identified several factors shaping labour market segmentation in Vietnam. In showing how migrants play a key role in private sector development, we argued that the dominance of self-employment among Vietnam's most marginal segment of the migrant population, the temporary (or seasonal) migrant, is best understood as the outcome of differences in social network structure and social investment strategies among the different categories of migrants. Unlike permanent and long-term migrants, temporary migrants draw on village-based social networks to secure a position within urban areas. History consequently repeats itself as one generation follows another in terms of specialisation. While this has led to a high correlation between a migrant's place of origin and urban-based economic occupation, it has come at the price of building extensive networks within the urban economy. As the next section shows it leaves these migrants far more subject to state policy changes than other migrants.

Our findings also suggest that the position of temporary migrants cannot be solely understood as a measure of capital shortage.[22] If that were indeed the case, we would be at a loss to explain the dramatic changes that have taken place in sending areas, including the construction of new and often elaborate homes, as well as the development of secondary labour markets to meet the demands of agricultural work. In each of the six rural sending areas we visited, these villages have well-developed agricultural labour markets. In one case, the labour market began in the early 1980s and has continued to this day. These labour markets raise an interesting challenge to demographic accounts of out-migration as a natural response to labour redundancy. After all, family members who remain behind do not always continue to engage in agricultural labour, but instead use income generated by other family members to pursue non-agricultural village-based occupations and to hire others from surrounding villages to work in agriculture.

These findings suggest that the key mechanism of labour market segmentation in Vietnam is not residency status but social networks. The impact of the household registration system is consequently best regarded as an artefact of limited social resources and social network structure. The latter two forces, far more than the household registration system, channel migrants into different forms of market participation in receiving areas and leave them subject to different levels of monitoring and vulnerability *vis-à-vis* the local state bureaucracy. The constraining effect of the household registration system, in other words, is restricted to specific segments of the migrant population, while the labour market more broadly has for some time been comprised of non-competitive networks of labour market participation. This is somewhat different from the Chinese case where the household registration system was until recently a central force in shaping labour market structure. Moreover, continued state subsidies to permanent urban residents in China resulted in the creation of a subculture of second-class citizens who faced clear hostility from both the local state and urban society.

The Vietnamese government, as part of its campaign against 'social evils', also singled out migrant communities as disorderly, just as its campaign to enforce traffic laws allowed urban residents to openly express their frustration with the most marginal segment of migrants who earn their livelihood on urban streets.[23] Nevertheless, the social composition of urban Vietnam is quite different from China. Not only do many permanent urban residents continue to maintain ties to their ancestors' places of origin, their more advantageous social networks and higher skill levels discourage any sense of direct competition from rural migrants. As the next section will show, subsequent state efforts to impose market transparency have worked to further discourage any threat from in-migration by strengthening the market position of urban residents *vis-à-vis* self-employed rural market participants.

THE FORCES OF RURAL SELF-EMPLOYMENT AND OUT-MIGRATION

The combination of labour supply glut, weakly developed small and medium-sized rural private and co-operative enterprises, as well as reliance on social connections, contributed to rural out-migration. But, taken alone, these factors do not explain why self-employment remains the most prevalent form of income generation among rural migrants in urban areas. To account for this division of labour, we also need to consider how the historical origins of rural–urban economic linkages, especially the role of the local state in facilitating underground trade, shaped network structure.[24] As we discuss in greater detail below, unorthodox historical divisions of labour are central to understanding why the state's effort to impose market order beginning in the mid-1990s unsettled the structure of power relations between rural and urban market participants.

As is well documented in the secondary literature, socialist transition in Vietnam was distinguished by a good deal of local-level resistance to the socialist organisation of production (Hy and Unger 1999; Kerkvliet 1995; Fforde 1989; Fforde and Paine 1987). Existing literature, however, has largely focused on resistance in terms of unsanctioned grassroots efforts to reorganise production through unofficial household contracting and the expansion of private plots. But, if we accept that unofficial decollectivisation was widespread and played a key role in shaping the process of reform, then how do we explain why some villages fared better than others after the official programme of economic reform began? To's (1995) earlier work on economic development within several Red River Delta villages offers some clues. He shows that villages that decollectivised earliest and *prior to Renovation* are the very same villages that were quickly classified as 'rich,' while latecomers continued to fall behind in terms of economic development. Although never stated, To's argument implies the presence of a core group of local level cadres who *continuously* supported bottom-up efforts to circumvent state rules. We can further hypothesise that if this group extended not just to production team level cadres but also included Commune-level (*xa*) administrative and party officials, then the range of tools available to households prior to economic reform may have gone well beyond the reorganisation of agricultural production to include underground trade and off-farm employment.[25] In other words, To's study offers insight into the possible sources of network variation that may have granted some rural locales an opportunity to develop rural–urban linkages in advance of others.

Our field research confirms as much. In each of the urban sectors studied, we found that the predominant group of migrants, measured in terms of place of origin, found in each sector correlated with the earliest dates of participation in the sector and a history of local cadres' assistance in facilitating off-farm activities. In what follows, we examine the conditions under which these rural–urban market relations first developed in the construction and petty trade sectors. Our aim here is to show how the policy context within which these networks emerged provided rural participants with a somewhat level playing field *vis-à-vis* their urban counterparts. The sections that follow examine how state policy increasingly unbalanced these relations in the mid-1990s.

Construction Sector

The construction sector has long been a conduit to urban employment for rural households. In the early years of socialist transition, state-owned construction companies looked explicitly for labour within villages historically famous for specialisations in carpentry and masonry. These villages are found mostly in the provinces of Ha Tay, Bac Ninh and Ninh Binh. In what follows, we discuss one such village, Noi Due, located in Bac Ninh province not far from Hanoi.

Noi Due, discussed briefly in Li Tana's (1996: 21, 32) earlier work on Hanoi's migrants, has a long history in the domestic construction sector. Prior to 1954, the village was famous throughout Vietnam for its skills in temple construction (Dang Uy 1992). Later, as contract labour for French-owned firms, some villagers as young as 10 headed off to Hanoi to work in construction. After 1954, villagers continued to work in this sector with a significant number of men leaving for work in state enterprises. Others worked unofficially in surrounding rural areas as house builders, in addition to meeting their agricultural responsibilities. On occasion, state companies also sought temporary workers in this village. Local rural cadres facilitated their participation, and, by all accounts, selection was fairly democratic with special preference given to households facing economic hardship. Work outside the village promised higher income than was possible through handicraft and agricultural work. Further, for families facing difficulties, the exodus of male household members meant that the state would provide these men with food allowances thereby lessening the household's burden.

By the 1970s, the nature of these relationships began to change as more households devoted attention to construction work away from home. As more residents sought contracts and income outside of the state system and away from the commune, rural cadres had to devise some means to meet production quotas. They did so by requiring departees to pay for their workpoints either in grain or money. This allowed local team leaders to meet their quotas and, if necessary, to purchase grain on the free market. In return, local cadres supported the departure of these men by providing an official letter of introduction. Certainly, not all villagers pursued this strategy. Others simply departed for work elsewhere, but in cases where they ran into difficulty, these men were more vulnerable to harassment from local cadres upon their return and especially if they encountered difficulties. Given the low cost of participation in the workpoint payment scheme, this institution emerged as a norm for all men leaving to work elsewhere.

By the early 1980s, Noi Due and the surrounding villages that comprise Tien Son district dominated the construction market in northern Vietnam. Much like a trademark, teams of construction workers from other villages began to claim they were from Noi Due in order to secure contracts. At the same time, state sector employees were still forbidden to engage in private sector activities. As a result, many engineers and architects forged alliances with rural builders and local party officials in Noi Due. The rural builders became the 'front men' of prototype private firms that were officially described as work teams belonging to the village's 'Unified Economic Co-operative' (*Hop Tac Xa Kinh Te Tong Hop*). Some households in Noi Due grew quite prosperous through this unofficial link with state firm employees who secured, often illegally, construction materials on their behalf in return for a portion of profits. More importantly, villagers gained access to a wider social network through state workers who ensured a steady flow of work throughout the late 1980s.

The role of local rural cadres during these years is quite unique in comparison with other areas of Vietnam, showing more in common with Chinese than Vietnamese rural development patterns. To begin, they used the 'Unified Economic Co-operative,' incorporating both textile handicraft workers within the village[26] and the growing number of men departing for work elsewhere, to sustain a managerial role for themselves in the outside economy. Further, by restricting letters of introduction to co-operative members, the local government set in place incentives for the remaining independent work teams to participate. By charging co-operative members for any paperwork completed on their behalf and by securing contracts on their own, local cadres further consolidated their managerial position.

Over time, the relationship between co-operative managers and co-operative members increasingly resembled employer–employee relations. In 1990, two years after decollectivisation, the international Comecon market for handicraft production declined, but by this point villagers were no longer dependent on the 'Unified Economic Co-operative' to protect their marketing activities. Women villagers consequently began to engage in petty trade, marketing textiles and other goods in Hanoi and elsewhere. The 'Unified Economic Co-operative' was then renamed the Noi Due Construction Co-operative (*Hop Tac Xa Xay Dung Noi Due*).

This co-operative continued to operate until 1992 when the state passed the law on small enterprises. Co-operative officials were then ordered by the province-level branch of the Ministry of Construction (*So Xay Dung*) to convert the co-operative into a registered private company (*cong ty tu nhan*). Certainly, the Noi Due Construction Co-operative by virtue of its hiring labour seemed not to operate as a 'co-operative' (*hop tac xa*). Villagers were also never fully regarded as shareholders, with profits distributed among the current and former local-level party officials who managed the organisation. In 1992, the co-operative was converted into a full-fledged private company, the Number One Noi Due Construction Company (*Cong Ty Xay Dung Noi Due I*). The declared capital used to establish this company, however, came from the co-operative. In other words, 'public' capital was privatised as the property of some key village officials in the creation of this company. Two other village-level private companies were created shortly thereafter, with villagers relying on all three firms for employment opportunities. These companies were however restricted under Ministry of Construction regulations to accept contracts only from Thanh Hoa province to the northern border. It was, in other words, illegal for them to work in the south. This ruling existed through 1997 when it was finally repealed. By this time, however, Noi Due had lost its competitive edge for reasons examined in the next section.

Petty Trade

The development of petty trade networks differs significantly. Not only do women dominate this sector, but it is rare to find any village that specialises in petty trade.[27] Some villages prior to 1954 specialised in commercial trade, but petty trade, owing to its small scale, was more or less open to anyone willing to engage in it (Nguyen 1993).[28] Consequently, whatever specialisations operate in this sector, in terms of the commodities traded, grew out of the initial choices of older villagers to produce and market one good rather than another.

Occupation was a matter of 'chance,' as Gourou (1936) explained in order to account for the seemingly irrational distribution of rural industrial development and specialisations in northern Vietnam. After 1954, however, the Vietnamese government pursued plans, not economic chances. During the campaign to transform the private sector (1958–60), independent small traders were organised into trading groups (*to buon ban nho*) in both rural and urban areas.[29] In addition, the campaign to develop supply and marketing co-operatives in rural areas at the district level and below was stepped up. In theory, both of these economic groups aided the expansion of state-controlled commerce through the purchasing and marketing of state goods. As was the case in other socialist systems, shortages left open plenty of space for underground trade. As early as 1960, the government launched campaigns against the growing number of farmers leaving agriculture to pursue work in commerce. Not only did these farmers market the surplus available from private plot production, they formed alliances with state commercial workers and others.

The number of 'private' petty traders in Vietnam continued to rise throughout the 1970s and 1980s, increasingly coming to include rural and urban residents – peasants, workers, soldiers and cadres. This spontaneous commercialisation of the Vietnamese planned economy sharply distinguishes it from the Chinese socialist experiment where the combination of strictly enforced mobility restrictions and continuous domestic campaigns waged in the name of class struggle made non-state and co-operative commercial activity, including small trade, politically hazardous throughout much of China's pre-reform era. The Vietnamese government instead waged campaigns against an invisible class of speculators, the *'bon dau co,'* and spoke of 'class struggle as unity', placing fault for the increasing number of independent small traders operating in Vietnam on 'objective' (*khach quan*) factors. These included weak bureaucratic management, natural disasters and the American War. Given rural households' widespread and increasing reliance on small trade, the role of rural cadres is central to understanding why some villages, but not others, came to occupy a key role in commercial networks. In what follows, we elaborate their role in facilitating non-state trade in the years prior to economic reform.

Rural cadres facilitated the development of specialised networks prior to economic reforms in several ways. In some cases, they made village-level state institutions, such as the supply and marketing co-operatives, available to villagers in ways contrary to central state policies of economic management. In other cases, they created systems similar to the workpoint payment scheme in Noi Due as a way to obtain rents from farmers who spent little time in agricultural work and to meet their production quotas. Others provided letters of introduction or simply turned a blind eye to activities at the grassroots level. Given the diversity of responses, there is no one village that can be classified as typical in this regard. But, Ninh Hiep Commune (*xa*), now part of suburban Hanoi and earlier belonging to Bac Ninh province, is a useful example of the kinds of unorthodox institutions that arose in the years prior to economic reform with the assistance of local cadres.

Ninh Hiep Commune, historically specialising in medicinal processing and textile production, is famous for its large and active marketplace. But, the origins of contemporary commercial networks did not grow out of this marketplace, *Cho Nanh.* Supply and marketing co-operative cadres instead had a central role in rebuilding marketing networks. As in other socialist states, supply and marketing cadres are at once a group envied for their easy access to state goods and despised for engaging in work considered somewhat unethical owing to its association with greed and profit. The latter Confucian stereotype was reinforced in the years of socialist planning as many supply and marketing cadres had earlier been independent peddlers better known for their bargaining skills and harsh tongues than their socialist ethics. Later, as the wives and daughters of local cadres occupied managerial positions in supply and marketing co-operatives, this institution of socialist commerce also became a symbol of socialist-type corruption where only those with connections were ensured a steady supply of goods.[30]

Ninh Hiep was somewhat different in this regard. The supply and marketing co-operative was used not only for personal advantage but also as a clearing house for the whole range of goods farmers brought to sell in exchange for higher value-added goods. Supply and marketing co-operative cadres also worked on their own account to secure goods outside of state channels. They did so through barter and black market trade in ration coupons. Not surprisingly, they initially specialised in medicinals and textiles. Through connections with both the Ministries of Foreign and Domestic Commerce, they sold medicinals in exchange for state goods, such as monosodium glutamate (MSG), thermos and other goods. These commodities were then sold to villagers who would take them to producing areas located in midland and upland areas where they would exchange them for medicinals. After processing these medicinals, they would either sell them to the co-operative or market them on their own.

As the co-operative paid prices based on demand and quality, villagers also developed marketing networks on their own and were in fact encouraged to do so. The village authorities aided them by providing cover against district-level tax, police and commercial cadres. People were on occasion arrested, but it seems whenever possible commune officials announced upcoming raids in advance, leaving each household to make its preparations.

The second leg of commerce, ration coupons, was built through the exchange of ration coupons for grain, money or other commodities. Cadres mostly focused their efforts on the acquisition of cloth and textile ration coupons that they exchanged in state shops. This trade was limited to cadres in the supply and marketing co-operative as they could more easily justify their mobility and bulk transport of commodities. Others could at best only move a small quantity of goods at a time.

Village-level cadres, through the agricultural co-operative (*hop tac xa nong nghiep*), also participated in commercial schemes. For example, they arranged for the barter of such goods as fertiliser and cattle in exchange for textiles, medicinals and Western medicine. Western medicine was obtained from state pharmaceutical companies, as well as through villages located near the Noi Bai Airport that established connections with Soviet pilots who exchanged Western medicine for silk and other precious local goods. Party officials cooperated in these schemes, appearing somewhat Janus-faced in their relations with higher levels. In an unpublished 1973 report written to provincial officials, the party secretary blamed Ninh Hiep's dismal agricultural productivity on farmers' continued participation in trade but claimed to be powerless. In our interviews with this retired leader, however, he acknowledged doing little to stop underground trade, as villagers would have been in dire poverty had they not pursued off-farm income opportunities.

In effect, all levels of commune government and economy in Ninh Hiep were integrated into a unified commercial system that simultaneously addressed problems of shortage within the village and encouraged villagers to participate in commercial work. By the late-1980s, Ninh Hiep villagers had opened stalls selling textiles in Dong Xuan Market in Hanoi and dominated the wholesale medicinal market in Hanoi. Soon after, a small number of villagers began to make trips to China to purchase Chinese medicinals and textiles, with some having travelled as far as Guangzhou without any official paperwork. This shift toward imports helped the village to maintain its competitive advantage as an increasing number of villages began to enter the urban market. By the early 1990s, Ninh Hiep ironically was celebrated by the national government as a showcase of rural development, enjoying a visit from the then general party secretary Do Muoi.

The experiences of Ninh Hiep and Noi Due villages go a long way toward explaining the prevalence of self-employment among rural migrants and rural market participants in Hanoi. As described above, the structure of business networks and self-employment cannot simply be interpreted as an outcome of capital shortage and limited opportunity for employment. They need instead to be set in the context of a policy environment that implicitly discouraged local level industrialisation in the years prior to economic reform. Not only were farmers wary of state-led forms of economic co-operation, but, as the cases of Ninh Hiep and Noi Due demonstrate, local cadres pro-actively changed local state institutions in order to obtain rents from activities already underway. In so doing, they not only sustained but also consolidated their economic and political legitimacy at a time when villagers were increasingly turning elsewhere to earn their livelihood.

While further research is needed, it is possible to hypothesise at this stage that village governments adopting this kind of co-optive, rather than predatory, strategy of economic management aided the long-term development of their villages. Contrary to To's argument, the timing of spontaneous decollectivisation in rural Vietnam may in fact be a less accurate predictor of economic success than the role played by local cadres. Other villages also sought off-farm opportunities in the pre-reform period but reported harassment by commune-level officials that stunted the development of commercial networks and perhaps encouraged the intensification of passive resistance on the part of farmers. Rural latecomers were subsequently denied easy entry into sectors already dominated by villages such as Ninh Hiep and Noi Due. They looked instead to unexploited sectors and, most typically, to their own village's special products.

By the mid-1990s, they began to encroach upon entrenched networks, such as those controlled by Ninh Hiep. But, by this time, state development policy was not working to the advantage of any particular group of rural market participants. The rules had changed for all through a series of policies that aimed simultaneously to encourage market development through rural enterprises and foreign direct investment, and to regain state managerial oversight through administrative reform, enhanced policing of cross-border trade and of private enterprises and population mobility.

In the early 1980s, villages, such as Noi Due and Ninh Hiep, benefited from high urban demand, weak development of the urban private sector, and social networks in state-owned enterprises. As described above, the policy environment encouraged fairly equitable relations between urban and rural market participants. In the case of Noi Due, state workers benefited from their alliance with rural builders at a time when they were restricted from overt market participation. With the growing demand for urban home construction in the early 1990s, Noi Due builders began to hire others from surrounding villages and secure contracts on their own. In Ninh Hiep, urban demand also allowed these villagers to set the conditions of trade to their advantage. It was largely a cash economy, with Ninh Hiep traders dictating whether or not to grant credit. Competition from other rural market participants was also scarce throughout much of the 1980s, but by the mid-1990s conditions changed dramatically. State policy had taken a turn against informal capitalism.

THE DRIVE FOR ECONOMIC REGULATION: RECONFIGURING THE STATE'S ROLE IN THE ECONOMY AND ITS IMPACT ON MARKET SEGMENTATION

The drive for economic regulation aims to strengthen the monitoring power of the central state over the economy. These campaigns have historically come in waves in socialist Vietnam. The set of policies introduced in the mid-1990s, however, were more comprehensive than preceding reform era policy changes, extending from the socio-cultural realm to the political and the economic. The totality of this policy movement shares its closest resemblance to the state- and socialism-building campaigns of the late 1950s. But, this time, the goals were different. In the 1990s, policies aimed toward the construction of civilised markets and a strong regulatory state.

In the socio-cultural realm, this translated into directives calling for the revival of traditional village covenants (*huong uoc*), the rule of law and an end to 'social evils,' such as gambling, prostitution and drug addiction. In the political realm, the National Assembly became a more vocal actor, pushing through new labour and civil codes. In addition, the state made a concerted effort to carry out administrative reforms. Finally, in the economic realm, campaigns against poverty, corruption, smuggling, counterfeit goods and for contracts, competitive bidding, business registration and tax collection all gained prominence by way of new laws and several key criminal cases that taught lessons through the published media. Today, the government continues to push through policies believed to enhance its regulatory power, never once forgoing its claim that the state sector must remain the leading sector of the economy.

The first effects of these policies are bewildering once compared to the state's other goals, such as strong central state regulatory capacity, a private sector, the elimination of poverty and labour rights. In this section, we consider two fields – rural development and the protection of workers – where the regulatory intervention of the state has altered networks that sustained rural market participants with effects that may be contrary to what was intended. By way of these topics, we also continue the story of Noi Due and Ninh Hiep Communes.

REGULATION AND RURAL DEVELOPMENT

Migrants, especially those working at the margins of the economy as construction labourers and petty traders, might in theory seem irrelevant to the broad policy changes described above. But the developmental trajectory earlier described for communes, such as Ninh Hiep and Noi Due, were leading to long-term changes in the allocation of labour in ways the state itself desired as part of its broader development goals such as poverty reduction. Not only were these villages recording dramatic shifts away from agricultural labour, the economic gains were taking shape with little investment on the part of the state. But, in forging changes in the regulatory environment, the state paid little heed to how macro-level policy changes might alter the structure of power relations within the social networks that initially allowed for such developments.

For example, in the state-owned construction sector, reorganisation, under the mantle of improving economic efficiency, granted subsidiary units of parent firms a more direct role in labour recruitment.[31] Not surprisingly, unit heads drew on their own social networks to recruit labour. Newcomers, often with little experience in the construction market, subsequently found entry onto some of the largest and most profitable construction sites in Hanoi and other major cities.[32] For Noi Due construction workers, this guaranteed exclusion from the construction boom of the mid-1990s on two grounds. First, many of these workers had over the past 20 years come to rely on the village-level co-operative to secure employment elsewhere. Now, reorganised as a company, Noi Due could no longer bid directly for contracts as it did not meet the capital requirements.[33] Second, Noi Due company managers had little interest in continuing relations with large state-owned construction firms as they could only obtain 'jobs' as sub-contractors. Their workers would be paid, but the firm itself would see little profit.[34] Instead, they shifted attention to border provinces, such as Lang Son and Cao Bang, where they could continue to work independently. Noi Due workers experienced a dramatic decline in status. Some continued to ally themselves with village-level companies. Others, securing contracts on their own, were still subject to making 'payment for paperwork' to these companies in cases where they secured contracts in need of bureaucratic approvals.[35] By the time of our fieldwork, 1996, the majority of Noi Due workers had retreated from Hanoi.

In the case of petty trade, the business registration campaign and increasing efforts to combat smuggling forced rural traders into new forms of co-operation with private and state sector firms. In the case of Ninh Hiep, the campaign against smuggling limited easy transport of medicinals and textiles into Vietnam. It did not, however, stop it. Instead, state companies began to sell their import quotas to villages, such as Ninh Hiep, who had become dependent on external markets and imports for their competitive advantage.[36] As in the construction sector, villagers who earlier worked independently of each other to secure goods in China banded together with state firms in a payment for paperwork scheme. While this allowed Ninh Hiep traders continued and safe access to the China market, state firms welcomed anyone to buy quotas. The village lost its competitive advantage, as other rural locales secured direct routes to China through other companies. In the abstract, such a scheme might appear to meet state regulatory interests, but the reality has been quite different. State firms, at least in the mid-1990s, had a competitive edge over private firms in smuggling. Moreover, state transporters had every interest in smuggling as villagers pay a set fee for quotas. This fee includes the estimated cost of import taxes. As such, any trucker savvy enough to evade customs keeps the difference.

At the level of street trade, textile and medicinal market prices remained stable owing to growing competition, but the relationship between rural suppliers and urban buyers changed dramatically. Urban residents, owning licensed shops in an environment that now allowed private trade, enjoyed an advantage over a growing glut of informal household enterprise-based suppliers such as those from Ninh Hiep. These urban shopkeepers subsequently began to demand credit as a condition of purchase. For Ninh Hiep, this change was a tremendous burden as they did not have credit relations with their suppliers in China and often had to wait as long as six months for Hanoi firms to pay their debts.[37] For younger generations in the village, market disenchantment led them to turn away from Hanoi, migrating instead to Ho Chi Minh City or shifting to higher value-added goods, such as electronics.

Both of these cases show how state policy produced unintended effects at the micro-level. The rupture of earlier relations of market segmentation through state regulatory campaigns has theoretically opened the urban economy to all rural entrants. But, for some, including the early market participants discussed in this chapter, the entry is as the virtual employees of state firms or as the unwilling creditors of urban merchants. This shift in status has negatively altered the possibility of many rural households finding the 'development' they seek in urban-based self-employment.

REGULATION AND THE PROTECTION OF WORKERS

The Vietnamese government has not resigned from its social welfare responsibilities, as has been the case in other countries after the dismantling of the central planning system.[38] State initiatives such as the reduction of working time in the public sector, plans to create an unemployment insurance programme and discussions about extending the pension system to farmers demonstrate that the government does not accept the full marketisation of social services. It aims not only to continue but to expand its role in the provision of guarantees and benefits to workers. Its political interest in ensuring equity in the labour market also accounts for the bold initiatives taken to protect labour, including the criminal prosecution of foreign nationals charged with violating the state's labour laws, the introduction of the Labour Code in 1994, and sector-specific regulations, as in the construction sector.

The construction sector has long operated as the nexus between state social welfare initiatives and economic development projects. In the early years of socialist transition, many farmers first found a place within urban areas through work as temporary contract workers in the construction sector. Others became permanent employees, literally 'building socialism' throughout northern Vietnam. In the early 1990s, the sector underwent significant changes that affected how labour was recruited. Specifically, subsidiary units within construction companies were converted into own-account subcontractors of parent state-owned firms.[39] As any given construction firm has hundreds of work teams (*doi*), it meant that market dynamics could play themselves out in a closed market setting. Teams informally bid against each other to get 'jobs' from the parent firm. And, while the parent firm recruited teams from within its own organisation, the unintended incentive was for these work teams to recruit casual labourers on short-term contract as a way to cut costs and guarantee their initial low bids to upper management.

Rather than enhancing the oversight of the parent firm, the change in enterprise organisation has instead limited managerial control over the labour process, including easy oversight of hiring and protection of workers. As a result, many state firms unwittingly do not adhere to the letter of the law. For example, construction sector specific laws and regulations include mandatory work safety training of *all* labourers, including short-term contract workers, the provision of insurance, the use of labour contracts and inspections by the local Labour Bureau to ensure that workers are properly equipped with hardhats and other safety equipment and enjoy formal written contracts with their employer. Upper management, especially those in foreign joint ventures, has an interest in meeting these requirements but often fails to do so.

The construction sector remains in Vietnam one of the most hazardous, with work-related accidents occurring not only on smaller-scale construction projects but also on large, internationally funded ones as well. Further, as short-term contracts with rural labour are typically arranged through their group's representative, labour contracts often do not conform to state law. Instead, labourers at best obtain a group contract that does not even list the names of work group members.[40] Moreover, the terms of payment, work hours and other arrangements are exclusively negotiated between a state-employed subsidiary unit team leader (*doi truong*) and a rural subcontractor who manages a group of workers as their leader (*to truong*). As a result, most workers are not individually insured, as the law requires. Instead, the parent firm just buys a number of policies that approximate the average number of workers on-site, using a random list of names that do not necessarily match the names of workers on the site. For workers engaged on small-scale projects, such as house construction, there is little monitoring by the Labour Bureau and rarely any instance where workers are provided either labour contracts or insurance.

Nevertheless, the Labour Code, and related laws and regulations, signal a degree of formalisation in labour relations. At this stage, however, such formalisation is limited mostly to regular employees. For example, in 1997, 82 per cent of wage labourers in Vietnam had a labour contract, written in 88 per cent of the cases (Henaff and Martin 1999: 61–63). But, the migration survey conducted in Hanoi in June 1996 shows that among the wage labourers, only 12 per cent of the temporary migrants had a written labour contract, while the proportion reached 75 per cent for permanent migrants.[41] This is partly due to the distribution of the temporary migrant labour force among the different forms of salaried employment. Most temporary migrants are short-term wage labourers or day/casual workers, whereas the other migrants are mostly long-term wage labourers. Consequently, the proportion of workers having a written contract is systematically lower for temporary migrants as compared to other migrants, no matter the form of salaried employment. As a result, temporary migrants are, on average, more vulnerable than the other types of migrants.

In fact, the data show that permanent migrants have more in common with non-migrants than with other individuals lacking a permanent registration at their place of employment. Both permanent in-migrants and non-migrants tend to benefit from written contracts, while temporary migrants, including seasonal migrants, secure some degree of labour protection largely through unwritten and thus not so easily monitored rules of custom. Further, as temporary migrants are more likely to engage in own account activities, pursuing their livelihood through petty trade and services, the reach of labour protection laws does not extend to them.

Turning to the behaviour of enterprises with respect to labour contracts, we can also see how the market is influencing the nature of hiring preferences and employment in Vietnam. Our 1999 enterprise survey shows that verbal contracts are far from occasional in use and that temporary labour is an important source of enterprise flexibility.

We found that even when contracts are signed, they are most often short-term contracts. Thus, 7 per cent of the enterprises surveyed employed more than half of their labour force through seasonal contracts (*hợp động thời vụ*), 38 per cent employed at least 75 per cent of their labour force on contracts of one to two years, and 33 per cent with contracts of less than a year.[42] Only state enterprises and joint state–private enterprises most often hired labourers with term-unspecified contracts (*hợp động không có thời hạn*).[43] Specifically, 40 per cent of state enterprises and 58 per cent of joint state–private enterprises hired more than 75 per cent of their labour force with these contracts. Conversely, the private sector avoids recruiting too many employees on such contracts. Most prefer instead to hire labourers on short-term contracts, with 84 per cent of the foreign enterprises, 73 per cent of the joint ventures and 63 per cent of domestic private enterprises employing more than 75 per cent of their labour force on these terms. Indeed, out of the total number of enterprises surveyed, we found that 90 per cent of the foreign companies, 84 per cent of the joint ventures between national and foreign companies, and 87 per cent of the private enterprises employ less than 25 per cent of their workers through permanent contracts.

The state sector also recruits workers with short-term contracts. Out of the total sample of state enterprises surveyed, 38 per cent had such contracts with their employees in 1999 and of these, 72 per cent hired more than three-quarters of their labour force with short-term contracts. Seasonal contracts are mainly used by private Vietnamese enterprises. We found that 3.4 per cent of our sample hired 50–75 per cent of their labour on the basis of seasonal contracts, with 8.3 per cent of this total hiring more than 75 per cent of their employees on such terms. Very few enterprises base their relationship with their employees on a verbal contract. Still, as many as 3.5 per cent of private enterprises and 2.4 per cent of the state–private joint ventures recruited their permanent labour on the basis of verbal contracts.

The opening up of the labour market and increased competition for employment are the consequences of state efforts to 'normalise' the labour market in order to monitor it more closely, extend social protection to larger sections of the population, improve Vietnam's integration in the region and more generally into the global economy.

The increasing prevalence of short-term contracts in this market might, however, be viewed as levelling the playing field between migrants and non-migrants as the conditions of employment deteriorate for non-migrants. And, so long as labour regulations effectively apply only to a small segment of the market, the general trend will be one of an increasingly precarious situation for *all* workers (Henaff and Martin 2000: 107-113). Indeed, the main characteristic of changes underway in the labour market is one of growing 'contingency' of the salaried labour force. The 1994 Labour Code, in other words, while introduced to protect workers by providing for fixed-term labour contracts, is allowing instead for employers to develop recruitment strategies that provide for as much labour flexibility as possible. Such recruitment strategies have been observed throughout Vietnam in all sectors, including the state and co-operative sectors (Henaff, 2002). Social networks, in other words, remain important in gaining access to the labour market, but the stakes are now decidedly different. We can see this not only in the terms under which labour secures employment but also in which it looks for opportunity. Today, migration from the rural to the largest urban areas has begun to decline in Vietnam, with migration to small- and medium-sized cities on the rise instead (Henaff and Martin, 2003).

CONCLUSION

Early on, the Vietnamese labour market was comprised of a multiplicity of mutually non-competitive networks. In this chapter, we have tried to provide some account of its genesis and impact on labour market dynamics. As we have shown, the nature of non-agricultural and non-state activities in the years prior to 1986, the crises of the late 1980s that produced a glut of labour supply and the limited employment opportunities in the private sector encouraged labourers to invest in own account activities. In the case of rural households, such activities took expression as out-migration, enthusiastic adoption of household farming, independent work as contractors, small traders and service providers. For this reason, among others, we saw a surge in the number of small household enterprises and self-employment in Vietnam in the early 1990s. As our discussion of the petty trade and construction sectors shows, the segmented networks that brought about these changes were not limited to labour market dynamics. They extended to other segments of the economy as well by providing information and opportunities to labourers, entrepreneurs and political leaders alike.

Our research also suggested that these networks, while segmented, worked to the mutual benefit of all labour market participants in the early years of economic reform. In this respect, Vietnam challenges existing portrayals of market segmentation, showing how it may arise under conditions of weak, rather than strong, market development and competition. We further argued that the ability of early market participants to expand and to maintain their position through the early 1990s cannot be understood apart from the head start they were granted through the support and co-operation of local village cadres in the years prior to economic reform. In effect, *early* labour market segmentation arose owing to reliance on social introductions, situational advantage and the different skill levels of job seekers, rather than to a deliberate effort on the part of employers to exclude any particular group to increase their returns or secure better control over their investment. To demonstrate our point, we examined the differing conditions of employment between migrants and non-migrants. As earlier reported, we found that only the most marginal segment of the migrant population, the temporary migrant, lacking the right connections, showed a marked disadvantage in terms of job placement, social insurance, labour contract and labour protection. In the latter portion of the chapter, we argued that this difference is diminishing as more salaried employees find themselves subject to similar terms of employment.

In this respect and others, the Asian financial crisis had only an indirect effect on labour and distribution markets in rural Vietnam, especially in the north. The overall share of employment in foreign-funded enterprises also remained too marginal in Vietnam to produce widespread shock in the labour market as seen in neighbouring Southeast Asian economies. Indeed, better-skilled employees, such as architects and engineers, who reaped the gains of Vietnam's construction boom in the 1990s, as well as those who benefited from corruption during these years, were more directly affected by the crisis than others. For farmers and other labourers in rural areas, the greater challenge has been and will continue to be how to take advantage of the government's growing support of the private sector.

In sum, the post-renovation years appear as a period of adjustment now giving way to normalisation. A variety of internal and external constraints and pressures, including apparent changes in the political will of the government, are important to understanding current processes unfolding in

Vietnam. The turmoil caused by war and reunification, and the adjustments engendered by the changing economic environment of the late 1980s are now gone. They have made way for a more stable, if not predictable, environment, one where the economy's integration into the regional and international economy will increasingly have a central role in shaping outcomes not only in the labour market but also in the private and public sectors, more broadly.

NOTES

1 We would like to thank Melanie Beresford, Adam Fforde, Andrew Hardy and participants of the Vietnam–China Workshop (Harvard University) for comments on earlier versions of this paper.

2 We date 'economic reforms' to 1979.

3 More recent approaches do away with these dichotomies by focusing on categories and forms of 'contingent' labour that can be found in both the formal and informal sectors. Our discussion of labour contracting and social benefits examines some common markers of 'contingency' found in both developed and developing economies. Our primary concern, however, is in understanding the institutional origins of the Vietnamese labour market and its effect on rural-to-urban migrants.

4 For an alternative argument, one that links segmentation to the voluntary choices of entrepreneurial types, see Maloney (1998).

5 'Own-account' activities and self-employment have equivalent meanings from different point of views: 'own-account' refers to capital (regardless of the size), while 'self-employment' refers to labour.

6 Anecdotal evidence suggests that the time required for setting up a business has dropped from 98 to 7 days.

7 Unless otherwise noted, the arguments made and data used in this paper draw on three surveys on labour, employment and human resources, conducted in 1996, 1997 and 1998 on 1,200 households in 12 provinces from north to south (see ORSTOM/MOLISA-CEPRH 1998: 9–17) , one survey on spontaneous migration in Hanoi conducted in June 1996 (1,000 migrants and 300 non-migrants) (UNDP project VIE /95/004, see Doan, *et al.* 1997: 5–10) and one enterprise survey on labour demand completed in October 1999 (IRD/MOLISA/IUED/WB project). The enterprise survey was conducted in October 1999 on 300 enterprises with at least ten workers. The sample for the enterprise survey was designed to allow for comparisons between different types of enterprise forms. The sample is thus balanced in terms of size, ownership and legal status, while the

number of enterprises interviewed in each province was determined by the distribution of enterprises throughout the country. The provinces selected for the labour, employment, human resource and enterprise surveys are: Hanoi, Hai Phong and Quang Ninh in the north; Da Nang, Ho Chi Minh City, Dong Nai, Binh Duong, Ba Ria-Vung Tau and Can Tho in the centre and the south.

8 Qualitative field research was conducted in five communes (*xa*), located in three northern provinces, including Hung Yen, Ha Tay, Bac Ninh, as well as Gia Lam district, a rural area belonging to Hanoi. Each area was chosen owing to its substantial economic links to Hanoi uncovered during interviews with shopkeepers, marketplace vendors, itinerant traders and employers in Hanoi in the construction, plastic goods, fruit, medicinal and clothing and textile sectors. The rural-based research entailed 900 hours of individual and focus group interviews with village officials and village elders on informal trade in the years prior to 1954, economic reform (*Doi Moi*) and current commercial activities. Where possible, all former Commune Party secretaries, agricultural co-operative chairman, heads of commune supply and marketing co-operatives, as well as craft co-operative leaders were interviewed. Production team leaders were by and large interviewed in focus groups where discussion centred on questions of labour management and economic policy implementation prior to economic reforms. In addition, a 450-sample survey of migrant itinerant traders in Hanoi was completed to map out family histories, credit relations, forward and backward linkages in the contemporary commercial sector, as well as the spatial distribution of commercial specialisations in the city. These data, as well as findings from the other three village studies, are not discussed in depth in this chapter. The qualitative research was conducted in 1994, 1996, 1997 and 1999.

9 The New Economic Zone programme began in North Vietnam in 1961.

10 There is no one Vietnamese study that discusses the working of the household registration system in great detail. Consequently, our understanding of it can only come from interviews and the relevant policies and laws. See for example, Cong Bao 1968, 1964); Pham and Tran (1986); Ty Cong An Ha Nam Phat Hanh (1958); Uy Ban Hanh Chinh Tinh (1958). For a discussion of the 1998 changes in the household registration system, see Bo Noi Vu (1997), Cong Bao (1997) and Hardy (2001, 1998). Good discussions of the origins and evolution of the household registration system in China can be found in Cheng and Selden (1994) and Solinger (1999).

11 As many southerners sent to New Economic Zones had connections with the prior regime, they were more closely monitored. Some did illegally return to Ho Chi Minh City, but many remained in the New Economic Zones until 1986.

12 The two wards, Phuc Tan and Phuc Xa, located along the Red River were popular resettlement locations. Returnees also settled along Dai Co Viet Street, located near the Technical University, building small shacks that remain to this day. Others settled in surrounding rural areas and the wards near the Vietnam National University.

13 During the period 1981–1985, 83 per cent of the demobilised soldiers turned to agriculture and 14.2 per cent to industry.

14 Net migration since 1986 is around 20,000 per annum in Hanoi and around 70,000–100,000 per annum in Ho Chi Minh City.

15 Existing studies of private enterprise in Vietnam do not distinguish the origins of enterprise owners or labourers, forgoing analysis of the important role of rural migrants in urban economic development in Vietnam. For a general study of private enterprise in Vietnam, see Ronnås and Ramamurthy (2001).

16 For example, see Ronnås and Ramamurthy (2001); Mallon (1999); Ronnås (1996).

17 The Vietnamese Communist Party Central Committee meeting of the Fifth Plenum, held in March 2002 voted that party members may engage in private sector activities. It did not, however, say that private sector actors may become party members. The decision, in other words, is fundamentally different from what unfolded recently in China where the Communist Party has decided to offer membership to 'capitalists'. It would therefore be a mistake to think that the Vietnamese Communist Party is simply imitating its counterpart in China with respect to the private sector.

18 Long-term temporary migrants who do not have some kind of membership in state organisations, such as students who maintain their registration at their places of origin, while studying at universities elsewhere, must renew their registration every six months. This typically includes individuals who work in factories, or on construction projects, as temporary labourers.

19 Seasonal migrants are required most frequently and directly to engage the local state bureaucracy. Their registration is limited to three months, but may be renewed. Other migrants, such as university students or temporary construction labourers, usually benefit from individuals who represent them and arrange paperwork on their behalf.

20 The question in our survey was multiple answer.

21 Li Tana (1996) reported the same in her study of migrants in Hanoi.

22 As earlier stated, capital shortage is one of the most common problems mentioned by private entrepreneurs.

23 By the mid-1990s, letters to the editor in all of the major papers included letters from disgruntled urban residents who described the cities of Hanoi and Ho Chi Minh as increasingly 'uncivilised' and 'unsanitary', owing to the activities of street traders, pedicab drivers and porters.

24 By underground trade, we do not mean 'second economy' activities as conventionally understood in the literature on socialist economic structure, referring as it does to state-sanctioned household plot and local marketing activities. We are referring instead to illegal activities, such as long-distance trade and trade in state-controlled commodities in the 'non-state' economy.

25 Dang Phong's Chapter 2 in this volume shows that the links reached in some cases to the central level. His account of how these connections facilitated market-orientated 'experiments' has parallels with processes of market reform in China. See Yang (1996).

26 Only one hamlet (*thon*) in Noi Due specialised in textile production and, subsequently, petty trade. All other hamlets specialise in construction. Interestingly, men from the 'textile hamlet' do not participate in construction and instead facilitate the work of their wives by remaining behind in the village.

27 Women can also be found in the construction sector, but they are often relegated to the most menial tasks. In the case of independent, roving work groups, a woman, usually a kin member of one of the male construction workers, assumes responsibility for cooking. In other cases, women are assigned jobs such as sweeping and, in the case of high-rise projects, unloading light construction waste basket-by-basket out of a building-in-progress.

28 Other Vietnamese historians dispute the idea of specialised commercial villages.

29 The political economic history of petty trade in northern Vietnam during the years 1954-98 is discussed in greater detail in Abrami (2002b).

30 It is important to note that the leadership of these co-operatives and trading groups (*to buon ban nho*) by individuals with the right political connections and political background was a deliberate policy of the Vietnamese government. It emerged after early investigations that the family members of soldiers, workers and cadres formed a significant

percentage of the small trader population, but that former capitalists and other suspect classes were dominating state commercial organisations. In 1960, the government ordered that all management committees (*ban quan tri*) be comprised of poor peddlers and these favoured classes. Suspect classes continued to maintain membership in these organisations, however.

31 This change came about informally and over time as state firms looked for ways to impose discipline on lower-level units within the firm. Although it cannot be confirmed, this change may be related to the creation of the conglomerate corporations (*tổng công ty*) in the 1990s.

32 For example, Binh Minh Commune, in Ha Tay Province that historically specialised in the production of fireworks, began to find work in construction through informal connections with state company foremen. These networks had lain dormant during the heyday of the fireworks industry but were employed after the industry was banned in the mid-1990s.

33 Contract bidding in the construction sector is based on the size of the project. Consequently, Noi Due either settled for building houses in Hanoi or moving out of this highly competitive market in search of more viable options elsewhere

34 A significant portion of enterprise profit in the construction sector comes from the materials market (e.g., cement and steel). Subcontractors in Vietnam, usually do not retain these rights, earning profits only through labour specialisation.

35 Payment for paperwork is common among unregistered businesses. They must rely on formal firms to obtain government clearances, such as building permits. Informal businesses, depending on the relations with the formal business, either pay a fee for this service or a percentage of the contract.

36 More accurately, they ‘rented’ the quotas, in that villages transported goods under the rubric of a state-owned company whose truckers pretended they were transporting goods for the firm.

37 Per Ronnås (1996) found few instances of credit in his study of private enterprises. In the cases we studied, it was extremely common but rarely in the form of money. Instead, individuals ‘lent’ commodities in a fashion somewhat similar to a truck system.

38 General discussion on social welfare issues in Vietnam is found in Litvack and Rondinelli (1999) and Dollar *et al.* (1998.) We limit our discussion to findings from our own research.

39 These changes and their impact on labour hiring and management are discussed in greater detail in Abrami (1997). For a critical account of the impact of these changes on the rule of law and corruption in Vietnam, see Pham (1996).

40 Interviews with Vietnamese team leaders on ten major construction sites, Hanoi, 1997. Half of these sites are joint-venture projects, with foreign project managers. The Vietnamese partner has responsibility for personnel issues, including hiring and the purchase of insurance

41 By permanent, we mean that the individuals have settled in the city and have no intention of returning to their former place of permanent registration

42 The term, 'seasonal contract' is used as defined in the labour code to refer to short-term contracted labour.

43 'Unspecified' here means longer than the longest of the 'short-term' contracts, that is more than three years, provided the employer and the employee are both satisfied. This type of contract is the most favourable to the employees. It ensures a certain stability in the employment as the conditions of breaking the contract are defined by the labour code.

REFERENCES

Abrami, Regina (1997) 'Kinh te Nong thon: Mot So Ghi Nhan ve Nhung Moi Quan he Xa hoi va Nghien Cuu Xa hoi Hoc ve Nhung Nguoi Laodong va Buon ban rong tai Hanoi [The Rural Economy: Notes on Social Relations and Sociological Research on Labourers and Itinerant Traders in Hanoi]. *Xahoi Hoc* [Sociology], vol. 4, no. 60.

—— (2001) 'Economies Under Different Commands: Socialist Era Norms and the Making of Market Power in Contemporary Hanoi, Vietnam and Chengdu, China.' Paper presented at the 2001 Annual Meeting of the Association for Asian Studies, Chicago.

—— (2002a) 'Just a Peasant: Economy and Legacy in Northern Vietnam.' In Pamela Leonard and Deema Kaneff, (eds), *Post Socialist Peasant: Rural and Urban Constructions of Identity in Eastern Europe, the Former Soviet Union, China, and Vietnam.* London, UK: Palgrave, pp. 94–116.

—— (2002b) Self-Making, Class Struggle and Labor Autarky: The Political Origins of Private Entrepreneurship in Vietnam and China. PhD thesis, University of California, Berkeley.

Bo Noi Vu. (1997). 'Thong Tu Huong Dan Thuc Hien Nghi Dinh So 51–Cp Ngay 10 Thang 5 Nam 1997 Cua Chinh Phu Ve Viec Dang Ky Va Quan Ly Ho Khau' [Ministry of Interior, Circular, Instructions on Carrying out the Government Regulation 51–Cp, Dated 10 May 1997, Regarding Household Registration and Management Work]. *Van Ban Phap Quy [Legal Register]*, no. 16, pp. 34–44.

Bonacich, Edna (1972) 'A Theory of Ethnic Antagonism: The Split Labor Market'. *American Sociological Review*, no. 37, pp. 547–59.

Bunce, Valerie (1999) *Subversive Institutions: The Design and Destruction of Socialism and the State.* Cambridge: Cambridge University Press.

Burawoy, Michael (1976) 'The Functions and Reproduction of Migrant Labor: Comparative Material from Southern Africa and the United States'. *American Journal of Sociology*, no. 81, pp. 1050–1087.

Cheng, Tiejun and Mark Selden (1994) 'The Origins and Social Consequences of China's Hukou System'. *China Quarterly*, no. 139, pp. 644–668.

Cong Bao [National Gazette] (1964) 'Nghi Dinh So 104–Cp Ngay 27-6-1964 Ban Hanh Dieu Le Dang Ky Va Quan Ly Ho Khau [Regulation Number 104–Cp, 6 June 1964, The Implementation of Household Registration Regulations and Household Registration Management], no. 28, 2 September, pp. 502–504.

——(1968) 'Nghi Dinh So 32–Cp Ngay 29-2-1968, Ve Viec Thong Nhat Cong Tac Dang Ky Ho Tich, Ho Khau Va Thong Ke Dan So [Regulation Number 32–Cp 29 February 1968, Regarding Unifying Household Registration, Census and Nationality Work], no. 3, 29 February, pp. 48–49.

——(1997) 'Nghi Dinh So 51–Cp Ngay 10-5-97 Ve Viec Dang Ky Va Quan Ly Ho Khau [Government Regulation no. 51–Cp 10 May 1997, Regarding Household Registration and Management Work].' no. 12, 30 June, pp. 799–803.

Dang Uy, UBND Xa Noi Due [Noi Due Commune People's Committee] (1992) *Lich Su Xa Noi Due* [History of Noi Due Commune], no publisher provided.

Doan Mau Diep, Nolwen Henaff, Trinh Khac Tham (1997) *Report on Spontaneous Migration Survey in Hanoi*. Centre for Population and Human Resources Studies. Hanoi: unpublished manuscript.

Dollar, David, Paul Glewwe and Jennie Litvack (1998) *Household Welfare and Vietnam's Transition*. Washington, DC: The World Bank.

Fforde, Adam (1989) *The Agrarian Question in North Vietnam, 1974–1979: A Study of Cooperator Resistance to State Policy.* Armonk, NY: M.E. Sharpe.

Fforde, Adam and Suzanne Paine (1987) *The Limits of National Liberation: Problems of Economic Management in the Democratic Republic of Vietnam.* London: Croom Helm.

General Statistical Office (GSO) (various years) *Statistical Yearbooks*, Hanoi: Statistical Publishing House.

Gourou, Pierre (1936) *Les Paysans du Delta Tonkinois*. Paris: Editions d'Art et d'Historie.

Hardy, Andrew (2001) 'Rules and Resources: Negotiating the Household Registration System in Vietnam under Reform', *Sojourn*, vol. 16. no. 2, pp. 187–212.

—— (1998) A History of Migration to Upland Areas in 20th Century Vietnam. Ph.D. Thesis, Australia National University, Canberra.

Henaff, Nolwen (2002) 'Enterprises and Employment in Vietnam: Towards globalisation?' Paper prepared for Euroviet V Transitional Identities, St Petersburg, Faculty of Oriental and African Studies, St Petersburg State University, 28–30 May 2002.

—— (2003) 'Migration et emploi, Évolution et tendances récentes'. In J.-L. Maurer and C. Gironde, Le Viêtnam à l'aube du XXIe siècle, Paris: Karthala.

Henaff, Nolwen and Jean-Yves Martin (1999) 'Labour and Human Resources Information System, Vietnam – Report on the Household Survey, Second round 11-12/1997'. Ministry of Labour, Invalids and Social Affairs, Research Institute for Development, Hanoi: Labour and Social Affairs Publishing House (also published in French and Vietnamese).

—— (eds) (2003) *Travail, emploi et resources humaines au Viêt-nam, Quinze ans de Renouveau*, Paris: Karthala.

Hy, Van Luong and Jonathan Unger (1999) 'Wealth Power and Poverty in the Transition to Market Economies: The Process of Socio-Economic Differentiation in Rural China and Northern Vietnam'. In Anita Chan, Benedict J. Tria Kerkvliet and Jonathan Unger (eds), *Transforming Asian Socialism: China and Vietnam Compared.* St. Leonards, NSW: Allen & Unwin, pp. 120–152.

Institute for Economic Research of Ho Chi Minh City (1996) *Migration, Human Resources, Employment and Urbanisation in Ho Chi Minh City, Project VIE/03/P02* Hanoi: National Publishing House.

Kerkvliet, Benedict J. Tria (1995) 'Village–State Relations in Vietnam: The Effect of Everyday Politics on Decollectivization'. *The Journal of Asian Studies*, no. 54, pp. 396-418.

Jowitt, Ken (1992) *New World Disorder: The Leninist Extinction.* Berkeley: University of California Press.

Lampland, Martha (1995) *The Object of Labor: Commodification in Socialist Hungary*. Chicago: University of Chicago Press.

Li, Tana (1996) *Peasants on the Move: Rural–Urban Migration in the Hanoi Region*. Occasional Paper No. 91. Singapore: Institute of Southeast Asian Studies.

Litvack, Jennie I. and Dennis A. Rondinelli (eds) (1999) *Market Reform in Vietnam: Building Institutions for Development*. Westport, CT: Quorum Books.

Mallon, Raymond (1999) 'Experiences in the Region and Private Sector Initiatives in Vietnam'. In Suiwah Leung (ed.), *Vietnam and the East Asian Crisis*. Northampton, MA: Edward Elgar, pp. 165–192

Maloney, William F. (1998) 'The Structure of Labor Markets in Developing Countries: Time Series Evidence on Competing Views'. World Bank, June, unpublished paper.

MOLISA (1997) *Status of Labour-Employment in Vietnam 1996*, Hanoi: Statistical Publishing House, 788 p.

—— (1998) *Status of Labour-Employment in Vietnam 1997*, Hanoi: Statistical Publishing House, 642 p.

—— (1999) *Status of Labour-Employment in Vietnam 1998*, Hanoi: Statistical Publishing House, 657 p.

—— (2000) *Status of Labour-Employment in Vietnam 1999*, Hanoi: Statistical Publishing House, 607 p.

Nguyen Quang Ngoc (1993) *Ve Mot So Lang Buon o Dong Bang Bac Bo trong The Ky XVIII–XIX* [Commercial Villages in Northern Vietnam in the 18th–19th Centuries]. Hanoi: Hoi Su Hoc Vietnam.

Oi, Jean and Andrew Walder (1999) *Property Rights and Economic Reform in China*. Palo Alto, CA: Stanford University Press.

ORSTOM-MOLISA/CEPRH (1998) *Hệ thống quan sát Lao động, Việc làm và nguồn nhân lực ở Việt Nam, Báo cáo điều tra hộ gia đình vòng 1, tháng 11-12/1996* [The labour, employment, and human resource monitoring system, report on the first cycle of household research, November–December, 1996]. Hanoi: Nhà xuất bản lao động-xã hội.

Pham, Hung and Quyet Tran (1986) *Lam Tot Cong Tac Quan Ly Ho Khau, Nhan Khau* [Do the Work of Household Registration and Population Management Well]. Ha Noi: Nha Xuat Ban Cong An Nhan Dan.

Pham, Viet Dao (1996) *Mat Trai cua Co Che Thi Truong (Dieu tra Kinh Te-Xa Hoi)* [The Negative Face of the Market System (A Socio-economic Investigation)]. Hanoi: Nha Xuat Ban Van Hoa-Thong Tin.

Population Council, UNDP, Ministry of Agriculture and Rural Development (1998) International Seminar on Internal Migration: *Implications for Migration Policy in Vietnam.* Hanoi, 6–8 May, Seminar Papers.

Reich, Michael, David M. Gordon and Richard C. Edwards (1973) 'A Theory of Labor Market Segmentation'. *American Economic Review*, vol. 63, pp. 359–365.

Ronnås, Per (1992) *Employment Generation through Private Entrepreneurship in Vietnam.* Hanoi: ILO.

—— (1996) 'Private Entrepreneurship in the Nascent Market Economy of Vietnam: Markets and Linkages'. In John McMillan and Barry Naughton (eds), *Reforming Asian Socialism: The Growth of Market Institutions.* Ann Arbor: The University of Michigan Press, pp. 135–165.

Ronnås, Per and Bhargavi Ramamurthy (2001) *Entrepreneurship in Vietnam: Transformation and Dynamics.* Copenhagen/Singapore: Nordic Institute of Asian Studies/Institute of Southeast Asian Studies.

Solinger, Dorothy J. (1999) *Contesting Citizenship in Urban China*, Berkeley, CA: University of California Press.

Stark, David and Laszlo Bruszt (1998) *Post-Socialist Pathways: Transforming Politics and Property in East Central Europe.* Cambridge: Cambridge University Press.

Stark, David, Victor Nee and Mark Selden (1989) *Remaking the Economic Institutions of Socialism.* Stanford: Stanford University Press.

To Duy Hop (1995) 'Some Characteristics of the Changing Social Structure in Rural Vietnam under Doi Moi', *Sojourn*, vol. 10, no. 2, pp. 280–300.

—— (ed.) (1997) *Ninh Hiep: Truyen Truyen va Phat Trien* [Ninh Hiep: Tradition and Development]. Hanoi: Nha Xuat Ban Chinh Tri Quoc Gia.

Truong Si Anh, P. Gubry, Vu Thi Hong and J.W. Huguet (1996) *Ho Chi Minh Ville de la Migration à l'Emploi.* Les dossiers du CEPED no. 40. Paris: Centre Français sur la Population et le Développement.

Ty Cong An Ha Nam [Ha Nam Police Bureau] (1958). 'Nhiem Vu cua Cong An Xa, Don, Trong Viec Thi Hanh The Le Di Lai' [The responsibility of commune- and base-level police with respect to issuing mobility passes]. pamphlet, unpublished document.

Uy Ban Hanh Chinh Tinh Hai Ninh [Administrative Committee of Hai Ninh Province] (1958) 'Dieu Le Tam Thoi ve Viec Khai Bao Ho Khau [Temporary regulations regarding declaration of household registration] (in Vietnamese and Chinese)'. Pamphlet.

Verdery, Katherine (1996) *What Was Socialism, and What Comes Next?* Princeton: Princeton University Press.

Viện kinh tế TP HCM (1997) *Báo cáo kết quả chủ yếu điều tra di dân tự do vào TP HCM*, Dự án VIE/95/004 [Final summary report on free migration into Ho Chi Minh City], May, unpublished document.

Woodside, Alexander (1997) 'The Struggle to Rethink the Vietnamese State in the Era of Market Economics' in Timothy Brook and Hy Van Luong (eds), *Culture and Economy: The Shaping of Capitalism in Eastern Asia*. Ann Arbor: The University of Michigan Press, pp. 61–78.

Yang, Dali (1996) *Calamity and Reform in China: State, Rural Society and Institutional Change since the Great Leap Famine*. Stanford, CA: Stanford University Press.

CHAPTER 5

Linking Growth with Equity? The Vietnamese Textile and Garment Industries since Doi Moi

Tran Ngoc Angie

INTRODUCTION

This chapter extends the analysis in my 1999 co-authored paper with David Smith (Tran and Smith 1999) in which we examined Vietnam's economic transition within the broader context of two competing theoretical perspectives on the role of the state. These were the popular Smithian/neo-classical advocacy of *laissez-faire* and the other perspective stressing the potential efficacy of developmental states. We supported the developmental state perspective and found, among other things, that Vietnamese state capacity, in relation to the ways in which East Asian Newly-Industrialised Economies (NIEs) led their economic development efforts, has played an increasingly important role since 1986.[1]

In this chapter, I further examine state capacity in formulating and implementing industrial policy, or linkage development in particular, by studying the Vietnamese textile and garment industries (VTGI). But how can these industries illuminate state capacity in developing linkages when integrating into a world of intensified competition? Developing both backward and forward linkages can be defined broadly in this context as greater connection between the labour-intensive garment industry and the more capital-intensive textile industry and other intermediate goods industries. I examine the extent to which governments can provide the initial push to help create linkages between industries that would not otherwise develop in the market system.

The Vietnamese textile and garment industry (VTGI) is a good case study to illuminate state capacity in developing linkages. It is the only manufacturing industry on the top ten export commodities list dominated by extractive (oil) and foodstuff (rice and food processing) industries. It is one of the top foreign exchange earners, having advanced to second place after oil and gas (1999 and mid-2000 data).[2] This sector has grown fast since reaching out to the capitalist markets beginning in 1993 (particularly in response to the collapse of the former Soviet Union and other Eastern European socialist markets): official statistics showed a consistent increase in the share of VTGI export in the total export value from less than 10 per cent before 1993 to over 15 per cent since 1995. The slight reduction in 1998 and 1999 may be due to the impacts of the Asian financial crisis (Table 5.1).[3] Moreover with at least 550,000 workers in over a thousand garment and textile factories throughout Vietnam, it is the top employer of manufacturing workers (MPDF 1999b: 44). However, an increase in VTGI export has been accompanied by high percentages of imported materials for sewing (Table 5.2). Since the early 1990s these have been over 30 per cent of all imported materials, except for 17 per cent in 1998 at the height of Asian financial crisis period. The imported component of materials for sewing grew markedly, from 63 per cent in 1999 to 74 per cent in 2000. The trend was consistent with imported fabrics in general, which increased from US$505 million (1999) to US$775 million (2000).

This topic is timely as Vietnam is at the crossroads of pursuing some critical industrial policies negotiated between various recommendations coming from both internal and external sources. The tension involves two contending development ideologies, leading to different recommendations. One view can be found in studies by international organisations, such as UNIDO, MPDF and CIDA, which argue against backward linkage development because the Vietnamese textile industry does not have comparative advantage (a static argument).[4] The other comes from VINATEX, the state textile and garment corporation, which argues for further state investment in the textile industry, including spinning, weaving, knitting and finishing. In fact, the Vietnamese industrial policies prioritising textile industry are a *fait accompli* since the late 1990s as discussed in later sections.

I argue that if Vietnam is to avoid the problem of 'enclave' development, in which garment production lacks linkages to the rest of the economy and is characterised by low value-added accumulation and heavy reliance on imported inputs, then the VTGI must develop more backward and forward linkages.[5] This argument is based on both primary and secondary sources from my fieldwork between 1993 and 2003, as well as relevant comparisons

Table 5.1: Textile and garment export 1981–2000 (millions of US dollars)

Year	VTGI export#	TOTAL Export#	VTGI export share#	VTGI export##	Share of VTGI export##
1981	30	401*	7.5*		
1985	58	699*	8.3*	27.5	7.9
1989	139	1,946*	7.1*	93.1	8.4
1990	215	2,404	8.9	118.5	7.9
1991	117	2,087	5.6	172.3	9.9
1992	190	2,581	7.4	396.8	15.6
1993	239	2,985	8.0	582.7	17.8
1994	496	4,054	12.2	799.4	17.8
1995	850	5,449	15.6	1,026.6	18.2
1996	1,150	7,256	15.8	1,338.2	19.8
1997	1,503	9,185	16.4	n.a.	n.a.
1998	1,450	9,360	15.5	n.a.	n.a.
1999	1,747	11,540	15.1	n.a.	n.a.
2000	1,892	14,483	13.1	n.a.	n.a.

* *Statistical Yearbook 1994*, General Statistical Office, Hanoi 1995, p. 278.
# *Statistical Yearbook* data.
UN data
Sources: VINATEX, April1997a; VINATEX, December 1996 and June 2000; US Consulate in Ho Chi Minh City, March 1998; *Statistical Yearbook 1999*, Statistical Publishing House, 2000, p. 274; *Statistical Yearbook 2001,* Statistical Publishing House, 2002, pp. 372, 376; Hal Hill 1998: 24.

with industrial development in Malaysia, South Korea, Singapore and Sri Lanka in the twentieth century and with developed countries in the nineteenth century. In the next section, I outline the two contending theoretical perspectives with empirical evidence from some Asian cases to provide a conceptual framework for subsequent discussion, and then examine the potentials and challenges for linkage development in the VTGI.

Table 5.2: Values of VTGI products (exported and imported) 1992–2000 (millions of US dollars)*

	1992	1993	1994	1995	1996	1997	1998	1999	2000
VTGI exports	190	239	496	850	1150	1503	1450	1747	1892
Imported fabrics for sewing	55 (29)	96 (40)	152 (31)	305 (36)	531 (46)	897 (60)	249 (17)	1096 (63)	1400 (74)
Imported fabrics	n.a.	n.a.	n.a.	109	n.a.	414	530	505	775

* From 1992 to 1994, the dollar values for imported fabrics are not available: only quantities (in metres) are given. Therefore, these statistics may underestimate the total value of imported inputs. Percentages in parentheses are the shares of imported inputs in total export values.

Sources: MPDF 1999b; General Statistical Office, December 1999; Hill 1998: 25; *Statistical Yearbook 1996*: 210, 214–215; *Statistical Yearbook 1997*: 274, 278–279; *Statistical Yearbook 1999*: 283, 169, 278; *Statistical Yearbook 2000*: 409, 410; *Statistical Yearbook 2001*: 379.

CONCEPTUAL ISSUES ON LINKAGE DEVELOPMENT

The two contending perspectives revolve around the concept of comparative cost advantage in deciding whether a country should develop certain industries during the industrialisation process. The first is based on static comparative advantage, demonstrated in the works of James Riedel and Hal Hill. The second is based on the work of Albert Hirschman, who argues for creating linkages between industries, or dynamic comparative advantage, as a development strategy. The works of Michael Porter and Gary Gereffi also support the creation of dynamic comparative advantage through linkage development, involving both production and distribution. Ample empirical evidence from economic histories of both Western and Asian countries supports this second view (Kelegama and Foley 1999: 1446–1447).

Some basic definitions are in order. In general, industries with backward linkages utilise inputs from other industries, whereas industries with forward linkages produce goods or services which then become inputs into other industries or end products reaching final consumers. In the VTGI context, backward linkages would create demand for and stimulate production of domestic inputs such as fabrics, cotton, synthetic fibres, dyestuffs, garment accessories (i.e., threads, buttons, zippers, shoulder padding) and industrial products such as machinery for textile and garment firms. Related processes include pattern design, spinning, weaving, dyeing, printing, stone-washing and finishing. Forward linkages would include establishing marketing networks and direct working relationships with foreign clients, product differentiation and quality enhancement. With fast-paced fashion changes, producers who can provide greater product varieties via small batches and respond quickly to buyers' specifications gain a competitive edge (Meyanathan and Ahmed 1994: 1, 10). Furthermore, indirect linkages, or consumption linkages, can be developed through wage earners' demand for consumer goods such as fabrics, apparel, processed foods and footwear (Gillis *et al.* 1992: 422).

The first perspective provides a case against linkage development. Riedel argues for linking the economy to the rest of world on the basis of static comparative advantage. In other words, domestic firms have cost advantages in producing labour-intensive goods and cost disadvantages in producing capital-intensive goods. He advocates participation in international trade to provide the economy with opportunities to specialise in and export products in which it has static comparative advantage, while importing intermediate inputs. In the context of the VTGI, he implies that Vietnam, with a surplus-labour economy should focus on labour-intensive products such as garments and buy inputs from the world market (Riedel and Turley 1999). Along the same lines, Hal Hill assumes that backward linkage analysis is based on a closed-economy framework. He argues that if the competitiveness of garment products is to be preserved and developed, firms must be able to secure inputs at internationally competitive prices. Hill doubts that Vietnam can develop an internationally competitive textile industry and argues against backward linkage development (Hill 1998: 42–43, 57).

The second perspective provides an alternative framework for conditions in which to create and develop backward and forward linkages. This can be beneficial to a country that does not necessarily have comparative cost advantage in those industries. Albert Hirschman advocates backward linkages since they can reduce the import intensity of the industry (textiles, for example) whose future growth may be conditioned on such import reduction (Hirschman 1958). He posits that it is possible for a developing country to jumpstart its industrialisation by relying on an 'unbalanced growth' pattern which concentrates resources on a few industries during the early stages of development and encourages their linkages with other sectors of the economy.[6]

The logic of this growth pattern firstly entails the development of some industries which require less capital and fewer skills (i.e., consumer goods such as foods, clothing and shoes). These industries will utilise inputs from other industries, therefore creating demand for intermediate and more capital-intensive industries, such as cotton, fabrics and machinery (Hirschman 1967). As such, some basic conditions must be met to engender linkage development. First is the existence of a domestic market large enough to absorb domestic intermediate and industrial import substitutes. Second, the export market for final products, such as apparel, should grow enough to enable economies of scale for input suppliers, such as fabric and machinery producers. Third, the export industry itself, the garment industry, should grow over time to continue serving as a market for input suppliers (Hirschman 1958; 111–113; Gillis, *et al.* 1992: 422).

Michael Porter, in support of linkage development, argues for the importance of the process of *creating* competitive advantage by way of lowering costs or manufacturing differentiated products that command premium prices. To sustain competitive advantage over time, firms must provide higher-quality products and services, or produce more efficiently. He stresses the important role of national attributes such as economic environment, institutions and policies in creating and sustaining competitive advantage of firms in particular industries. Localised processes and state policies continue to play a significant role, contrary to arguments that the role for nations has diminished under intensified global competition (Porter 1990: 2–3, 18–21, 29–30). He focuses on the interconnectedness, the mutually advantageous symbiotic relationship, between local input suppliers and garment firms (input users producing end products) to determine the competitiveness of garment export firms. Domestic suppliers can attend to frequent garment fashion changes, quality and delivery schedules more easily than foreign ones. With on-time supply, garment producers can ensure on-time delivery, reduce transportation costs, obtain inputs in instalments and begin production quickly rather than waiting for input shipments from abroad that could result in late delivery of final products. Moreover, the established relationships between garment producers and domestic local input suppliers can facilitate frequent check-ups on input samples to ensure consistent quality and better meet 'just-in-time' orders (Kelegama and Foley 1999: 1450, 1455).

In support of linkage development, Gary Gereffi argues for the improvement of value added by industrial upgrading (moving up the production chain) and producing inputs domestically. His 'buyer-driven commodity chains' structure for the global market[7] examines unequal power relationships among different actors in terms of how financial, material and human resources are allocated within such a production chain. Large retailers and trading companies in developed countries control the designs, specifications and brand names (Gereffi 1995: 115–117). The East-Asian NIEs moved up the production chain, developed backward linkages, by becoming input producers and exporters, moving out of assembly operations and into original equipment manufacturing (often in the case of electronics industry). They produced inputs such as fabrics and other accessories for the garment industry or electronic boards for the electronics industry domestically (or increasingly in cheap labour countries like Vietnam), based on buyers' designs and specifications. While many Western corporate buyers still control the final marketing of these products, the East Asian suppliers have become 'package suppliers' to these buyers, and accumulated larger value added for their inputs (Kelegama and Foley 1999: 1456–1459).

Actually the neo-classical analysis of *dynamic* comparative advantage recognises a role for government in market intervention to promote national and local R&D activity, and to provide an initial push for 'infant industries' (Grossman and Helpman 1997; Krueger 1993). In particular, the work of Grossman and Helpman on policy hysteresis, referring to the permanent effects of a temporary policy, took into consideration the prominent role of history in determining long-run trade patterns and output growth. They argued that a country beginning with a greater stock of knowledge capital enjoys an initial advantage in the research lab and can perpetuate its technological lead. For developing countries, they supported government intervention over a given period of time, in order to eliminate the initial disadvantage in knowledge and technology. A temporary policy, e.g., state subsidies in national and local R&D activities, implemented with a pre-announced termination date, could have permanent effects and enhance national welfare. With government support, a developing country can gain research experience until the accumulated stock of knowledge surpasses that of its trading partners. Once this has been accomplished, the subsidy is no longer needed to ensure an adequate incentive for continued research.[8]

Relevance of Asian Cases for Vietnamese Linkage Development

Economic histories of many developed and developing countries provide evidence for this multi-stage industrialisation process and for the roles of the state and markets (both domestic and foreign) in facilitating linkage development.[9] This pattern of industrialisation took place in Australia, New Zealand,

France, Chile, Brazil, South Africa and Japan in the late nineteenth century and in some Asian countries in the late twentieth century. With state support, the (now) industrialised countries worked their way backward from the 'final touch' stages of garment and food processing industries (assembling) to domestic production of intermediate inputs (fabrics, accessories, etc.) and finally to the basic industrial materials (machinery, synthetic fibre, cotton, etc.). At the end of nineteenth century, the French domestic market supported production of fine cloth, ribbons and flannels. After World War I Japan, already in the second stage of industrialisation, used imported raw cotton to produce processed cotton for home consumption. Brazil in 1927 produced cotton for home consumption and India in the late nineteenth century produced finished cotton goods for the home market (Hoffmann 1958: 111–123, 140).

Vietnam's emphasis on state-led development in a market setting lends itself more towards the state-led economic development models of East and Southeast Asia than the Western models. The Vietnamese state continues to uphold its socialist ideals that are reflected in official pronouncements such as 'rich people, strong country, civilised and equitable society' and 'socialist market-oriented economy under state guidance' even after *doi moi* in the mid1980s. With ample evidence of Vietnamese engagement in industrial policies to develop linkages to intermediate goods production, the following Asian experiences provide a good framework to assess the VTGI case.

A large literature on the state role in East and Southeast Asian countries demonstrates that proactive state policies can create dynamic comparative advantage in industries which otherwise would not develop in the market system. The arguments put forward are consistent with Hirschman's linkage development, Grossman and Helpman's policy hysteresis, Gereffi's industrial upgrading and Porter's connectedness between local input suppliers and garment firms. Over the past three decades the states in Singapore, South Korea, Malaysia and Sri Lanka have invested in developing industries in which they did not originally have comparative advantage (Kuruvilla 1992: 7-9; Kim 1994: 185–188). They created and developed backward and forward linkages through incentive structures which were subject to clearly-defined performance conditions and time limitations; to receive these privileges, firms were required to develop specific domestic input industries within a given period of time.[10]

These proactive states created various incentive structures to promote export-orientated industrialisation (EOI) strategies in the late twentieth century for global integration, foreign investment stimulation and job creation. They intervened to move their economies from low-cost EOI to higher value-added, advanced EOI. They encouraged partnerships between universities and businesses (local and global), R&D and skills development programmes (which encouraged employer contributions to a general training fund from which they received refunds for approved employee-training programmes). For instance, the Singapore promoted advanced EOI by attracting higher value-added foreign investment and investing in skills enhancement and training via the Skills Development Fund established in 1982. Singapore advanced to computer assembly and semiconductor manufacture in 1980 and subsequently to higher value-added goods and services such as finance, banking, ports and oil refining in the late 1980s.

Hirschman's linkage development theory speaks to the case of South Korea. The Korean state combined financial, industrial and trade policies in proper sequence to develop the textile industry, first creating a demand for textile machinery and then assisting with the development of the machinery industry.[11] First, it established the Textile Modernisation Fund in 1981; second, it formulated the Industrial Development law in 1986 to provide low-interest loans for small and medium-size companies gradually to replace old textile machinery (hence creating demand for new machinery) and to shift to higher value-added products. Third, between 1987 and 1991, the state financed the development of a domestic textile machinery industry via low-interest loans, preferential tax and depreciation policies, which effectively increased machinery self-sufficiency from 36 per cent to 55 per cent. Concurrently, it used import protection and licensing policies in the 1980s within a four-year transition period (1986–1989) for these policies to take full effect. In particular, to encourage domestic fabric and apparel production the multi-tier import policies were implemented with lower tariffs on textile inputs (10 per cent duty on fibres) and higher tariffs on finished products (30–35 per cent on fabrics and 35–50 per cent on clothing). The orderly expansion of textile production capacity, closely monitored by licensing, prohibited new entrants into the textile industry and allowed inefficient firms to exit gradually with little disruption.

Gereffi's industrial upgrading argument also finds support in the case of South Korea where there was a shift from mass-produced, low-quality garment and textile products to higher-quality, value-added goods. This shift enabled Korea to achieve two main objectives: (1) to transcend the quota restrictions of the Multi-Fibre Agreements imposed by the United States and the then European Community; and (2) to cope with fierce competition from other lower-wage Asian producers. These objectives were achieved by investing in flexible production technology appropriate to smaller batches of diversified products, for diverse export markets such as Europe, the Middle East, Hong Kong and Africa (Meyanathan and Ahmed 1994). Korea also established many technical and research institutes to integrate textiles with other sectors in the economy. For instance the Korea Advanced Institute for Science and Technology and the Textile Technology Promotion Centre helped develop high-tech intermediate goods such as porous polyester fibre and flexible polyester fabrics (an integration between the textile and petrochemical industries). In addition, the Korea Federation of Textile Industries promoted design and high quality garments through various state-sponsored events such as Textile Week and International Designers' Fair.

The Malaysian state in the early 1990s also actively combined financial, industrial, foreign investment and skills training policies to build forward and backward linkages (Kuruvilla 1992: 11–12). The government tied financial incentives to domestic content requirements to integrate their export sector with other sectors of the economy. In 1991, 30 per cent domestic sourcing and 20 per cent domestic value-added conditions were imposed in return for certain financial incentives (Rasiah 1997: 131, 138–139). The government's Vision 20/20 industrial strategy restructured the investment incentives to attract foreign technology-based investment and skills training. For instance, it attracted Japanese investment in R&D (with operations located in Malaysia) in higher-end semiconductor and chip design phases of the electronics industry. Porter's argument finds support here; the Malaysian state helped build domestic industrial structure by encouraging linkages between local electronic parts suppliers and computer manufacturers. As in Singapore, Malaysia also focused on skills development and training programmes. The Skills Development Fund (SDF) was developed in 1992; 1 per cent of firms' payroll costs are matched by the government to subsidise training costs; each firm can receive a refund of up to 60 per cent of its SDF contribution. Partnerships were promoted between business and universities (the Federation of Malaysian Manufacturers and the University of Science and Technology), and between domestic and foreign firms (Penang Skills Development Centre developed by multinational corporations (MNCs) and local firms).

The Sri Lankan case provides evidence for Porter's ideas on the importance of partnerships among local suppliers, local manufacturers and MNCs in linkage development. Sri Lankan local suppliers, having cultivated trusting relationships with MNCs over the years, were able to supply simple inputs such as shoulder padding and corrugated cartons that met garment fashion demands and avoided high freight costs (Kelegama and Foley 1999: 1449, 1455–1457). They have supplied inputs for both the local export-orientated garment industry and MNCs' garment production sites in other countries. Moreover, local garment manufacturers shifted from mass-produced, standard products to differentiated products characterised by higher quality and lower volumes, using technological innovations such as computer-aided design (CAD) systems made available by these partnerships. These technologies can facilitate grading patterns (for different sizes) and replace manual cutting techniques with accurate computer-guided cutting systems.

Some studies in Vietnam, based on static comparative advantage arguments, opposed textile development and recommended adoption of a free-market framework. The basic argument is that upstream textile development is costly because Vietnam does not have advantage in that industry; therefore the state should not invest in it. They found the most significant areas of weakness related to the lack of consistent input quality and availability, and product design (backward linkages), as well as inadequate overseas distribution and poor access to the internet (forward linkages). They summarised those problems rather succinctly: 'suppliers cannot supply the right types of inputs with the required quality at the right time' (Institute of Economics-IDRC/CIDA 2001a: 21–29).

While they pinpointed a reasonable diagnosis of the problems, their recommended solution is partial and reflects an emerging interest in the state sector vouching for state investment in information technology and the internet. They advocated the deregulation of the telecommunications and internet service sector in the hope that lower costs for these services would increase usage and lead to more direct access to clients, and sources for inputs and machinery (Institute of Economics-IDRC/CIDA 2001a: 40–41). Another study argued that moving away from subcontracting (CMP) towards FOB[12] exports involves additional capital, which is scarce in Vietnam. So they argued that shifting towards FOB exports improves cost effectiveness only if firms can improve their competitiveness, which means higher managerial skills, better access to information and to a wider range of input suppliers (domestic and foreign) (Institute of Economics–IDRC/CIDA 2001c: 52–53).

While access to information is a useful component for the development of VTGI, it is hardly sufficient in light of positive results from proactive state policies in creating comparative advantages in the 1980s for Singapore and South Korea, and in the 1990s for Malaysia and Sri Lanka. As a caveat, however, these policies took decades to materialise and had negative implications for workers at the lowest level of subcontracting as discussed in the next section and in other studies.[13] In light of those Asian lessons, the relevant question is to examine the effects of Vietnamese industrial policies on export performance and workers' conditions within the context of a restructuring VTGI to which I now turn.

SETTING THE CONTEXT: PRODUCTION, TRADE, LABOUR AND LINKAGE INSTITUTIONS

A Changing Structure

The combination of domestic economic reforms and a changing international politico-economic environment resulted in major restructuring of the VTGI, that has various implications for linkage development.[14] Increasing global integration brought about a rise in foreign investment and control in the VTGI, and a relative decrease in state production. As one of the most rapidly expanding manufacturing sectors over the past decade, the VTGI has increasingly served the growing domestic market, but garment export still relies on imported inputs resulting in low value-added for domestic producers and workers. Figure 5.1 demonstrates the growth of VTGI since the early 1990s,

Figure 5.1: Vietnamese textile and garment exports, 1981–2002 (in millions of US dollars)

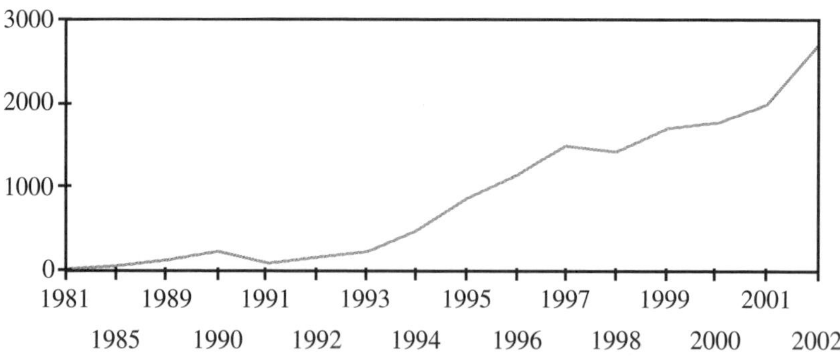

Note: Data between 1995 and 1999 are at constant 1994 prices, between 1990 and 1994 are at constant 1989 prices, between 1981 and 1989 are at constant 1980 prices. I took these different constant prices into consideration by choosing 1989 as a base year for the whole series. The lack of growth between 1997 and 1998 may be due to the Asian financial crisis. 2002 statistics estimate only.

Sources: VINATEX Publications, Statistical Yearbooks 1990, 1995, 1999, 2000, 2001, 2002.

punctuated by two landmark years. First, in 1991 Vietnam began reaching out to capitalist markets in the EU and Japan. Second, effective since 1995, the Vietnamese government made some significant consolidations in order to streamline the state sector; VINATEX emerged, signifying the ascension of the textile interest concomitant with the linkage development policy. Moreover, in trading with the former socialist countries, the symbiotic relationships between public and private sectors have facilitated both backward and forward linkage developments, as will be discussed in the next section. In effect this symbiosis blurs the boundaries, often conceived by the neo-classical framework, between state and private firms.

Direct state control over the VTGI diminished over time and stabilised after state consolidation took effect in 1996. But the interesting trend was the rise in production from foreign-invested firms with consistent contribution from Vietnamese private producers (Tables 5.3 and 5.4).[15] It is clear that the state sector is strong in textile production (around 50 per cent of output), whereas the Vietnamese non-state sector has a strong hold in garment production (around 45 per cent), mostly for low value-added CMP exports. After 1996, the state sector supplied about 50 per cent of total textile products, and

Table 5.3: Share of gross textile values by ownership types, 1995–2000 (%)

Sector	1995	1996	1997	1998	1999	2000
State	59	58	50	50	54	51
Domestic non-state	26	26	34	23	25	23
Foreign-invested	15	17	16	27	21	26

Sources: *Statistical Yearbook 1997:* 166, 202; *Statistical Yearbook 1999*: 177, 193, 203; *Statistical Yearbook 2000*: 255, 268, 292, 314; *Statistical Yearbook 2001*: 246, 258, 270, 276; Hill (1998, citing the Government Statistics Office): 17.

Table 5.4: Share of gross garment values by ownership types, 1995–2000 (%)

Sector	1995	1996	1997	1998	1999	2000
State	37	36	34	33	33	32
Domestic non-state	50	49	45	45	44	43
Foreign-invested	13	15	20	22	23	25

Sources: As for Table 5.3

around one-third of garment products. There has been an increasing role for foreign firms over the second half of the 1990s: 15 to 26 per cent of output in textiles and 13 to 25 per cent in garments; while the Vietnamese private producers maintained around 25 per cent in textiles and 45 per cent in garments. This trend is consistent with the rise in foreign investment in textile and garment industries, that, paradoxically, posed both challenges and opportunities to Vietnam's linkage development as discussed further.

Consolidation of the state bureaucracy in late 1995 streamlined the management of state-owned textile and garment firms. After state consolidation, only four ministries oversee the VTGI: the Ministry of Industry (consolidating the former Ministries of Light Industry, Heavy Industry, and Energy Industry), the Ministry of Trade and the Ministry of Finance. The Ministry of Industry approves the general development strategy for the textile and garment industries; the Ministry of Trade allocates export quotas (primarily for the EU and Canadian markets, and for the U.S. market after the signing of the Bilateral Textile Agreement in May 2003); the Ministry of Finance allocates low-interest loans to state firms, negotiates with foreign sources for funds and audits all central state firms; and the Ministry of Planning and Investment oversees foreign investment in the VTGI as well as in other industries.

Also in 1995 an 'umbrella' state corporation called VINATEX was created by the prime minister to oversee all central–state owned textile and garment firms and to foster greater integration between state textile and garment firms.[16] By 2000, VINATEX had the same number of textile and garment plants, 25 plants in each sector out of a total of 61 member firms (although the restructuring plan discussed later would change this ratio). The rest are service firms: one finance company, four mechanical-repair and spare-parts enterprises, one research institute for textile and garment products, one fashion design institute (FADIN established in 1997), one cotton research institute and three vocational training schools (VINATEX brochure 2000). While maintaining a leadership role, the contribution of VINATEX to total production and export of the VTGI remained about 30 per cent (Customs Department 1998a). Yet its member central state firms received a large amount of EU quotas (about 70 per cent of total VINATEX exports were destined for the EU) (interview Tran Van Quyen, June 2000; interview Nguyen An Toan, June 2000; Customs Department 1998b).

The VTGI still relies on imported machinery. By 2000, the domestic textile and garment machinery industry supplied only about 2 per cent of total machinery and spare parts. The rest were imported from developed countries such as Germany, Japan, South Korea, Italy, Switzerland, France and the United States (interview Tran Van Quyen, June 2000). Additionally, many East Asian representative sales offices in Vietnam have sold machinery and parts to Vietnamese firms (MPDF 1999a: 98). There are two ways to finance this imported machinery. First, the most common payment method is long-term amortisation to be paid off by deducting a certain percentage from the subcontracting prices (or CMP as explained in the section on labour issues) over a period of time. Second, foreign machine manufacturers assist Vietnam in obtaining loans from foreign commercial banks.

But it is encouraging that the VTGI has increasingly served the growing domestic market of over 76 million Vietnamese. This domestic market has generated consumption linkages to intermediate goods, such as fabrics and other accessories. Both state and private producers supplied about 70–75 per cent of the domestic garment market. About 10–15 per cent were smuggled from China; 5 per cent were legally imported from South Korea, Singapore, the EU and the United States; the rest were 'left-over' products from CMP firms and second-hand clothes donated by international humanitarian organisations (Figure 5.2) (MPDF 1999b: 8; *Asia Pulse* 2000). Most Vietnamese consumers are concerned about prices and, to some extent, fashion when buying clothes. Of course, the upper and middle class consumers pay more attention to product quality and the brand image of certain apparel companies. During fieldwork in 2000, I interviewed several enterprising private producers in Nam Dinh (the bastion of Vietnamese textile industry) who have been successful in competing with cheap and mostly poor quality Chinese products. These private producers used domestic fabrics and adapted popular designs from South Korea, Thailand and the EU to serve domestic needs, especially in the provinces, rural and mountainous areas (interview Tran Van Duoc 2000; interview Vu Phuong Sao 2000). Interestingly, I recognised many people of different age groups in Nam Dinh and Hanoi wearing affordable yet fashionable shorts and T-shirts, with adapted 'Adidas' designs, made by the private producer whom I interviewed in Nam Dinh.

Export Types and Linkage Development

Further global integration since the mid-1990s gave rise to structural change in the export markets, increasing export to capitalist countries. In 1999, two major capitalist markets, the EU and Japan, dominated the scene,[17] accounting for over 70 per cent (US$700 million and US$500 million respectively) of total VTGI export value (US$1.747 billion). The rest was distributed among Canada (US$100 million), the Middle East (US$100 million), the U.S. (US$20

Figure 5.2: The Vietnamese domestic garment market by product source

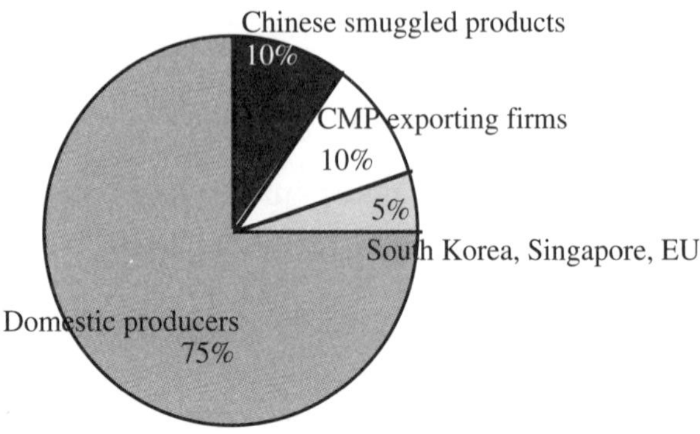

Sources: MPDF 1999b; *Asia Pulse* 2000

million), and Eastern Europe (EE) (US$50 million) (Ministry of Trade and VINATEX, June 2000). However, after the signing of the Bilateral Trade Agreement with the U.S. in 2001, exports to the U.S. market rose sharply from US$47 million in 2001 to US$970 in 2002 (Ministry of Trade, October 2003).

Interestingly, the type of export to capitalist markets (CMP) is not conducive to linkage development in comparison to the type of export primarily to the former socialist trading partners (free on board, FOB). In principle, under FOB trade, Vietnamese subcontractors are responsible to buy inputs, assemble them and deliver the final products. This enables the use domestic inputs (i.e. fabrics) for garment products, hence facilitating linkages with other Vietnamese economic sectors. However, in practice, this potential depends on negotiations with foreign corporate buyers who may want to dictate where to buy inputs (Interview Hoang Minh Khang, 2003). Two types of FOB trade are explained further below. On the other hand CMP trade requires the use of imported fabrics and accessories in garment exports. There is a trade off, however, between these two types of trade deal in terms of the risk involved. The import-dependent CMP trade provides less risky subcontracting orders with imported inputs (purchased by corporate buyers) and guaranteed export markets. The potentially better-integrated FOB trade, on the other hand, requires money advanced to buy necessary input that often poses a difficulty for cash-strapped Vietnamese firms (they do not always get reimbursed for money already invested if the final products are rejected for any reason). As time progresses, more FOB deals were developed although official statistics tended to underestimate and refer to them as '*tieu ngach*', or FOB deals made mostly between private entrepreneurs and the EE buyers. Official statistics mainly accounted for official export including CMP exports to the EU and other capitalist countries, and official FOB trade between state firms and the EE markets. Official FOB deals in 1999 accounted for about 35 per cent of total export value (the rest were CMP deals) compared to almost none previously (interview Tran Van Quyen, June and July 2000). However anecdotal evidence revealed that *tieu ngach* trading amounted to about US$262 million in 2000. (*Vietnam Courier* 1995; *Thoi Bao Kinh Te Saigon* 1997: 36; interview Tran Van Quyen, June and July 2000). Next I will discuss how these two export types have different implications for linkage development.

Historical conditions facilitated trade with the socialist countries, that helped build both backward and forward linkages in Vietnam. The legacy of the Soviet-era in providing education and training for fellow communists has left about 50,000 Vietnamese in Russia, including about 5,000 scientists and students; the rest were guest workers (to repay Vietnam's debts to these socialist countries) and traders. Private entrepreneurs were able to transcend the difficulties in FOB trade and established informal backward and forward linkages.[18] My interviews with both state officials and firm owners in the north and south between 1995 and 2000 provide evidence for this dynamism; many private, enterprising and resourceful managers in both regions either served in the army or were guest workers (for instance, Tien Long in the south and HEPRO in the north). They have maintained personal business contacts and connections to obtain garment orders, using domestic inputs, subcontracting to domestic factories (state and non-state) as well as homeworkers throughout Vietnam and selling directly to EE consumers via containers transported by commercial liners. Their direct forward linkages with small-scale local retail stores and/or kiosks in these EE countries provided them with valuable market information about final consumers' tastes and preferences.

FOB deals with the EE markets had undergone major restructuring. Trading relationships with Russia, the former East Germany and Czechoslovakia commenced with counter trade via inter-governmental agreements (*hiep dinh chinh phu*) in the late 1980s and turned into cash-based exchange after the collapse of these countries' socialist regimes in the period 1989–91.[19] Until recently, state efforts in re-establishing formal commercial relationships with these EE markets (especially with Russia) were plagued with difficulties due to their political uncertainties, unstable currencies and widespread mafia problems (interview Tran Van Quyen, July 2000). A commercial agreement signed between Vietnam and Russia in September 2000 stipulated the terms for Vietnam to repay its 1.7 billion debt, based on a mutually agreed value of the rouble, and to facilitate trade.[20] This agreement also facilitates formal banking relations including the establishment of the necessary Letters of Credit (LC) for FOB trade between the two countries (FPT 2000).

Different types of FOB trade have different implications for linkage development. In 1999 total FOB trade consisted of 15 per cent *unconditional* deals (approximately US$262 million), whereby garment manufacturers are free to select input suppliers, and 20 per cent *conditional* deals in which Vietnamese counterparts must buy inputs from specific suppliers specified by foreign corporate buyers (the rest were CMP trade). It is the unconditional FOB trade that allows Vietnamese producers more leeway to use domestic inputs hence facilitating further backward linkage.[21] Most state officials and firm managers that I interviewed prefer unconditional FOB exports since they can supply inputs from their own sources (either produced in Vietnam or sourced from outside). In this case, Vietnamese contractors can obtain roughly 10–20 per cent profit margin (interview Nguyen Thuy Huong, June 2000). About one half of these unconditional FOB exports utilised fabrics made by well-known state textile plants such as Thang Loi, Phong Phu, Viet Thang and Nam Dinh. The other half used domestic fabrics and accessories sold in commercial markets such as Dong Xuan and Phung Khac Khoan (in the north), and Soai Kinh Lam and An Dong (in the south). Private weavers in the Nga Tu Bay Hien weaving centre in Ho Chi Minh City (HCMC) and small weavers in the north have supplied domestic fabrics and accessories for these markets. But for consistent product quality, many garment firms rely on East Asian fabric sources such as the 100-per-cent Korean-owned cotton fabric plant, PANGRIM, or other Asian fabric distributors in Vietnam (interview Tran Van Quyen, July 2000).

Moreover, symbiotic relationships between state and non-state sectors in FOB trade facilitate further backward linkages. Interviews conducted between 1996 and 2000 demonstrated multi-level subcontracting among domestic firms. Most large state firms obtained EE orders from the state (via intergovernmental agreements); they either carried them out in their own plants, or subcontracted to smaller state or private garment firms who may in turn subcontract down to household production units. Most large state textile plants used their own fabrics in apparel production for EE markets in this process. My 2000 fieldwork in Nam Dinh, the oldest 'textile town' in Vietnam, confirmed this trend. Three garment plants of Nam Dinh Textile have been using Nam Dinh cotton fabrics (jean, solid and checked) to manufacture children's shirts and trousers for export to Canada and some EE countries (interview Pham Van Tuan, July 2000).

Vietnam has actively reached out to capitalist markets to compensate for the loss of its traditional socialist markets. It signed a major trade agreement with the then EC in December 1992 which established the system of gradually rising export quotas in 151 garment categories with restrictions on both quantity and value.[22] Access to this relatively large market was crucial to the survival of the VTGI, especially in light of the then US trade embargo (lifted in July 1995), which isolated Vietnam from the biggest and richest pool of consumers in the world.[23] Overall the Vietnamese producers face many challenges and uncertainties both in terms of structure and potential markets. The triangular subcontracting framework provides a static characterisation of the trading structure with the EU markets. It reflects the unequal power relationships between the three main actors: the Vietnamese garment producers and workers (assembling inputs); the middlemen (from East Asian countries such as Taiwan, South Korea, Hong Kong and Singapore who provide all inputs); and the capitalist corporate buyers (from the EU, Japan, Canada, Norway and the United States who place orders).[24] Over time I found that the triangle has become flatter as more corporate buyers deal directly with Vietnamese producers to gain greater value added and cut out the middlemen's costs, and the middlemen would move up the subcontracting ladder to become corporate buyers themselves. But from the Vietnamese perspective, CMP trade does not facilitate backward linkages (inability to provide inputs by themselves) or forward linkages (no direct marketing links to final consumers) (MPDF 1999a: 11). The corporate buyers and middlemen still had primary control over sources of inputs via the use of letter of credit (LC), a common financial instrument.[25] Moreover, fluctuations in export markets also affected VTGI trade performance. The Japanese economic downturn in recent years has negatively affected VTGI exports. Also East European producers, a viable competitor to Vietnamese producers, have attracted more EU firms due to lower transportation costs (proximity advantage) and low labour costs (MPDF 1999a: 10–11).

Labour issues: structure, pay, working conditions

Garment workers have played a vital role in the industrialisation process of developing countries, in the 1970s in Taiwan, South Korea and Singapore, in the 1980s in Malaysia and in the 1990s in Vietnam. However, they have not received equitable benefits resulting from EOI strategies (Deyo 1997: 212, 222) and have borne some negative consequences. Most of export manufacturing sectors have been non-union (Deyo 1997: 214; Rasiah 1993: 3–23;

Bonacich *et al.* 1994: 9, 11), while all of these states have, in varying degrees, suppressed labour movements in exchange for political stability to attain those EOI objectives.

Workers have faced similar impacts of the multi-level piecework subcontracting system: poor working and living conditions and gender expectations to increase productivity and flexibility in this global industry.[26] As experienced in other developing countries, most workers in the VTGI are women who earn low piece rates for assembling garment products. They face low-skilled, dead-end and insecure jobs, and engage in self-exploitation to assemble as many pieces as humanly possible to make ends meet. Moreover, I found a prevalent gender division of labour, in which men workers are assigned to work with machines because of their supposedly 'male' characteristics, while most women workers are stuck in simple manual tasks due to their 'female nature'. This took place irrespective of technological evolution of the Vietnamese garment industry in which current technology no longer justifies such a gendered division of labour. The socially constructed gender roles of female and male workers facilitate and perpetuate these expectations which then translate into hiring decisions, differential on-the-job training and pay levels, consistently along gender line benefiting males over females. Moreover, there is evidence of many explicit and implicit forms of workers' protests to improve their working conditions in both state and non-state firms.

Multi-level subcontracting has weakened state capacity to enforce the progressive Vietnamese labour laws. The piece-rate system renders labour policies ineffective and unenforceable since workers tend to engage in self-exploitation. The remuneration system entails that the more clothing pieces workers assemble, the more they receive. The piece rate is a part of the CMP price negotiated between foreign corporate buyers and Vietnamese subcontractors. As of summer 2000, the national average hourly rate in the VTGI was about 25 US cents, or between 3,300–3,500 dong.[27]

Important labour stipulations on work hours, minimum wage, and overtime pay are non-binding and not respected by many owners or managers. As noted in one study, 'Workers do not generally protest if not properly paid, as they are willing to take normal rate in extra-working time. This situation is mainly due to high competition for work' (Institute of Economics–IDRC/CIDA 2001b: 51, 54). While it is true that workers are allowed to strike and women are entitled to take breaks when they are pregnant, nursing or menstruating, they exploit themselves by not taking these breaks since they would lose earnings under the piece rate system.

Unequal power characterises the relationships between MNCs and workers. MNCs are effectively monopsonists who are at the top of the subcontracting ladder. They have a credible threat to shift production from Vietnam to other developing countries. Workers are at the bottom of the chain for both CMP and FOB deals and have very few choices: earning very low wages, under-employment or unemployed. Their limited 'power' is to compete with similarly placed workers in other developing countries, hence effectively maintaining the low wages from which the MNCs benefit.

In all the pro-market literature, labour is considered as one of the production costs, the lower the better since it contributes to the 'comparative advantage' of an industry. At present, Vietnamese labour cost remains among the lowest in East Asia. Before the onset of the Asian financial crisis in 1997, Vietnam's textile wage rates were about 20 per cent below some major low-income exporters such as China, India and Indonesia and about one-third those of Thailand (Hill 1998: 22–23).[28] Rapid currency depreciation in Thailand and Indonesia at the height of the Asian financial crisis temporarily pushed their wages below those in Vietnam thus making their CMP export products cheaper than Vietnamese products. However, this was only a temporary condition since by 2000 Vietnamese wage rates were still among the lowest in East and Southeast Asia (interview Nguyen Thuy Huong, July 2000). As the financial crisis had significant impacts on Asian countries in 1998, labour productivity in those countries fell dramatically while that in Vietnam and China were less affected and continued to increase. But this does not mean that Vietnamese workers received higher wages as the labour share of the value-added remains low (Institute of Economics-IDRC/CIDA 2001b: 27–28).

Domestically, garment wages are still lower than other industries' average and only higher than the agricultural average. Statistics in 1998 showed that the monthly average income of a garment worker is 650,000 dong (about $50), for a textile worker it is 801,000 dong (about $62) and the industry average is about $53, compared with service sector wages of about $55, and in agriculture of about $48. Foreign-owned firms tended to pay more: 900,000 VND/month (or about $69) (Institute of Eco-nomics-IDRC/CIDA 2001b: 49–51).

In terms of distribution of value added to owners of labour and capital (as value added is defined as including labour and capital incomes), I found that the owners of capital and wage earners in other countries reaped the lion's share of the value added, not the Vietnamese workers and producers. Distribution of revenues among different actors involved in the context of CMP trade has remained the same since 1996: only about 4 per cent for the Vietnamese counterparts. My 1996 estimates of income distribution in the manufacturing and marketing of a boy's dress shirt (Table 5.5) are supported by a 1998 study on the income distribution of men's shirts. For a men's shirt assembled in Vietnam and sold in the United States for $15, Vietnamese producers obtained about 4 per cent (60 cents); the middlemen accumulated 15–16 per cent of the retail price ($2.30); while about 80 per cent went to the Western buyers (Pham Quang Ham 1998; *Lao Dong*1997). Both of these cases demonstrate that, if Vietnamese producers can supply the inputs themselves (as in FOB trade), they can capture at least 10–15 per cent of the retail price.

My econometric model (details in Appendix 5.1) provided an accurate snapshot of conditions in the mid-1990s by identifying significant factors such as export types (CMP), foreign investment, ownership type, firm locations (northern or southern region) and export policies that affected total sales. My finding about the negative relationship between CMP exports and value added remains true at the time of writing. Over the period of 1993–2002, while trade promotion policies have increased total trade value, the value added accumulated by domestic producers and workers remains very low.

Table 5.5: Allocation of income to factors of production and distribution (data from retail price of a boy's dress shirt)

Total retail price = $10 per shirt	**Income Allocation to Factors of Production and Distribution**
Domestic share (**4% of retail price**) = US$0.40 (This is also total CMP* value)	Vietnamese workers' wage: ca. 53% of total CMP Vietnamese entrepreneurs' wages, rents, normal profits and instalments paid to foreign machine manufacturers: ca. 47% of total CMP
Middlemen's share (16% of retail price) = US$1.60	East Asian input producers' incomes East Asian managers' wages
Corporate foreign buyers' share (80% of retail price) = US$8.00	Designers' wages Profits to retailers, incomes to service providers (such as transportation/shipping and insurance)

* Structure of CMP value includes these components: (1) Vietnamese workers: wages (estimated from piece rates); (2) Vietnamese sub-contractors/entrepreneurs: salary, normal profits, operating costs; (3) Instalments paid to foreign machine manufacturers.
Source: Field research in Vietnam (1996–97).

This model, however, does not capture some dynamic factors arising since Vietnam's further integration into the world market. These include an increase in foreign investment in the textile industry, a relative decrease in state production, a growing domestic market for Vietnamese fabrics, a steady demand for export-related inputs and the symbiotic relationship between state and non-state firms especially in manufacturing for the EE markets. There has been an increase in the use of domestic fabrics (over 50 per cent were produced by the private sector) in manufacturing apparel for the EE markets in Russia, Poland, Hungary and Czechoslovakia from late 1980s to late 1990s. Future research can incorporate several indicators to capture the effects of this symbiotic relationship: the share of domestic fabrics in total inputs used in FOB trade, the magnitude of subcontracting or quota sales/transfer between state and private firms.

Institutional Support for Linkage Development

Vietnam has a rich variety of institutions aimed at supporting linkage development but their real contribution was limited to trade promotion and export market diversification. While there exist many state, para-statist and private service providers claiming to offer a wide array of services (such as training and education, marketing, production-related services, design, information, financial, research, procurement and investment consultancy), institutions for genuine backward linkages are still sorely missing.[29]

The partnerships between research institutes and textile promotion centres as exist elsewhere in East Asia are lacking. VINATEX training schools and over a dozen private centres primarily focus on training in basic assembly skills, *not* higher-skilled activities (such as clothing design, R&D in intermediate inputs, technical know-how, marketing and management skills) that would empower workers to negotiate for higher value-added jobs (MPDF 1999a: 44). Technical universities and research institutes, such as Hanoi Polytechnic University, Ho Chi Minh City Economics University, the four state-owned R&D institutes on textile and garment technology, materials and designs tend to operate independently from each other and from firms in the VTGI (MPDF 1999a: 92–7).

Institutional focus was still limited to trade promotion and export market diversification. The existing trade-promotion institutions are business-orientated and offer a variety of services to protect intellectual property (such as patents, trademarks and copyright) and to seek out export markets via trade fairs.[30] The largest and most established is the Vietnamese Chamber of

Commerce and Industry (VCCI), a para-statist institution with 3,500 member firms from all industries with an equal share of members from both private and state sectors.[31] It has a new, professional-looking headquarters in the International Trade Centre building in Hanoi and a website to promote its activities in relation to small and medium enterprises (interview Pham Thi Thu Hang, July 2000). The second is VITAS (Vietnam Textile and Apparel Association), another para-statist institution established in 1999 with VINATEX as a member and as of 2003 consisting of about 500 members including about 120 firms with foreign investment.[32] VITAS's main goal is to promote trade, diversify export markets, and serve as a bridge between member firms and the ministries (Interview Le Van Dao, 2003).[33] The third one represents private interests of southern textile and garment firms, the Association of Weaving, Clothing, Knitting and Embroidery (*Hoi Det May Theu Dan*) formed in 1993 in HCMC; its membership increased from 82 to 187 by 2000.[34]

The state can adapt much more from the relevant East and Southeast Asian experiences discussed earlier. It needs to initiate the establishment of a skills development fund to develop higher-order skills such as cognitive, technical and analytical skills. A cost-sharing scheme between the state and participating firms, as in Singapore and Malaysia, would be appropriate. The state also needs to create a clear incentive structure to facilitate partnerships among factories, research institutes and universities (domestic and foreign) as in South Korea. Relevant ministries can foment partnerships among the large foreign-owned textile firms in Vietnam, Vietnamese R&D institutes and factories, for transfer of technology, as well as technical know-how and know-why, as in Sri Lanka.

EFFECTS OF EOI AND LINKAGE DEVELOPMENT POLICIES (1993–2000)

The Vietnamese state has already engaged in both trade and industrial policies to go back to intermediate goods production, but there is a big gap between the formal intentions of policies and their implementation and enforcement. While Vietnam has all the linkage development policies and export-orientated-industrialisation (EOI) policies, the necessary disciplinary conditions, notably performance criteria and time limitation, demonstrated in the East Asian cases, were lacking in Vietnam. The state firms receiving these privileges were not subject to clearly defined performance criteria and their track records were not made available for public scrutiny. Moreover there was no time limit as to when state support would stop after the initial kick-start. While EOI and progressive foreign investment policies led to an increase in foreign investment, especially in 100 per cent foreign textile plants, there is no evidence of transfer of knowledge and technology between domestic and foreign firms, as will be discussed next.

Export-Orientated-Industrialisation Policies

Since *doi moi*, the Vietnamese state has introduced a series of EOI policies, regarding customs procedures, import and export taxes, financial, quota allocation and foreign investment. Thus far, export promotion policies have tended to increase VTGI exports in the low value-added CMP trade, rather than the higher value-added FOB trade.

Streamlined trade bureaucracies and procedures, commencing in 1995 and more prominent since 1998, eliminated export licenses, export registration and customs procedures. These reforms helped increase total VTGI export sharply after 1995 (Table 5.2) and enabled timely manufacturing and delivery, crucial to CMP trade. Moreover, the Minister of Trade permitted local trade and customs departments (*so thuong mai dia phuong*) to directly manage and oversee trading activities of local firms (state and private). Customs procedures were complicated but have been improved over the years, and their impacts were mainly an irritation to export firms. Export tax exemption to promote export of final textile/garment products has been applied as well as import taxes (of 35–40 per cent of invoice prices of fabrics and accessories, and over 50 per cent on apparel) to protect domestic producers (Institute of Economics-IDRC/CIDA 2001b: 53-54; NXB Thong Ke 1997: 270–283).

Quota allocation policies illuminate state equity and poverty alleviation goals. They reflect state concerns for rural–urban equity, but in practice resulted in unintended reinforcement of structural inequity between SOEs and private firms. Quota allocation is based on firms' previous year performance (an efficiency goal), while a certain amount is supposedly reserved for firms in poor and mountainous provinces (an equity goal). In implementation, the longer-established large state firms have a natural advantage over private firms and continue to receive more quotas. Firms in poor, rural and mountainous provinces tend to subcontract for large state firms in big cities.

State bureaucracy to manage EU quota allocation remains cumbersome. Representatives from three ministries formed the Inter-Ministerial Quota Consortium [*To quota*].[35] This consortium was supposed to allocate quotas in March of each year, and check up on firms in mid-year to see how they had utilised their quotas, then make adjustments by shifting some quotas from inefficient firms to the more efficient ones, to prevent the practice of selling quotas (Institute of Economics-IDRC/CIDA 2001a: 66–67; Institute of Economics-IDRC/CIDA 2001b: 53–54). However, quota transfer and borrowing/lending among firms is allowed (Interview Le Van Thang, 2003).

EU quotas only satisfy about 35–50 per cent of total VTGI export.[36] In practice, about 90 per cent of the EU quotas were allocated to state firms.[37] But the private sector probably accounted for more than 10 per cent through subcontracting for SOEs and purchasing quotas unofficially from them.[38] These underestimated underground activities illustrate the symbiotic relationship between SOEs and private firms.

There were efforts to promote the use of domestic inputs and market diversification, development of backward and forward linkages by linking a trade bonus incentive system with local content requirements. Firms that used domestic fabrics and delivered all allocated EU quotas on time in the previous year, or exported to non-quota markets, received bonus EU quotas on popular items such as jackets or shirts. Large state firms ended up receiving these bonus quotas because most of them already used domestic fabrics. So greater policy fine-tuning is needed to overcome the structural inequity between state and private firms.

Over time, quota allocation policies have become less distorting due to reform of the quota allocation mechanism and the rising share of Vietnam's non-quota markets (Institute of Economics-IDRC/CIDA 2001c: 66–67; Institute of Economics-IDRC/CIDA 2001b: 53–54). In 2000 the government experimented with a more market-based quota auction policy to make quotas available to the non-state sector, albeit only a small part was auctioned. The pilot project auctioned the 20 per cent annual increase of seven EU quota categories in December 1999; the rest were still based on the previous year's performance (Tran Manh Thu, July 2000). The purpose was to curtail the corrupt common practice of '*xin, cho*' [asking, giving], and to promote transparency of the quota distribution process. In the first auction the private sector represented 44 per cent of the bidders, but only 26 per cent of the winning bids (Institute of Economics–IDRC/CIDA 2001c: 66–67). Each bidder paid the auction price plus 30 per cent to contribute to the 'insurance fund' to be refunded after delivery of the order (interview Tran Manh Thu, June 2000).

Based on lessons learned from the 1999 quota auction, the government made some policy adjustments to improve the auction policy. First, the policy did not achieve the equity goal since most high bidders were large private firms from HCMC with more capital and better infrastructure (interview Tran Manh Thu, June 2000). Consequently small and provincial firms continued to subcontract for large state and private firms. Second, since most bidders, operating below capacity, actually delivered their auctioned EU quotas on time, the Quota Consortium decided to eliminate the 'insurance fund'. (It imposed an unnecessary burden on cash-strapped firms and may have unintentionally encouraged bribery and misuse of funds in the process of collection and refund of the insurance fund.)

The state has not tied financial privileges with accountability and discipline from SOE recipients as in other Asian countries. This area requires rigorous reforms if Vietnam seeks to learn from the more successful Asian models. In general, state firms have more access to state financial sources, including low-interest loans and state investment than private firms (Institute of Economics-IDRC/CIDA 2001b: 53). Also they are not subject to transparent performance criteria or 'sunset clauses'. I was unable to obtain any clear performance criteria from interviews with state officials in various ministries and ended up inferring the main criteria from the list of remaining state firms after the VINATEX restructuring plan (2000–05). They related to job saving/creation and fixed assets (capital already invested in state firms which are mostly large firms in major cities).

State firms have access to more diverse sources of capital while most private firms rely primarily on private capital sources, hence SOEs have more chances to engage in machinery upgrading, new projects' investment, workers' training, and R&D activities. In principle, the state Fund for Cooperation and Development, established and administered by the prime minister and three ministries (Industry, Finance, and Planning and Investment), allocates low-interest state loans to all sectors based on risk analysis, financial status and debt repayment ability.[39] In reality, VINATEX is able to secure low-interest loans for its member firms. While state firms have access to all capital sources such as the state budget (the largest source), official development assistance (ODA) and commercial banks,[40] most private firms can only obtain loans from private commercial banks and the MPDF (MPDF 1999a: 117; MPDF 1999c: 9–11).

The evolution of foreign investment policies since the inception of *doi moi* demonstrates that the state recognised potential benefits of foreign investment in job creation, capital investment, transfer of technology and technical expertise. The Vietnamese foreign investment legal framework is very liberal compared to many other developing countries. As early as 1987 wholly owned foreign firms FDI and joint ventures at the inter-governmental level were approved; several amendments in 1990 effectively expanded and permitted many possible variations of joint ventures at both firm and individual levels, domestically and globally.[41] East Asian firms have ranked the highest in their investment in fabric and apparel production, with Taiwan and South Korea being the top two countries during 1997–2000.

Overall while the majority of foreign-invested firms' textile production was for export, they have made inroads into the Vietnamese textile market by supplying for both domestic use and garment export. The government should be more conscious of this development and proactively encourage partnerships between local Vietnamese plants and foreign-invested plants for transfer of technology and knowledge as in Sri Lanka and Malaysia.

FDI in the VTGI contributed to job creation and to a smaller extent, supplied the domestic market. By 2000, all foreign-invested firms employed about 50,000 people (or 10 per cent of total workers in the VTGI), and paid them a minimum monthly wage ranging from $30 to 55, although in big cities like HCMC and Hanoi the rates are higher.[42] For the domestic market wholly foreign-owned textile firms supplied about one-third of their total fabric sales, and textile joint ventures with Vietnamese firms provided about 50 per cent. On the other hand, most garment outputs from foreign invested firms were for CMP export and only about 10 per cent for the domestic market (Table 5.6). Consistently good quality is one of the main reasons why export orientated garment factories have utilised outputs from foreign-invested factories. For instance, many domestic firms (state and private) use cotton fabrics from Pangrim (wholly South Korean owned), high-quality threads from Coats-Tootal Phong Phu (a British-SOE joint venture), polyester padding from Hanoi-EVC (an East Asian-SOE joint venture) and sewing machines and accessories from Viet Tien-Tung Shing (a Hong Kong-SOE joint venture).[43]

Vietnam, as a latecomer, must confront a more competitive environment, as there are more world textile and garment producers now than when the NIEs embarked on EOI strategies in the 1960s, 1970s and 1980s. Under the Vietnamese Foreign Investment law, owners of wholly foreign-owned firms are able to accumulate the majority of value added and repatriate profits after paying wages to workers and rents and taxes to the Vietnamese state. Moreover, in light of industrial upgrading and deepening, quite a few East Asian corporations engaged in a strategy of establishing both backward and for-

Table 5.6: Market shares for outputs from foreign invested firms, 1988–99

	Textile		Garment	
	Export %	**Domestic %**	**Export %**	**Domestic %**
Total FDI	66	34	88	12
Wholly owned	71	29	87	13
Joint ventures	56	44	90	10

Source: *MPI 2000.*

ward linkages in Vietnam to take advantage of cheap labour there and supply their fabrics for both Vietnamese and world markets.

Many foreign-invested factories in Vietnam are subsidiaries of big corporations headquartered in South Korea, Taiwan and Japan; these subsidiaries utilised (often used) machinery and technology from their 'mother' corporations while absorbing cheap Vietnamese labour. For instance, Asian companies, such as the Korean Choongnam Spinning Ltd, invested in large and sophisticated wholly owned textile plants making industrial inputs (such as yarns and synthetic fibre) in Vietnam, while also forming smaller joint ventures with Vietnam to utilise these inputs in manufacturing fabrics for both domestic and foreign markets (as a form of backward and forward linkages for those Asian corporations). Choongnam invested over $50 million in its Choongnam Vietnam Textile Ltd to manufacture yarns in Vietnam and at the same time formed a US$7.5 million joint venture, Choongnam-Viet Thang, to make fabrics (VINATEX 1997: 393–394).

Wholly foreign-owned textile plants invested more in backward linkages and intermediate goods production than did joint ventures. More than 20 wholly foreign-owned textile plants with total investment of over $1 billion produce a wide variety of high-quality cotton, polyester and synthetic fabrics with high-tech production processes (fibre filament, weaving, dyeing, finishing). The largest investment of $470 million came from the Taiwanese Hualon Corporation. On the other hand, joint ventures with Vietnamese counterparts were much smaller; they invested about US$71 million and produced simpler textile products such as cotton, denim, silk and knitted fabric with less sophisticated technology.

Industrial Policies

Since the late 1990s the Vietnamese government has prioritised investment in intermediate goods, such as fabrics, over apparel manufacturing. By 1999 it had invested almost three times more in textiles ($42 million) than in garments ($15 million).[44] The overall rationale for focusing on textile development is justified by the ability of the garment industry to survive by itself due to increasing private investment, whereas the textile firms, left to market forces, could not compete with the wholly foreign-owned firms operating in the country. There is support for that rationale. As shown in Table 5.7, foreign investment in the garment industry has grown faster than in textiles, although foreign investment in the more capital-intensive textile industry is absolutely larger while total investment in the garment industry was only about a quarter of that in textiles. Between 1997 and 2000, foreign investment's share in the garment industry has increased from 18 to 22 per cent, while that in textiles decreased from 82 to 78 per cent.

However, there was no co-ordination among the relevant state institutions in the planning process of the three grand policies to prioritise backward linkage development: the VINATEX 2010 Plan, the Restructuring Plan and the Textile Zone Plan. It appeared that all three plans were conceived

Table 5.7: Structure of FDI disbursement in textile and garment industries

Sector	**Cumulative to 1997**		**Cumulative to 2000**	
	$m.	**(% of total FDI inVTGI)**	**$m.**	**(% of total FDI inVTGI)**
Textile	503	82	605.8	78
Garment	112	18	173	22

Sources: MPI Reports on FDI in the VTGI, 1997 and 2000.

independently in various offices of the MOI without consultation with the MPI or other technical and research institutes. Also there is no evidence that the VINATEX 2010 Plan and the Textile Zone Plan took into consideration the existence of over 30 foreign textile plants in the VTGI which, as discussed above, have provided both challenges and opportunities for linkage development in Vietnam. Moreover, none of these plans addressed the basic industries such as machinery and synthetic fibre. With over 90 per cent of domestic demand for textile and sewing machinery and spare parts fulfilled by imports (domestic machinery accounted for only 2 per cent of the needs), the state could further develop the existing VINATEX mechanical repairing and spare-parts enterprises, as well as Vietnamese machinery (such as cutting machines used in many state factories). As for synthetic fibre demand, much more transfer of knowledge and technology can take place through partnerships with these existing foreign textile plants in Vietnam.

The VINATEX 2010 Plan, approved in 1998, was intended to attract foreign and domestic capital for cotton production, weaving and dyeing in Vietnam (VINATEX, April 1997).[45] The results were not positive two years after its inception: by 2000, Vietnamese cotton production did not support domestic needs (there was only one raw cotton plant in HCMC) and it is still cheaper to import raw cotton from more efficient producers such as the United States, India and Russia. Moreover, this plan did not create partnerships between Vietnamese firms and foreign textile plants to engender transfer of technology and knowledge, or connections with export markets. Part of the challenge was that most foreign investment in textiles was wholly owned with only a few joint ventures with VINATEX member firms, as discussed earlier.

The Restructuring Plan (2000–2005) and the Textile-Zone Plan (2001–2005) were more market-based and reflected a clear priority to the textile industry through equitisation and consolidation of state firms.[46] They planned to maintain advanced textile plants while equitising most state garment plants, leaving only large firms employing a lot of workers in both north and south. First, the Restructuring Plan proposes to equitise two thirds of VINATEX by 2005 and prioritise textile firms over garment firms. The ratio of textile to garment firms will be shifted from 1:1 in 2000 (25 in each industry) to 2:1 by 2005 (14 fabric and raw materials firms to seven garment firms).[47] Of the existing garment firms only the seven most productive will remain. In the textile industry, most intermediate inputs plants will remain, including 11 of the existing textile firms, three raw materials firms (cotton, wool, jute) and one finance company. Second, the Textile Zone Plan aims at using the expertise of the remaining state firms to establish ten autonomous textile modules/zones in major cities of Vietnam. These zones include spinning, weaving, finishing, knitting and waste-water treatment facilities, subject to free market competition.[48]

Tran Van Quyen, the then head of the VINATEX Investment Department, submitted the plan for the ten textile zones to the government in 1999 and a revised version at the beginning of 2001. The main objectives are creating thousands of new jobs and making use of existing infrastructure in industrial zones throughout the country (four in the north, four in the south and two in the centre). He obtained approval in April 2001 and put this plan into effect with VINATEX member firms playing the leading role.[49] The ten zones will be built in two phases: 2001–05 and 2006–10 with a total state investment of about $4.3 billion. As of April 2001, VINATEX had started to construct the first textile complex in Pho Noi (Hung Yen) near Hai Phong port. However, lack of funding has delayed this process as explained later.

The Textile Zone Plan poses many potential problems in light of the Asian experiences. First, it lacks clearly defined performance criteria as conditions for granting state loans to create these zones. Second, it does not stipulate any time limit after which the zones must be able to operate independently. Third, the zones will have to compete with over 30 existing foreign textile plants with sophisticated technology and expertise, as well as many East Asian sales offices and trading companies which for years have supplied fabrics, accessories and machinery to Vietnamese firms. Therefore, the government needs to facilitate partnerships between the existing foreign textile firms and the fledgling Vietnamese plants for transfer of technology and market connections to take place. Moreover, the state should encourage synergy among domestic actors themselves via some incentive structure making funding, for instance, conditional upon establishment of links between factories and universities and research institutes during the planning and implementation phases of the zones.[50]

Potentials and challenges for linkage development

What are some implications of those policies for Vietnam's linkage development *vis-à-vis* a new set of realities within a world of intensified competition? The relative position of Vietnam in the world economy with an additional layer of the NIEs in the global subcontracting system poses challenges to linkage development in Vietnam, not confronted by those NIEs during their industrialisation in the 1970s and 1980s. Many East Asian corporations invested in the Vietnamese textile industry and became input producers and exporters. As in a flying-geese model, they moved up the production chain and accumulated higher value added in Vietnam rather than in the lower value-added assembly operation stage of the 1960s and 1970s.

Over two decades after the industrialisation of those Asian countries, the Vietnamese state must confront the challenge of balancing both efficiency (job creation and foreign investment) and equity (pay and working conditions). Export promotion policies have increased trade volume and employment but not improved the value added accumulated by the Vietnamese; the pay and working conditions in general have been appalling for workers, and even worse for female workers in the lowest level of the subcontracting ladder.

Progressive FDI policies resulted in an influx of foreign-invested enterprises in the VTGI that created jobs (about 10 per cent of total workers in the

VTGI) but most were low skilled and low paid (minimum monthly wage ranging from $30 to 55 as discussed above). Especially the ascension of wholly foreign-owned textile plants in the VTGI has posed both challenges and opportunities for Vietnamese linkage development. On the one hand, these plants became viable competitors to domestic fabric manufacturers and fulfilled the needs for high quality fabrics, especially synthetic fibre, a vital input for fabric production. For instance, the three largest wholly foreign textile plants (all made fibre) supplied over $100 million worth of fabrics to the domestic market in 1999,[51] while the three largest joint ventures supplied only around $85 million (an assortment of fabrics and fibre).[52] On the other hand, there is still neither an incentive structure nor any stipulation to form partnerships between these sophisticated textile plants and local Vietnamese firms for transfer of technology, knowledge and skills.[53]

Conceptually, the reality of intensified world-wide competition faced by Vietnam calls for different interpretations of the linkage development arguments put forth earlier. The competition that Vietnamese fledging input industries must face is not so much from imports, as envisaged by Hirschman's idea of backward linkage growth being conditional on import reduction, but more from inputs manufactured *inside* Vietnam from the wholly-owned foreign textile plants. The recommendation is not, however, to inhibit healthy competition between local and foreign firms but to institutionalise and reward linkage building with the existing foreign firms to develop economies of scale, to gain technical knowledge and higher value-added skills, as well as to facilitate timely response to changing input demands by the world market.

The Vietnamese reality, in particular, demonstrates that the basic conditions to foster linkage development were ripe. First, the domestic market has grown large enough to absorb domestic intermediate and industrial goods, which could substitute for imported products. The demand of the Vietnamese market and foreign markets such as the EU and EE is large enough to enable economies of scale for Vietnamese input industries. The export industry, the garment industry, has grown in the market system with increasing private investment to serve as a market for input suppliers (fabric manufacturers), and in turn provide final products (apparel) for both domestic and foreign markets. Second, Vietnam's fuller integration into the world system has diversified export markets for final products and that factor should enable economies of scale for input suppliers such as fibre, fabrics and machinery.

Third, on achieving industrial upgrading, existing domestic institutions should be more proactive in upgrading product quality and design. The emerging clothing design efforts of both state and private sectors need to address more varied social demands beyond the two extremes: fashion shows catering mainly to the middle and upper classes and simple products for all walks of life.[54] Other Asian countries have invested in sending their talented people abroad to designer schools to improve their skills and to enrich their understanding of diverse consumer tastes. Similarly, VINATEX can strengthen the capacity of FADIN, the state-owned fashion design institute, by selecting the best members and sending them to international design schools to enhance their clothing design skills and knowledge. So what can the state do in light of these realities? The Asian cases mentioned above demonstrated the value of the 'carrot and stick' policy using discipline together with a combination of financial, industrial and trade policies to develop their textile industry and backward linkages. In the case of Vietnam, greater co-ordination among relevant ministries is needed to balance the goals of efficiency and equity; in this regard, quota allocation reforms were on the right track. However financial policies need rigorous reforms, and industrial policies need clear performance criteria and time limitation as conditions for firms that receive state assistance. The state must seriously take advantage of the wealth of existing foreign expertise in large East Asian textile firms in Vietnam to realistically develop and implement linkage development policies. Moreover, the state needs to develop an incentive structure to reward partnerships between foreign and local input producers, technical universities and research institutes to develop products such as machinery, machine parts, dyestuffs, cotton and synthetic fibre (as in South Korea and India) so the VTGI can truly integrate with the rest of the economy.

CONCLUSION: ASIAN FINANCIAL CRISIS AND FUTURE CHALLENGES

This chapter argues that by continuing to rely on existing comparative advantage, Vietnam would be 'stuck' in the vicious circle of low-wage, low-skilled CMP subcontracting arrangements. While short-term EOI policies have increased total export value, they have not led to an increase in Vietnam's share of the value added. On the other hand, proactive and co-ordinated state policies to foster forward and backward linkages can bring about greater value added.

Considering the larger picture of Vietnam's noble goal of fostering growth with equity, there seem to be two simultaneous equity issues at work: unequal power relations between domestic and foreign actors in the multi-level CMP subcontracting system, and that among domestic actors (state versus private firms, and large versus small firms). But the unequal power relation between international capital and domestic actors tends to outweigh the inequity among domestic actors. On the one hand, multi-level sub-contracting has weakened state capacity to enforce Vietnam's progressive Labour Code. MNCs have a credible threat to pack up and relocate their production lines in other developing countries, and have the power to source inputs based on factors which at times may have nothing to do with input quality. They can use their own international networks of input sourcing and buying offices, their bargaining power *vis-à-vis* other developing countries or their long-term relationships with input suppliers. Workers at the lowest level of the subcontracting ladder are immobile and bear the greatest burden in order to deliver flexibility and productivity for the global market in exchange for very low wages.

Future research can examine the symbiotic relationships reflected in *domestic* arrangements between state and non-state sectors and in FOB trade, relying on both statistical and qualitative evidence. One can make an argument that jobs were created by state sector to non-state enterprises (and also from private to state factories, especially for exports to the EE markets), hence compensating to some extent the preferential treatment enjoyed by SOEs. The neo-classical blueprints (for privatising all state firms and levelling the playing field) tend to focus on the negative aspects of state firms and (incorrectly) to frame state and non-state sectors as competitors (Beresford, Chapter 3 this volume); such blueprints do not capture the nuances of intimate connections between state and private firms which remain underestimated in official statistics.

The ramifications of the Asian financial crisis (mid-1997 to late 1999) underscore the exposure of a national industry such as the VTGI to the vicissitudes of the global market. This financial crisis had negative impacts on both CMP and FOB exports. Rapid currency depreciation in Indonesia temporarily pushed wages there below those in Vietnam, making their CMP export products cheaper than Vietnamese products. Moreover, the Asian crisis spread to the EE countries (i.e., Russia, the Baltic countries, Poland, the Czech Republic) and caused a further drop in demand for Vietnamese products. At the same time, currency devaluations alongside lower transport costs in Eastern Europe made their clothing products more appealing to EU consumers, creating another source of competition for Vietnamese producers.

Other challenges point to the urgency of having a well-co-ordinated and concerted state effort to develop linkages for sustainable development. The ending of the quota system under the Multi-Fibre Agreement in 2005, and Vietnam's full membership in AFTA by 2007, will lead to even more intensified world competition in the textile and garment industries, especially with Vietnam's neighbouring exporters. Moreover, China's membership in the WTO in 2001 has afforded it a competitive edge over Vietnam in terms of textile and garment exports to the diverse US market. Finally, as mentioned earlier, the Bilateral Trade Agreement with the United States resulted in spectacular growth of VTGI export, but the Bilateral Textile Agreement with quota imposition has many ramifications for the development of the VTGI. This topic will be further explored in another study (Tran and Smith, forthcoming).

I believe that the challenges of backward and forward linkage development are not insurmountable. Major economic restructuring and linkage development take time to succeed. Other Asian countries took decades to restructure their industries and to consciously develop their domestic linkages. On the other hand, the Vietnamese state has just embarked on this process since the mid-1990s, hence it needs time, focus, co-ordination and sustained commitment in order to contribute to national development with growth and equity.

APPENDIX 5.1: ECONOMETRIC MODEL

My econometric model (using 1993 data) presented significant institutional factors that affected total sales, that primarily reflected the VTGI export value to the EU market since all other markets (including domestic) were then very small. The model used a Cobb–Douglas production function. After many statistical tests, I found some significant factors accounting for different levels of output, measured by total sales during 1993. These factors included share of CMP export (an indicator of level of linkages), export incentives (an indicator of export promotion policies), ownership (an indicator of industrial policy), capital embodied in machinery and foreign capital (indicators of industrial policy), labour and regional impacts (historical, socio-economic factors).

Transparent and consistent customs procedure, or longer time to use up all imported inputs for garment exports (an extension from 30 to 90 days) with no import taxes, facilitated more sales.[55] The net effect of being a state firm still positively contributed to total sales.[56] Most foreign investment continues to concentrate in HCMC.[57]

lnSALES = 12 + (0.31) lnK + (0.55) lnL + (0.36) XINCMP + (-1.52) CMP/EXP + (0.72) REGFOR + (1.42) REGION + (1.28) OWNER + (-0.84) REGOWN
Rsqd = 0.93 n = 58 firms

Definitions of significant variables

lnK: natural log of capital. Most capital came from non-communist countries.

lnL: natural log of labour. Most labour assembled clothes for CMP-based export.

CMP/EXP: the share of CMP export, in total VTGI export value. This reflected the share of wages, rents, interests and normal profits paid to Vietnamese workers and managers (as discussed in Table 5.5) with continuous values between 0 and 1. Its coefficient (b-value) is negative meaning that it negatively affected total sales.

REGION: location of firms. The south, or HCMC in particular, was very significant in light of its past history of capitalism, better infrastructure (in terms of nearby port and productive facilities) which attracted more orders for export to non-communist markets.

OWNER: state firms endowed with special privileges such as the use of land and facilities, access to low-interest state loans and export quotas, and ease of customs procedures. These privileges gave them a further competitive edge over private firms in getting work orders, foreign investment and technical know-how. At the time of writing, most SOEs got more CMP orders from large foreign corporations than did private garment firms because of their established connections and privileges.

REGFOR (REGION x FORCAP): any southern firm that had some foreign capital added to total sales. Values are 1 for any southern firm (state or non-state) that received some foreign capital and 0 otherwise. My expectation that most foreign corporations would prefer to form partnerships with southern firms rather than with firms in other regions was correct (see note 57).

REGOWN (REGION x OWNER): Values are 1 for state firms in the south (with privileges as stated above) and 0 otherwise. Its coefficient (b-value) is negative, hence negatively affecting total sales.

XINCMP (XINCEN x CMP/EXP): export incentives (XINCEN) aimed at promoting CMP export to the EU markets (CMP/EXP). Its values are continuous, between 0 and 1. This variable reflected the positive effect of simplified customs procedures.

LIST OF INTERVIEWEES

Mr Hoang Minh Khang (2003), Manager of Planning Department, May 10 Garment Company, Hanoi, October.

Mr Pham Quang Ham (1998) Development Strategy Institute, Ministry of Planning and Investment.

Mr Tran Van Duoc (2000) a private garment manufacturer in Nam Dinh.

Ms Pham Thi Thu Hang (2000) the deputy general director of VCCI, July.

Mr Nguyen Xuan Hoa (2000) chairman of VITAS, June.

Mr Nguyen Hoan (1994) chairman of Weaving, Sewing and Knitting Association, November.

Ms Nguyen Thuy Huong (2000) Department of Foreign Investment, Ministry of Planning and Investment, June and July.

Mr Tran Van Quyen (2000) Technical and Investment Department of VINATEX, June and July.

Ms Vu Phuong Sao (2000) textile/garment instructor at Nam Dinh Vocational School, July.

Dr Phan Thi Thanh (2000) director of Research Centre for Female Labour, Institute for Labour Sciences and Social Affairs, Ministry of Labour, Invalids and Social Affairs (MOLISA), June.

Mr Tran Manh Thu (2000) vice chairman of the Planning and Investment Department - Ministry of Industry, June.

Mr Nguyen An Toan (2000) Technical and Investment Department of VINATEX, June.

Mr Pham Van Tuan (2000) a worker in Nam Dinh Garment, July.

Mr Pham Van Tuyen (2000) Technical and Investment Department, VINATEX, July.

Mr Le Van Dao (2003) General Secretary, Vietnamese Textile and Apparel Association (VITAS)

Mr Le Van Thang (2003) Deputy General Director of Export and Import Management Department, Ministry of Trade

NOTES

1 We also found evidence that the Vietnamese state was relatively autonomous in formulating policies, both proactive and reactive to the popular fence-breaking and bottom-up initiatives since the late 1970s, and that the state and non-state sectors have co-existed since the mid 1980s.

2 Its 1998 export performance was even better: it ranked the highest, above crude oil and gas (Tran Van Quyen July 2000).

3 The United Nations' trade data system, from partner reporting, demonstrated that the official Vietnam statistics may underestimate the real VTGI trade values since a portion may have gone through other intermediary Asian countries. It showed an even higher percentage: over 15 per cent since 1992 (Table 5.1).

4 Mekong Project Development Facility (MPDF) is a multi-donor programme set up to support the growth of the private sectors in Vietnam, Laos and Cambodia. It is managed by the International Finance Corporation (IFC), the private sector arm of the World Bank Group. Donors to MPDF include Australia, the EU, Finland, the IFC, Japan, Norway, Sweden, Switzerland and the United Kingdom. See also the studies made by the Institute of Economics which were commissioned by IDRC/CIDA (Canadian International Development Aid).

5 Value added is defined as income accumulated at a particular stage of production (Gillis *et al.* 1992: 37). In the context of the VTGI, value added is equal to the payments to the factors of production, such as wages, profits, interest, capital depreciation, rents and taxes.

6 This pattern, at first glance, might be seen as the opposite of the balanced-growth pattern which advocates the development of a wide range of industries simultaneously, the big push approach, in order to achieve sustained growth (see the works of Ragnar Nurkse and Paul Rosenstein-Rodan). When stated in less extreme forms, they can be seen as opposite sides of the same coin; the very concept of creating linkages with the rest of the economy suggests that the imbalances will eventually lead back toward a more balanced path (Gillis *et al.* 1992: 66–67).

7 He conceptualises the world economy in terms of global commodity chains defined as the links between successive production phases from raw material supply, manufacturing, distribution, to marketing final products (Gereffi 1995: 43–44, 47).

8 They argued that a policy intervention can tip the equilibrium from one steady state to another such that state intervention need not be invoked on a permanent basis (Grossman and Helpman 1997: 231–233).

9 Hoffmann 1958: 2–4, 100–101. The four-stage industrialisation process starts with consumer goods industries, followed by intermediate and industrial goods industries which will develop faster than the first group. In stage 1, consumer goods industries are the most important with their net output on average five times larger than that of capital goods industries. In stage 2, net output of consumer goods industries reduces to about 2.5 times larger than that of capital goods industries. In stage 3, net output of the two groups are about equal, and finally in stage 4, capital goods industries outgrow consumer goods industries.

10 A case study of Gujarat state, India, showed that the state tied financial assistance and subsidies to plants, which were able to upgrade their technology and quality, indicated by the attainment of the ISO 9000 certificate within a time limit. Textiles, chemical and petrochemical industries, producing dyestuffs and synthetic fibre, received the major share of state loans. Backward linkages among these industries were encouraged based on their proven track record. If they did not operate effectively, they were given time for 'rehabilitation'. If they still did not recover within that period, such a unit will be sold to another party interested in pursuing this line of business. (Lalitha 1997: 7, 21–23, 31, 37).

11 Kim (1994: 185–188). Another example, of the Korean heavy and chemical industries (HCI), shows that after a slow start in the mid-1970s, the HCI development plan took off. These industries are now major Asian exporters of heavy-industry products such as ships, steel and automobiles.

12 CMP stands for 'cutting, making, packaging'; FOB is 'free on board'. Some studies use the term CMT for 'cutting, making and trimming'.

13 See, for instance, Deyo (1989).

14 For an historical perspective, see Tran (1996) which analysed in depth the evolution of the VTGI in three main periods: pre-1986 under a command economy; 1986–1995 when Vietnam engaged in consistent market reforms and responded to impacts from the collapse of the Communist regimes of the former Soviet Union and the Eastern European countries; and 1995–present when Vietnam must respond to both opportunities and challenges arising from the global garment and textile markets.

15 Time series for trade data by ownership type (state and non-state sectors) are unavailable.

16 The prime minister appointed the top management of VINATEX: chairman and general director, and nominated the deputy general director (to be approved by the Minister of Industry). See Tran (1996) for more history of this consolidation. Local state firms remain under jurisdiction of provincial people's committees.

17 Between the two, the Japanese market grew faster: exports to Japan were doubled from 16 per cent to about 30 per cent, while those to the EU market dropped from 50 per cent to about 40 per cent. (Ministry of Trade and VINATEX, June 2000).

18 See Tran (1996) for a detailed discussion on how FOB exports with the Eastern European countries added variation to the buyer-driven production chains and highlighted the significance of domestic integration in the sense of forward and backward linkages.

19 Interestingly, this counter trade was similar to a subcontracting arrangement, in which Vietnam received raw materials, such as cotton, to weave

into fabrics, part of which were used domestically, the rest being delivered to the socialist countries as a form of payment. These negotiations enabled the exchange of textile and garment products for machinery and technical assistance (interview Tran Manh Thu, June 2000; *Ministry of Light Industry Journal*, July 1993: 13).

20 Cash payment accounts for only 10 per cent, while commodities and investment opportunities are worth about US$70 million annually.

21 Compared to Sri Lanka, Vietnam was still very much behind in unconditional FOB deals: in 1999 Sri Lankan producers made about 15 per cent CMP deals, 55 per cent conditional FOB deals and 30 per cent unconditional FOB deals (Kelegama and Foley: 1999: 1451).

22 This quota system absorbed only about 30–35 per cent of total VTGI production capacity, while annual increases in several quota categories did not meet the supply (Tran 1996).

23 However, even with the bilateral trade agreement between Vietnam and the U.S. (effective in 2002), the long-term net impact remains to be seen since the lower tariff rates to the U.S. market lasted only one year, after which the United States imposed various quotas and restrictions via the Bilateral Textile Agreement effective in May 2003 (Pietro P. Masina, unpublished manuscript critiquing the ideology of free trade in Vietnam, July 2000; interview Le Van Thang, 2003).

24 For a more detailed analysis, see Tran (1996) and Gereffi (1995: 118–119).

25 Most LCs stipulated that over 60 per cent of their value must be used to purchase inputs from East Asian sources; as a consequence few backward linkages are developed. Vietnamese producers obtained LCs from the national banking system (such as the VIETCOMBANK) with credit issued by East Asian overseas banks (such as Japanese banks). Once the East Asian middlemen have opened a 'master LC', the Vietnamese producers can then open 'back-to-back baby LCs' to pay wages to Vietnamese workers and supervisors and to buy inputs from East Asian sources.

26 For a more detailed analysis from workers' perspectives, see Tran (2001) and Tran (2002).

27 The conversion from piece rate to hourly rate was based on an average monthly wage of 600,000 VND for 24 work days per month and 7.5 hours per day with a 30-minute lunch break or US$30, the minimum monthly wage in firms with foreign investment. All calculations were adjusted for purchasing power parity (PPP) (MPDF 1999a: 1). This statistic was confirmed by phone interviews with Phan Thi Thanh, June 2000.

28 In terms of *production costs per hour* (without transportation costs) in Asia, Vietnam and Bangladesh were still the lowest: US$4.8 per hour,

compared to US$5.4 in China, US$6.0 in Indonesia, US$7.2 in India, US$9.0 in Sri Lanka, US$9.6 in Thailand, US$11.4 in Hong Kong, and US$12 in Taiwan (MPDF 1999a: 11).

29 MPDF 1999a: 44, 60, 69, 74, 80, 85, 90, 92, 98, 112.

30 For example, VIETEXPO was held in the United States in December 1994. Also, VINATEX and Hong Kong International Exhibition & Fair Company have co-operated to organise annual international textile–garment exhibitions since 1998 to expose domestic garment and textile firms to modern technology and know-how and to a range of products and supply sources (equipment, machines, spare parts, materials). The Saigon Expo in April 2002 attracted about 300 manufacturers from 23 countries and regions (*Saigon Times Daily* 1998; VINATEX, n.d.).

31 Members of the Board of Directors include party members and state officials (VCCI Publication, June 2000).

32 Interview Nguyen Xuan Hoa, June 2000. Interestingly one of the vice chairmen was head of the privately-orientated Association of Weaving, Clothing, Knitting, and Embroidery in the south. Also, as of 2003, Mr. Le Quoc An is the chairman of both VINATEX and VITAS (VINATEX and VITAS brochures, 2003).

33 There are some other para-statist associations: VICOOPSME (a co-operative association), Foreign Trade Development Corporation (managed by the People's Committee of HCMC).

34 Interview Nguyen Hoan 1994; MPDF 1999a: 85. This association was established by Mr. Hoan, a private firm owner in the south. He was keen to find ways to gain more private membership, and improve the organisation and leadership. The general concerns when I talked to him in late 1994 were with policies dealing with production and export activities, such as loans, taxes, land-lease, and the EU quotas.

35 They included the Planning Department of MOI, the Import-Export Department of MOT, and the Industry Department of MPI. The EU framework allows for some flexibility: 'swing' between categories, carry forward and carry over of some quota categories to the following year to utilise the maximum number of quotas granted. However, as of 2003, MPI is no longer in the quota group, so the structure is further streamlined.

36 About 70 per cent of EU quotas are commercial quotas granted directly to the Vietnamese state; 30 per cent are Outward Processing Traffic quotas, granted to the EU producers who must use EU inputs in final products, which are to be assembled in Vietnam and re-exported to the EU.

37 Since none of my interviewees were willing to provide the list of these affected firms, I had to deduce these statistics after several visits to the EU

department of the Ministry of Trade (MOT) in June and July 2000. While the MOI statistics indicated that 50 per cent of quotas were allocated to private firms, more reliable data from the MOT/EU Department showed that SOEs accounted for about 90 per cent of the total 1998 EU export value, and 10 per cent from private firms, mostly large ones in HCMC.

38 Interview with an official at the Industry Department of MPI, June 2000.

39 Interview with Tran Van Quyen, July 2000.

40 There are two types of ODA depending on types of project: over 25 per cent grants and low-interest loans (of 1–5 per cent per year). They come from bilateral negotiations with donor countries including Japan, China, Spain, Germany, Holland, France, Italy and Belgium.

41 See Tran (1996) for more details and SCCI (1994).

42 This explains the high average monthly wage in foreign-invested firms, about $69 per month, mentioned earlier 3.3.

43 Fieldwork in summer 2000.

44 List of projects from VINATEX member firms approved for state investment in 1999 (interview Pham Van Tuyen, July 2000).

45 This plan was approved by the prime minister in 1998 in consultation with MPI and MOI.

46 Equitisation is the Vietnamese concept for privatisation, reflecting their sensitivity to the ideology of building a market system within socialism.

47 According to Tran Van Quyen (2000), 22 central SOEs are slated to remain, although some of these SOEs will be equitised later on. At the time of the interview, VINATEX was collecting and reviewing these firms' long-term development proposals.

48 In the first year, 2001, one to two pilot projects were to be built with expertise from the 16 remaining SOEs. These zones would concentrate in major industrial centres of Vietnam: Hanoi, Hai Phong, HCMC, Thanh Hoa, Da Nang. Each zone is to employ between 2,600–3,000 workers and produce around 20 million m^2 of fabric per year and 1,500 tonnes of knitted goods. To achieve this, the plan requires state budget support of US$120 million per zone at the low annual interest rate of 7 per cent (interview Tran Van Quyen, June 2000). But as explained further in note 50, financial shortage and unfulfilled expectations of entering the U.S. market left these zones unfinished and nonoperational.

49 At least in principle, the rationale for these textile zones is logical; there is a need to concentrate textile plants in non-residential areas such as industrial zones to utilise existing infrastructure, especially waste treatment facilities. Moreover, concentration can facilitate specialisation and co-operation among allied industries (Industry, no. 11, 2001: 8–9 Hanoi: Ministry of Industry).

50 Capital shortage seems to be one of the main reasons that slowed down this broad-based and ambitious industrial policy, especially in building backward linkages. According to Mr. Mai Hoang An, General Director of VINATEX, at present VINATEX needs about 300 billion VND to implement that industrial policy (e-mail communications with Ms. Nguyen Thuy Huong at MPI, June 2003). VINATEX has been seeking a state subsidy but has not yet received any positive news. Consequently, VINATEX member firms do not have adequate capital to expand production as planned. Moreover, evidence showed that after two years of implementing this plan, only 7.3% of total planned budget (about 898 billion dong) was disbursed as of 2003 (*Saigon Giai Phong* newspaper, April 24, 2003). This led to serious funding shortage to build basic infrastructure (such as waste water treatment) prerequisite to those planned textile complexes and spinning plants (*Vietnam News*, 'Textile, garment projects fail to stitch up necessary investment', November 27, 2002).

51 Pang Rim Yoochang (Korean, making fibre, weaving and dyeing in Phu Tho, north Vietnam), Hualon Corporation Vietnam (Taiwanese, making fibre, weaving and dyeing in Dong Nai, south Vietnam), and Formosa Textile (Taiwanese, making fibre, weaving, dyeing and manufacturing garments in Long An, south Vietnam) (MPI 2000).

52 The three largest joint ventures between three major state textile plants and East Asian firms are Choongnam-Viet Thang Textile (South Korean and Vietnamese, making fibre, weaving and dyeing, HCMC), Dong Nai-Bochang (Taiwanese and Vietnamese, making cotton towels in Dong Nai, south Vietnam) and Saigon-Joubo Textile (Taiwanese and Vietnamese, making denim, HCMC) (MPI 2000).

53 Partnerships can be achieved on an individual basis. A few enterprising Vietnamese private owners were able to reach out to final consumers and upgrade to higher value added by partnering directly with the foreign corporate buyers. A private firm owner in the south, for example, began by assembling CMP sports shirts and anoraks for export to the EU market via a Taiwanese middleman. Through this subcontracting relationship, he was eventually able to form a partnership with his European customers. He then learned to broaden his product range and contributed to CAD product design. On the other hand, the European buyers regularly visited his factory, consulted on product design, training and machinery, and provided technical expertise. In short, his direct relationship with the final buyers has enabled that owner to earn four times more than he could have under the multi-level CMP contracts (MPDF 1999c: 46).

54 Minh Hanh, a fashion designer based in HCMC, is well known for her eclectic designs for *ao dai*, the Vietnamese traditional long dress. But only middle- to upper-class urban consumers can afford these products.

55 There is a small positive effect of policy XINCMP on total sales: 0.36.

56 The negative REGOWN *reduces* the positive effect of OWNER a little: 1.28-0.84=0.44.

57 There was positive contribution of foreign capital in the south (represented by REGFOR) to total sales since many firms in the south (represented by REGION) were exposed to the capitalist system before 1975 and have obtained technology mostly embodied in foreign machinery (represented by variable FOR). My 1993 sample data showed that *all southern firms (state and private) have higher capital endowment (total capital per labourer)*: about $2,800 per southern worker compared to $1,700 per worker in other regions. Also, the contribution of technology (K) to total sales was rather small: for 1 per cent increase in capital input, there is only 0.31 per cent increase in total sales, holding the labour input constant.

REFERENCES

Bonacich, Edna *et al.* (1994) *Global Production: The Apparel Industry in the Pacific Rim.* Philadelphia: Temple University Press.

Deyo, Frederic (1989) *Beneath the Miracle: Labour Subordination in the New Asian Industrialism.* Berkeley : University of California Press.

—— (1997) 'Labour and Industrial Restructuring in South-East Asia'. In Garry Rodan, Kevin Hewison and Richard Robison (eds), *The Political Economy of South-East Asia: An Introduction.* Melbourne: Oxford University Press.

FPT (2000) FPT Internet Corporation *Internet Newsletter*, November.

Gereffi, Gary (1995) 'Contending Paradigms for Cross-Regional Comparison: Development Strategies and Commodity Chains in East Asia and Latin America'. In Peter H. Smith (ed.), *Latin America In Comparative Perspective: New Approaches to Methods and Analysis.* Boulder, CO: Westview Press.

Gereffi, Gary and Miguel Korzeniewicz (1994) *Commodity Chains and Global Capitalism.* Westport, CT: Greenwood Press. P. 4

Gillis, Malcolm, Dwight Perkins, Michael Roemer and Donald Snodgrass (1992) *Economics of Development.* New York: W. W. Norton.

Grossman, Gene M. and Elhanan Helpman (1997) 'Dynamic Comparative Advantage' and 'Hysteresis'. In *Innovation and Growth in the Global Economy*. Cambridge, Ma: the MIT Press.

Hill, Hal (1998) *Vietnam Textile and Garment Industry: Notable Achievements, Future Challenges.* Report prepared for Development Strategy Institute of Ministry of Planning and Investment, and Medium-term Industrial Strategy Project, United Nations Industrial Development Organisation, July.

Hirschman, Albert O. (1958) *The Strategy of Economic Development.* New Haven, CT: Yale University Press.

——. (1967) *Development Projects Observed.* Washington, DC: The Brookings Institution.

Hoffmann, W.G. (1958) *The Growth of Industrial Economies.* London: Manchester University Press.

Kelegama, Saman and Fritz Foley (1999) 'Impediments to Promoting Backward Linkages from the Garment Industry in Sri Lanka'. *World Development*, vol. 27, no. 8, pp. 1445–1460.

Kim, Ji-Hong (1994) 'Restructuring of the textile and garment industry in Korea'. In Saha Dhevan Meyanathan (ed.), *Managing Restructuring in the Textile and Garment Subsector: Examples from Asia.* Washington, DC: World Bank.

Krueger, Anne O. (1993) 'Impact of Government on Growth and Trade', in Wilfred Ethier, Elhanan Helpman and J. Peter Neary (eds), *Theory, Policy and Dynamics in International Trade.* Cambridge: Cambridge University Press.

Kuruvilla, Sarosh (1992) *Industrialization Strategy and Industrial Relations Policy in Malaysia.* Ithaca, NY: Institute of Collective Bargaining, School of Industrial and Labor Relations, Cornell University.

Lalitha, N. (1997) 'State Level Reforms to Promote Industrialisation: A Case Study of Gujarat', *Working Paper*, no. 82, Gujarat Institute of Development Research, March.

Meyanathan, Saha Dhevan and Jaseem Ahmed (1994) 'Managing Restructuring in the Textile and Garment Subsector: An Overview',in Saha Dhevan Meyanathan (ed.), *Managing Restructuring in the Textile and Garment Subsector: Examples from Asia.* Washington, DC: World Bank.

MPDF (1999a) 'Private Companies in Vietnam: A Survey of Public Perceptions'. Mekong Project Development Facility, no. 7. Hanoi, July.

—— (1999b) 'Vietnam's Garment Industry: Moving Up the Value Chain'. Mekong Project Development Facility, no. 9. Hanoi, January.

—— (1999c) 'SMEs in Vietnam: On the Road to Prosperity'. Mekong Project Development Facility, International Finance Corporation (IFC the private sector arm of the world bank group). Hanoi November.

MPI (2000) Ministry of Planning and Investment, Department of Foreign Investment Management, *Reports on Foreign Projects in Textile and Garment Industries*, Department of Foreign Investment, MPI. Hanoi October.

Nguyen Dinh Tai (1999) 'Social Impacts of the Asian Financial Crisis on Vietnam'. In Institute of Economics, *Vietnam's Socio-Economic Development.* Hanoi: National Centre for Social Sciences and Humanities, Summer.

Pham Quang Ham (1998) Development Strategy Institute, Ministry of Planning and Investment.

Porter, Michael (1990) *The Competitive Advantage of Nations.* New York: Free Press.

Rasiah, Rajah (1997) 'Class, Ethnicity and Economic Development in Malaysia'. In Garry Rodan, Kevin Hewison and Richard Robison (eds), *The Political Economy of South-East Asia, An Introduction.* Melbourne: Oxford University Press.

—— (1993) 'Competition and Governance: Work in Malaysia's Textile and Garment Industries'. *Journal of Contemporary Asia*, vol. 23, no. 1.

Riedel, James and William Turley (1999) 'The Politics and Economics of Transition to an Open Market Economy in Viet Nam', Paris: OECD

Tran, Ngoc Angie (1996) 'Through the Eye of the Needle: Vietnamese Textile and Garment Industries Rejoining the Global Economy'. *Crossroads: An Interdisciplinary Journal of Southeast Asian Studies*, vol. 10, no. 2.

—— (2001) 'Global Subcontracting and Women Workers in Comparative Perspective'. In Claes Brundenius and John Weeks (eds), *Globalisation and Third World Socialism: Cuba and Vietnam.* London: Macmillan.

—— (2002) 'Gender Expectations of Vietnamese Garment Workers: Viet Nam's Re-Integration into the World Economy'. In Jayne Werner and Daniele Belanger (eds), *Gender, Household, State: Doi Moi in Viet Nam.* Ithaca: Southeast Asia Program, Cornell University Press.

Tran, Ngoc Angie and David A. Smith (1999) 'Cautious Reformers and Fence-Breakers: Vietnam's Economic Transition in Comparative Perspective'. *Humboldt Journal of Social Relations*, vol. 24, No. 1 and 2.

—— (Forthcoming) 'Sewing for the Global Economy: Thread of Resistance in the Vietnamese Garment Industry'. In Richard Appelbaum and William Robinson (eds), *Critical Globalization Studies*, London: Routledge

OFFICIAL PUBLICATIONS, MAGAZINES AND NEWSPAPERS

Asia Pulse (2000) 'Vietnam Textile Makers Focus on Domestic Market', 16 May, 2000.

Customs Department (1998a) *Statistics of Textile and Garment Exports and Imports in 1998.* Hanoi.

—— (1998b) *Trade Values of Vietnam's Textile and Garment Products in 1998.* Hanoi.

General Statistical Office (GSO) (1994) *Vietnam Living Standards Survey 1992–1993.* Hanoi: Statistical Publishing House.

—— *Statistical Yearbooks* (1994, 1997, 1999, 2000, 2001) Hanoi: Statistical Publishing House.

Institute of Economics–IDRC/CIDA (2001a) 'Analysis of Qualitative Factors Affecting Competitiveness of Textile and Garment Firms in Vietnam', Project on 'Trade Liberalisation and Competitiveness of Selected Manufacturing Industries in Vietnam'. Hanoi, January.

—— (2001b) 'Textile and Garment Industry in Vietnam'. Project on 'Trade Liberalisation and Competitiveness of Selected Manufacturing Industries in Vietnam'. Hanoi, May.

—— (2001c) 'Analysis of Competitiveness of Textile and Garment Firms in Vietnam: A Cost-Based Approach'. Project on Trade Liberalisation and Competitiveness of Selected Manufacturing Industries in Vietnam. Hanoi, September.

Lao Dong [Labour] (1997), March 27.

Ministry of Industry, *Cong Nghiep* [Industry], various issues in 2000 and 2001.

Ministry of Light Industry Journal, July 1993.

MPI (2000), *Report on FDI projects in Textile Industry*. Hanoi: Ministry of Planning and Industry, Department of Foreign Investment Management.

NXB Thong Ke (1997) *Bieu Thue va Danh Muc Xuat Nhat Khau* [English translation]. Hanoi: Statistical Publishers.

Saigon Times Daily (1998), 17 March.

SCCI (State Committee on Co-operation and Investment) (1994), *Luat Dau Tu Nuoc Ngoai tai Vietnam nam 1987, Cac Van Ban Phap Luat ve Dau Tu Nuoc Ngoai tai Vietnam* [Law on Foreign Investment in Vietnam 1987, Legal Documents on Foreign Investment in Vietnam]. Hanoi: National Political Publishers, January.

Textile and Garment Industry in Vietnam, May 2001.

Thoi Bao Kinh Te Saigon, 15 August 1996 and 30 January 1997.

Vietnamese Chamber of Commerce and Industry (VCCI), including Constitution and Bylaws, Prime Minister's Decree in 1993, Organization, Offices and Branches, 2001.

Vietnam Courier, 22–28 October 1995.

VINATEX (Vietnam National Textile and Garment Corporation) (1997a), 'The General Plan of VTGI Development to the Year 2010'. Hanoi: VINATEX, Ministry of Industry, April.

—— (1997b), *Vietnam Textile-Garment Industry: the Present and Future*. Hanoi: Ministry of Industry.

—— (2001), June. http://www.vinatex.com/textile/s02texlist/LISTCOUN.html

CHAPTER 6

Rural Diversification: An Essential Path to Sustainable Development for Vietnam

Bui Van Hung

INTRODUCTION

Background

Agriculture plays a fundamental role in many developing countries, but the important role of agriculture has been seen particularly clearly in Vietnam, where a whole nation's survival has been based on it. Today, agriculture remains very prominent in Vietnamese production, with a quarter of aggregate GDP in 1999–2000 (GSO 2001: 69), generating more than a third of its export value and employing over two-thirds of its labour force. Moreover, the income of about 76 per cent of the population depends mainly on agricultural earnings. Agriculture not only has a direct impact on the country's daily economic life but will also be decisive in long-term development. For these reasons, agriculture has been a permanent concern of the Vietnamese government and has led it to focus its reform efforts first of all on agriculture.

The government intends to build on its success and has ambitious medium-term development objectives, including achieving GDP growth of between 7 and 8 per cent annually and building a modern industrialised economy within 20 years. At the heart of the government's medium-term objectives is ensuring that this rapid growth and transformation of the economy occurs in parallel with a significant reduction in poverty and greater equity. This will demand a pattern of economic transformation that generates higher productivity and employment opportunities for a rapidly growing labour force, particularly in the rural areas, where over three-quarters of the Vietnamese people still live.

Although the government has a stated goal of rapid industrialisation and modernisation, it recognises the important role of agriculture as a building block for the sustainable development of the country and as an engine for broad-based poverty reduction and income growth. In particular the government considers agricultural processing and non-farm rural service activities as an important way of achieving its long-term development goals.

Economic reforms have so far recognised that farm households are a key unit of production, privatised land-use rights and liberalised decision-making about trade in agricultural inputs and outputs. These changes, in combination with technological progress, have brought about higher agricultural productivity and output. As a result, agricultural GDP has grown steadily by 4–5 per cent annually since 1989. The agricultural sector has been performing well despite the slow-down in the national economy during 1997–99. Indeed, agricultural production hit record levels in 1999 and 2000 (GSO 2001: 110). Vietnam has moved from being a net food importer in the mid-1980s to being the world's second largest exporter of rice. Exports of rice increased from 1.4 million tonnes in 1989 to 4.5 million in 1999 (GSO 2001: 407). At the same time, the number and proportion of people in absolute poverty declined considerably, in spite of continuing annual population growth of nearly 2 per cent.

Despite these achievements, farmers' incomes remain low and vulnerable, unemployment and under-employment are still the rural hot problem, and the gap between rural and urban incomes has widened. The emerging rural–urban income gap indicates that although radical institutional and technological changes have taken place in the agricultural sector, its productivity is much lower than that of the urban industrial sector. Moreover, diversification of farmers' incomes is limited, most rural people are dependent on agriculture, forestry and fishing. They suffer extreme uncertainties, particularly climatic instability and insect infestation, which contribute greatly to the riskiness of agriculture in general and of rice cultivation in particular. The lives and livelihoods of the Vietnamese rural population are vulnerable to frequent natural disasters, such as storms, floods and drought. 'Nobody on the farm will get rich by growing rice' is a popular saying in Vietnam.

The core government aim in rural development is to create a wide range of employment opportunities and increase farmers' incomes so as to close the rural–urban gap and restore balanced and sustainable development. How can more employment opportunities and incomes be created in rural areas in the context of industrialisation and modernisation? An answer to this question can be found in rural diversification, which can provide a wide range of activities, covering both expansion of off-farm occupations (in industry, construction and services) and diversification of farming activities. These general avenues are in part not just a goal but also a strategic essential to shifting a growing number of farmers from farm production to off-farm activities and from rice cultivation to higher value crops. The development of rural industry and services will not only create more jobs for rural areas but also implicitly increase farming productivity by withdrawing excess labour from farms, thereby improving farmers' incomes. An increase in rural household incomes through the development of off-farm employment will generate socially and economically sustainable development in rural areas.

Rural industrialisation and diversification

In rural areas there exist two ranges of activities: farm and non-farm. 'Farm' activities, as Saith (1992) defines them, refer to a set of economic activities including crop-cultivation and auxiliary activities such as fishing and aquaculture, dairying and husbandry, poultry rearing and beekeeping. 'Non-farm'[1] work not included in this range of activities can involve manufacturing, processing, handicrafts, construction, trades and services.

The concept of rural industrialisation is understood differently in different countries. In many Western countries rural industrialisation is associated with capital-intensive farm technology and has resulted in loss of rural jobs and the creation of ghost towns. The phrase 'rural industrialisation' means something different in countries like Vietnam and China, where there are manufacturing, processing and handicraft industries in rural areas in which technologies are labour-intensive. These industries are the main source for what these countries call 'rural industrialisation'. Rural industrialisation is a measure to change the rural socio-economic structure by expanding rural industries and related services (trade, credit and technology transfer, for instance). It is a process of shifting an increasing proportion of the labour force in the rural sector from farming to work in rural enterprises that process, store, transport and market from farm gate to the point of domestic or export sale.

Rural diversification has a broader meaning and refers to a wider range of activities, including diversification of farming activities and non-farm occupations in industry, construction and services. Rural diversification is an alternative to the rice-cultivation that now predominates in Vietnam. It is crucial to rural employment creation, income diversification and generation, restriction of excessive out-migration, sustainable poverty reduction and overcoming the relative stagnation of agricultural development.

Diversification of farming activities is a change in the structure of agricultural production away from rice to other more highly valued crops. It makes for better use of Vietnam's rich endowment, that is, an impressive range of natural habitats and ecosystems. Additional incomes in the rural sector will be generated by diversification to higher-value crops such as flowers, vegetables and fruits, as well as livestock. As rising agricultural incomes do create more demand for industrial goods and services, they can therefore promote job creation in non-farm activities.

Many off-farm jobs could be created in traditional handicrafts involving bamboo, wood, pumice lacquer, stone, silk, paper, textiles. Carpet, embroidery, and ceramic production are resurgent in some areas of Vietnam, meeting the demand of both domestic and foreign markets. About a thousand traditional handicraft villages in Vietnam currently employ about ten million workers and obtain over US$3 million in export value. (A $1 million increase in handicraft exports is associated with the creation of 3,000 rural jobs.) Labour-intensive industries in clothing, footwear, travel bags, toys, supply of agricultural inputs, transport, storage, equipment repairs, primary processing of agricultural products and financial and marketing services are additional ways to absorb rural labour and create more business opportunities in both rural and urban zones.

The experiences of the newly industrialising countries in East and Southeast Asia are of particular relevance given some of the initial similarities between their economies and the Vietnamese economy. In Southeast Asia success has come through the comparative advantage in having one abundant resource – labour. The experience of other developing countries has been that diversification of farming activities and growth in off-farm employment both assist labour absorption and increase rural incomes. In rural industrialisation for off-farm employment China is a pioneer. The rapid growth of industrialisation in the countryside, particularly the development of the township and village enterprise (TVE) sector has been a key factor in the success of China's economic reforms, which started in 1978. The output of China's TVE sector has grown at an average annual rate of 15 per cent since 1978 and TVEs now employ about 130 million people, keeping large numbers of what might have become surplus agricultural labour in the rural areas. Since TVEs have also increased farmers' incomes, they have been one of the main forces narrowing the rural–urban income gap over the last two decades.

In China, non-farm incomes now make up around 35 per cent of rural household incomes, whereas a decade earlier their share was only 15 per cent.

In the Republic of Korea, the share increased from 18 to 50 per cent between 1975 and 1995. In Thailand, the proportion of off-farm income in total income of farm households rose from 46 per cent in 1971–72 to 59 per cent in 1982–83 (World Bank 1998).

Rural incomes and employment opportunities can, therefore, grow through a diversity of rural activities where labour-intensive industry and services hold a greater promise for employment-generation in Vietnam than agriculture does and should be seen as a key part of the national development strategy. In the following sections we examine Vietnam's progress in the direction of rural diversification as well as the physical, policy and financial constraints, which need to be removed if it this development is to be sustained.

REALITIES OF THE VIETNAMESE RURAL SECTOR: THE WIDENING INCOME GAP

Vietnam has experienced remarkable economic growth and development in the post-reform period. The pattern and quality of this growth is, however, uneven. There have been limited employment generation and a widening income gap, as evidenced by persistent poverty, particularly in rural and upland areas.

Unemployment is emerging as a major problem in Vietnam. Although there has been high growth in terms of GDP in the agricultural, industrial and service sectors since 1988, urban and rural non-agricultural employment creation is not fast enough. From 1990 to 1997, employment in the industrial sector grew by less than 1 per cent a year (from 3.4 to 3.6 million) and employment in agriculture, forestry and aquaculture increased by 2 per cent a year (from 21.6 to 24.8 million) (CIEM 1998).[2] More recently job creation has been negative in industry, due to a sharp 60 per cent reduction in foreign investment since 1997 due to the onset of the Asian financial crisis, and only modestly positive in agriculture and the mostly informal services. With low growth of employment in the three main sectors, Vietnam cannot cope with a fast increase in its labour force. Unemployment and underemployment, already serious, are growing. In the Red River Delta unemployment was 7.3 per cent in 2000. In Hanoi it was 8 per cent and in Ho Chi Minh City, the fastest economic growth zone, 6.5 per cent (GSO 2001: 61).

Under-employment, due to the seasonal nature of agricultural production, is also expanding. Outside of harvesting or planting time, there is relatively little to be done. While the official unemployment rate is relatively low, at 3.9 per cent, three-quarters of the rural population are considered underemployed.

Available working time used in 2000 was only 74 per cent and the rate has been falling since 1996 in all the northern rural areas (GSO 2001: 62). Due to their generally low incomes, farmers are reluctant to take time off and, of the 30 million rural people of working age; 8.6 million are either unemployed or underemployed. Thus job creation in agriculture simply increases underemployment. Farmers, particularly women, in rice monoculture areas are more affected than those in diversified areas. Men have more mobility and can move to other jobs outside the village during the off-season, while women stay at home with their children and without a job. Yet, in more diversified areas, such as the handicraft and trade villages in Bac Ninh province, both men and women are employed year round.

The main reason for the existence of unemployment and under-employment is that state-sector industrial expansion has, in the past, been relatively capital-intensive. It has therefore provided fewer employment opportunities than agriculture and the informal sector, where production is more labour-intensive and far less productive. Vietnam adds about one million to its labour force annually, most of them taking up agricultural work. Yet adding more and more people into an already over-populated agricultural sector has meant declining productivity growth and hence slow growth of rural incomes. To accommodate the increased labour force, marginal lands have been opened up for cultivation and holdings have diminished in size. These factors have not only widened the rural–urban income gap, resulting in significant social conflicts, but also increased environmental degradation.[3] Creation of off-farm employment through the development of rural industry and related services could ameliorate this situation by drawing off a significant amount of labour.

Paradoxically, there are some negative unintended consequences of more equitable land allocations, such as land fragmentation, which aggravate low agricultural productivity. Vietnam is well known as a country with scarce arable land. Per capita availability of cultivated land is 0.12 hectares (GSO 2001: 14, 35). Of the 33 million hectares of land, only 9.3 million is used for agriculture and there is little scope for extension. Given the existing ratio of people to land and population growth rate, there are no prospects to increase farmers' incomes by expanding the land area devoted to agriculture. Land fragmentation, resulting from the rather equitable land allocations after agricultural decollectivisation, aggravates land limitations. Farmers in the rice-growing areas of the Red River Delta are farming an average of eight to nine non-contiguous plots as small as 300 square metres each. This fragmentation has not only prevented farmers from applying technology in tilling the fields, pumping water and harvesting crops quickly, but also reduced the efficiency of labour and capital as farmers spend significant amounts of time travelling and moving supplies and equipment between plots. Fragmentation is much worse in the north of the country than in the south and significantly limits the earning potential of farmers. For example, a rice-farming household that has an average-size farm of 1.2 hectares and obtains an average yield of 6.1 tons per hectare will earn a yearly net income of about VND6.6 million ($470) (World Bank 1998). Since most rural households now work on smaller farms and obtain well below average yields, they are therefore significantly worse off. So an increase in rice yields will not be enough to lift farm households out of poverty.

Though it is important to capitalise on the potential for productivity growth and diversification in farming, the agricultural sector has limited capacity for employment-generation in the long run. As the rural labour force continues to grow, the rural–urban income gap will only be reduced significantly by the creation of substantial non-farm employment opportunities.

Absolute poverty, in which people cannot control the basic necessities such as food, shelter, education, health care and, therefore, choices and opportunities, can be seen particularly clearly in remote and mountainous areas of the country and in the north-central coastal provinces (Table 6.1). Interestingly, contrary to common expectation, the more fertile Mekong River Delta did not improve as much on poverty reduction as the Red River Delta.

Table 6.1: Incidence of poverty by regions, 1993–98 (%)

Region	1993		1998	
	Total poverty	Food poverty	Total poverty	Food poverty
Northern Uplands	84.22	41.64	65.81	33.27
Red River Delta	71.67	30.09	33.33	8.46
North Central	76.91	37.79	51.76	20.72
Central coast	59.15	26.52	39.96	20.64
Central Highlands	72.96	32.02	48.39	24.84
Southeast	45.82	15.17	14.37	3.51
Mekong River Delta	51.92	19.74	42.98	13.99

Source: GSO 1999.

Despite a doubling in per capita income from $200 to about $400 and a significant reduction in poverty as a result of economic growth over past decade, Vietnam remains one of the poorest countries in the world. Most of the poor are found in rural areas and the incidence of poverty is significantly higher among those who derive their livelihoods solely from farming. In remote and mountainous regions infrastructure is weak and the land is less productive due to severe deforestation and erosion. While other crops may be more suited to these areas, farmers have to concentrate on rice production for food security. Few opportunities exist for diversification of livelihoods beyond subsistence agriculture.

There are many causes of poverty, but most of the poor themselves attribute the direct causes to lack of information, low education, limited health care and lack of production resources such as land and capital. Other causes come from natural disasters, poor quality of infrastructure and demographic factors. Families with large numbers of children are common in rural areas and often have high dependency ratios. Lack of adult labour means lack of both land and labour that can bring income from non-farm activities. Thus families with high dependency ratios are more likely to be poor (GSO 1999). This constitutes a vicious circle of poverty: the poorer the production resources, the more farm hands needed to till the land, hence further poverty.

Despite agriculture's rapid growth of 4–5 per cent a year since 1988, urban incomes rose faster and the urban–rural income gap has increased. Indeed, urban incomes rose twice as rapidly as rural incomes (60 per cent versus 30 per cent) between 1993 and 1998 (World Bank 1999). In 1998 annual per capita income in rural areas was about $182, less than a third of the city level of $647 (Le Du Phong 2000). Whereas in 1995 the top 20 per cent earned 6.8 times more than the bottom 20 per cent, by 1997 they were earning 7.3 times more (World Bank 1998).

A major contributor to the increasing rural–urban income gap is that food prices have fairly consistently risen more slowly than prices of non-food goods and services (GSO various issues). In 1996, for example, food prices rose by 0.2 per cent, while those of non-food items increased by 4 per cent. The terms of trade had diverged even further by 2000.

Decollectivisation has broken the safety net formerly provided by farm co-operatives and made the poor more vulnerable. Farmers have now had to pay higher fees for their public goods such as education and health care, because of a sharp contraction of government subsidies. Farmers have to pay agricultural tax, irrigation and school fees as well as contribute to the agricultural co-operative, electrification and road funds of local authorities. As the incomes of many farm families are insufficient to cover public services, they may keep children out of school or sell property, such as land and buffaloes, to pay hospital fees. Families who wish to send children for tertiary education will find a very large share of their income going on tuition fees.

In cities, where even before economic reform urban incomes were higher than in rural areas, *Doi Moi* has created higher incomes. Industrial workers are better off because industrial productivity is well above that in agriculture. In addition, urban-based industry has undergone a high annual rate of output growth of 13.5 per cent in 1990–2000 (GSO 2001: 251), thanks in large measure to the impact of foreign direct investment (FDI). The urban services sector has also developed rapidly and brought about more jobs and higher incomes. Higher urban wages have in turn encouraged rural–urban migration. In 2000 the average monthly income in rural areas of the Red River Delta was about VND 81,000, while in Hanoi it was VND 550,000. Around 700,000 people have moved each year from rural to urban areas since the 1980s.[4] According to the Ministry of Labour, Invalids and Social Affairs (MOLISA), the number of labourers from rural areas seeking casual jobs in Hanoi was about 12,000 in 1992 and over four times that in 1998. Rural out-migration benefits employers in fast growing cities by increasing the labour supply and helping to keep wage rates lower but is also a burden in causing urban overcrowding. As noted above, urban population growth is greater than urban employment growth, leaving new immigrants more vulnerable than older inhabitants, forcing them to accept insecure casual labour at relatively low wages (see Abrami and Henaff, Chapter 4 this volume).

Currently, the migration-absorbing capacity of large cities such as Hanoi and Ho Chi Minh City has been exhausted because job creation in their industrial sectors has stagnated. Living facilities in these cities are, although better than in rural areas, primitive and limited. Overcrowding causes these cities many problems, not just rising unemployment but pollution, increased congestion, housing shortages, inadequate social services and insecurity.

The pattern of agricultural growth over ten years has also created an income gap within rural areas. According to the Ministry of Agriculture and Rural Development (MARD), Vietnam has a group of farmers in non-rice areas, in cash crops such as coffee and cashew, that is much better off. There are about 115,000 of these farms and they average 6.63 ha. They are located mainly in hilly and mountainous regions and have incomes much higher than those of rice farmers. These farms hold a significant amount of land and capital stock, for example, $8,000 per farm in the north, $29,885 in the south and $35,350 in the Tay Nguyen (central highlands) region. On average each farm can earn about $5,800 a year and wages are over $1,000 a year, 5.5 times more than the earnings of a rice farmer (Le Du Phong 2000). Most of these farm holders have either been officials or are local cadres whose position and social relations bring them many benefits. Some, for example, were offered a piece of land in the city, as part of the privatisation of land-use rights: since the price of urban land rose rapidly, they could sell it and buy a large farm with the proceeds.

Besides the existence of large landholdings, the other reason for income disparity is that a proportion of rural households has shifted early to new activities, or forms of rural diversification, with higher income such as transport, trade, construction and diversified farming activities. For example, the export value of 1 kg of shrimp is known to be equal to that of 100 kg of rice or 300 kg of salt. In the Nam Dinh coastal districts shrimp farms are therefore replacing salt fields, while farmers in the Khanh Hoa coastal zone earn higher incomes by growing shrimp and sea crabs. Others have been induced to grow high-value pepper crops for export.

The rural income gap also appears to widen with differences in living location, working position, age, gender, ethnicity and assets. Some regions have an advantage in geographical conditions, which favour a shift to higher-value crops. But age, education and gender play a key role in the market-orientated areas. The majority of farmers who have succeeded in their farm and/or off-farm businesses are men aged from 30 to 50. Women and the less educated find it very hard to shift to other crops and new off-farm businesses because they lack social contacts and other access to information which would increase their capacity, while they are also more likely to be risk averse. Female householders and the aged are also more likely to experience labour shortage. As a consequence, low income and low economic diversification of these households are widespread in rural areas. Before identifying major constraints on rural diversification, let us first take stock of some development in this area.

PROGRESS IN RURAL DIVERSIFICATION: A CASE OF UNEVEN DEVELOPMENT

The most important potential for Vietnam's rural industrialisation and diversification lies in the country's endowments of abundant cheap and relatively skilled labour and remarkably diversified natural resources. The valuable labour resource holds huge potential for development of labour-intensive industry and services, while the diversity of natural resources holds much potential for more profitable types of production.

As incomes have increased recently, especially in the cities, people have changed their tastes and tended to diversify their consumption. This in turn induces rural diversification. For example, there will be a move away from rice to wheat products and to increased consumption of higher-value foods, such as meat, organic vegetables, fruits and dairy products.[5] Such diversification is already taking place on city fringes. So far, however, the rise in demand is limited. Broader growth of the domestic market is needed for rural diversification to take off, generating more employment in sale of farm inputs, equipment repairs, financial services, primary processing of agricultural products, marketing services, manufacture and repair of consumer goods. Such jobs are more likely to interest young, educated people. At present, there is little incentive for high school and higher education graduates to remain in the countryside because skilled jobs are scarce there.

A further potential advantage is rapid integration into the world and regional economies, which increases Vietnam's access to new labour-intensive technologies. Effective use of imported and local technologies will steadily increase labour productivity. The combination of cheap and relatively skilled labour and high productivity will help Vietnam hold its unit labour costs below those of its competitors (see Table 6.2) for a substantial period of time, even as incomes rise.

Table 6.2: Monthly wage rate of garment workers in some Asian countries (US$)

Countries	Monthly Wage
Vietnam	40.00
Indonesia	83.00
Thailand	100.00
Malaysia	120.00
Singapore	415.00
Hong Kong	612.00
South Korea	767.00
Taiwan	772.00

Source: Credit Lyonnais, cited by Vo Phuoc Tan (1998: 12).

Vietnam has good potential for rapid growth of a variety of export-orientated, labour-intensive industries in non-urban locations, although production facilities do not necessarily have to be located in villages. They can cluster near transportation routes and locate in smaller population centres within easy reach of cities and ports. Once the Ho Chi Minh Highway, which runs parallel with the National Highway One, and a number of roads linking the two are completed, the distance from any point in Vietnam to major roads will be shorter and offer a better chance for mountainous areas to develop their economy. This could help Vietnam easily realise a more balanced development of its rural economy, if its policies are well made.

A start has been made in diversifying the economy. Agriculture's share of GDP fell from 36 per cent in 1986 to 24.3 per cent in 2000 (GSO 2001: 69). Other regional countries have undergone a similar transition. In Thailand, for instance, agriculture's share of GDP fell from 31 per cent in 1974 to 10 per cent in 1996. That in Indonesia fell from 31 to 16 per cent over the same period, while China's declined from 27 to 20 per cent between 1986 and 1996. (World Bank 1998). Vietnam is on a similar transition path to more diversification even though agriculture still accounts for over 70 per cent of total employment.

In recent years, in line with the rapid development in agriculture, non-farm industries and services have developed in many rural areas. The major trends are:

- restoring traditional cottage industries and trades of different localities;
- developing new handicrafts and products;
- promoting trade and services that are related to both farm and non-farm production.

According to a survey by the General Statistics Office (GSO 1996), some 2.2 million rural households (18 per cent) were engaged in industrial crafts, construction, commercial, service or other non-agricultural activities in 1994. Of the total rural labour force of around 30 million, eight million have some off-farm employment. The non-farm sector in rural areas now consists of about 4,500 state-owned enterprises (SOEs), 24,000 private firms as well as the 2.2 million household enterprises mentioned above (McKenzie 1998). Most of the private and household enterprises are small and are involved in activities such as handicrafts, agro-processing, tanning, paper production, brick making or production of other construction materials, non-ferrous metallurgy and provision of services to agriculture.

Private companies are concentrated mainly in trade (50 per cent), industry (35 per cent) and construction (10 per cent). Within the manufacturing sector, private firms are chiefly involved in the resource-based subsectors, such as food processing and beverages, mineral and non-ferrous products, wood and stone processing and rubber. These private companies are smaller than their urban counterparts in number of employees. Whereas the urban private sector employed an average of 80 workers per firm in 1999, the average in rural private firms was 26, while non-farm households averaged only three workers.

There are about 1,000 specialised villages across the country as well as numerous individual household enterprises in manufacturing. The specialised villages are mostly located in the Red River Delta, while other household manufacturing is found in the southeast and the Mekong River delta. Xuan Tien Mechanics Village (see box) illustrates labour and income generation, as well as a positive linkage between state and non-state sectors. However, rural enterprises associated with transport, storage, processing and, especially, the marketing chain from the farm gate to the point of domestic or export sale, have been slower to develop.

Xuan Tien Mechanics Village

This village is one of eight villages in Nam Dinh province, 130 km south of Hanoi, specialising in the production of mechanical equipment. The villagers inherited skills in metal work from the nineteenth century. Their vocation went into decline, due to lack of a market, under collectivisation. Agricultural reforms, however, brought increasing demand from rural households for small harvesting and husking machines. Because they are well designed, the village's products are famous for high quality, strength and convenience and therefore its market is expanding, mainly in surrounding districts. The industry not only provides more jobs and additional incomes for villagers but also offers some employment to neighbouring villages in collection of scrap metal. Today, Xuan Tien manufactures new products for use in the construction industry, lifting materials or mixing sand, gravel and cement. In making its machines, the village uses engines supplied by state-owned enterprises.

However in general linkages are as yet thinly developed: the specialised villages have few connections with each other, while there are also weak linkages to urban firms,[6] especially in terms of production co-ordination. Markets are often limited to the immediately surrounding areas. Subcontracting to larger firms in the city is beginning to develop, especially for export goods because small rural firms lack the capacity to export directly. This situation is similar to the early stage of TVE development in China, when few linkages to the urban sector existed. In contrast with Vietnam, however, development of the Chinese urban economy generally lagged behind that of the TVEs, at least in the 1980s. The growth of Shanghai's economy, for example, was very modest until 1992, while the TVE sectors in Zhejiang and Jiangsu experienced much more rapid growth. In Wenzhou municipality of Zhejiang province – one of the pioneers in TVE development – there was virtually no major urban industrial sector (World Bank 1998). Vietnam's urban sector, on the other hand, boomed first and has been slow to develop linkages with rural industries.

The resurgence of the specialised villages has not been the result of any deliberate policy decision, but rather farmers' response to market-orientated economy. First, therefore, there has been an absence of policies that encourage the retraining of farmers, especially women and youth, with the aim of shifting their careers to off-farm employment. Second, there has been a shortage of investment funds due to a low level of rural savings and weak performance of the rural financial system (see also Smith, Chapter 7 in this volume). Third, the lack of access to inputs such as credit, land, materials and technology and access to output markets are crucial barriers to rural industrialisation.

In rural areas, food crops account for about half of farm output. Rice, the main crop, provides two-thirds of the country's food energy and about one-sixth of the national income. Rice production in 1998 was 31.7 million tons, compared with 11.6 million tons in 1980 and accounted for nearly 90 per cent of total grain output and 70 per cent of total sown area. Maize, potato and cassava are the other staple food crops. Livestock, industrial and other crops (such as fruit and vegetables) have maintained a fairly constant share in value of production. Thus rapid agricultural growth is occurring with limited diversification. Table 6.3 illustrates this point.

The reasons for limited diversification in agriculture lie in both government policies on agricultural development and the rice cultivation habit of farmers. Vietnam is a well-known rice-growing nation, but it was also a food-importing country for a long period. The supreme goal of past policy was to achieve self-sufficiency in food and then create a rice surplus for export. Today,

Table 6.3: Structure of Vietnam's agricultural production, 1990 and 1996

	1990		1996	
	Value VND bn	**Share (%)**	**Value VND bn**	**Share (%)**
Total Value	14.3	100.0	20.0	100.0
Grains	7.4	51.7	9.9	49.5
Other crops	3.7	26.4	5.5	27.5
Livestock	3.2	22.4	4.5	22.5

Source: Official data.

this goal has been met and it is therefore time for a change of policy toward more agricultural diversification.

Insofar as such diversification has taken place, the trend varies among regions. Expansion of tree crops, such as tea, coffee, pepper and rubber, has taken place in the central highlands and in the southeast. In the northern uplands, feed production for the livestock sector has expanded, mainly to cater for the needs of the neighbouring Red River Delta. A shift towards commercial products can be seen in many coastal districts and in the vicinity of major cities, where both domestic and foreign markets can afford the higher prices. Farmers in these areas have moved into production of shrimp, sea crab, livestock and livestock feed, organic vegetables and fruits and cut flowers. As noted above, those who have been able to diversify have often been those whose position and social relations have enabled them to derive benefits from the privatisation of social capital.

The government's efforts to diversify agricultural production are illustrated by the development of plantations in the south and some parts in the northern mountain region. Its objectives have included increasing income for both landholders and workers, diversifying products, providing additional goods for domestic and export markets and, finally, greening deforested hills. However, these plantations have also caused a widening income gap within rural areas, which has led, in some instances, to social divisions that will have a negative impact on rural development in the long term. Such conflicts are compounded by competition for water between prawn farms and other citizens in several coastal districts. Government diversification policy has, therefore, done little to date to offset the tendency towards a widening income gap as those who are more advantageously situated (that is, with better social connections) have taken up the opportunities afforded by the market economy. Indeed its encouragement of large-scale ventures such as plantations could have the opposite effect.

In the two decades since the latest agricultural reform began in Vietnam, the agricultural economy has changed impressively toward rice and coffee export. However, this change has not been enough to transform most farmers' lives and livelihoods. A new direction in the rural development programme to both accelerate and broaden the base of rural diversification is needed. In the case of Vietnam, there is considerable evidence that farmers have historically responded to market signals by adjusting their cropping patterns and enterprise mixes, unless constrained by political, physical, agronomic, financial and marketing factors. Removing constraints, with varying levels of state assistance in some, but not all, sectors, will be a key to enhancing the rural economy.

CONSTRAINTS ON RURAL DIVERSIFICATION

Rural diversification, for all its potential, currently faces many challenges and constraints. Typically among these are lack of investment funds, officials' capacity and willingness to implement public development programmes, access to inputs and information, and weak purchasing power due to low rural incomes. Underlying these various constraints, we can identify four major elements inhibiting further rural diversification – rural finance, the SOE–private sector relationship, inadequate rural infrastructure and lack of education. All four areas are highly amenable to government policy interventions. Removing these constraints will open many opportunities for a large proportion of the rural population to shift their careers confidently to non-farm occupations, creating more jobs and increasing their incomes.

Rural Finance

The rural financial sector will play a crucial role, not just in agricultural growth but also in Vietnam's success in rural industrialisation. However, shortage of investment funds in rural areas is often cited as a major constraint to rural development in general and to the smallholder farmers and rural business enterprises in particular. In the Ministry of Agriculture and Rural Development survey, 40 per cent of respondents identified lack of capital as their main constraint (Johnson 1998). This shortage of investment funds can in part be traced to deficiencies in the financial system, chiefly immaturity of the financial sector and government interventions that distort credit markets.

The rural financial sector can be broadly divided into three categories (Johnson 1998; Smith, Chapter 7 this volume):

- An informal financial sector – an unregulated financial service provision mainly by family and friends, traders or private moneylenders;
- A formal financial sector – financial institutions such as the Vietnam Bank for Agriculture and Rural Development (VBARD), the People's Credit Fund system (PCFs), and the Bank for the Poor (VBP) under the supervision of the State Bank of Vietnam (SBV); and
- A semiformal financial sector – organised but largely unregulated financial activities involving non-financial organisations. These include savings and credit schemes operated by mass organisations or government ministries and non-government organisations (NGOs).

Of the three categories, the informal sector is generally considered to be the largest. It provided funds for 50 per cent of rural households in 1997 (Johnson 1998). The formal sector is still underdeveloped, although there has been major growth since 1988. Most poor rural households in Vietnam cannot, or do not wish to, use the formal sector. The rural financial system has been liberalised significantly by a resurgence of informal financial markets and the entry of large number of semiformal financial institutions in rural areas since 1989. Because the formal sector is still underdeveloped and contributes little to finance in the poorest areas, the informal and semiformal sectors are a necessary supplementary force. However, fund mobilisation and credit provision remain weak and inefficient in all three sectors. This can be seen in the fund-mobilisation performance of the PCFs, a competent financial institution belonging to the VBARD. After three years of operation, in April 1997 total savings mobilisation of the system, VND 764.7 billion, amounted to 62 per cent of its total assets. The PCF system was one of very few financial institutions achieving this high ratio.

Although PCFs have been relatively successful in savings mobilisation, their inertia is indicated by the fact that deposits are substantially short-term (less than one year) (Nguyen 1998). Almost no funds of more than one year have been mobilised, leading to a severe shortage of long-term funds to meet the demand of members. The formal sector cannot mobilise medium- and long-term savings because low and vulnerable incomes make savers unwilling

Table 6.4: Lending pattern of Vietnam's banking system, October 1997

Type of bank	outstanding loans	*of which*:	
	(total VND m.)	short-term loans	long-term loans
		%	%
State-owned commercial banks	52,766,241	76.00	24.00
Urban joint-stock banks	9,666,567	87.00	13.00
Rural joint-stock banks	423,816	99.67	0.33
PCF system	1,289,240	100.00	0.00
Financial companies	125,507	98.18	1.82
Foreign banks	17,198,908	60.40	39.60
Joint-venture banks	1,878,968	65.92	34.08
Total	83,351,528	74.34	25.66

Source: Nguyen 1998.

to make long-term deposits. Moreover, due to low fund mobilisation of the banking system, which has led to a weak capital base, banks found themselves adapting short-term loans to rural areas and these loans did not, in the end, support development of rural industry and services. This situation is common to many rural financial institutions in Vietnam today.

Private moneylenders and many of the international NGOs operating in Vietnam have actively promoted commercial loans to smaller clients. The NGOs either provide technical assistance to a mass organisation (such as the Women's Union) that acts as an agent of the commercial banks, or provide capital and technical assistance to a mass organisation that acts as a financial intermediary. The experience to date has been mixed, and no sustainable approach has yet been found. The problems include uncertainty about policy and legislation, lack of clarity about accountability and institutional responsibilities and the mass organisations' limited capacity for financial management. If both these sectors could act as a supplementary force to the formal sector to provide small funds for the mass of rural people to run their small farming businesses, the formal sector would be able to shift its lending pattern toward bigger and longer-term loans. Otherwise rural households will be prevented from investing in larger projects like off-farm businesses devoted to processing, storage, transportation, manufacturing and construction. In reality, almost all funds lent by Vietnam's banking system are still short-term, 74.3 per cent, while long-term loans are about 25.7 per cent and urban-biased (Table 6.4)

Overdue loans are a problem facing Vietnam's banking system, making it financially fragile. Bank overdues appear to have risen quite substantially since the end of 1995, reversing the decline that occurred in the early 1990s (Table 6.5). As of 1997, loan losses had the potential to wipe out over half of the system's total capital (Nguyen 1998). The average ratio, about 12 per cent, of overdues to outstanding loans, coupled with a weak capital base, leaves the state-owned commercial banks highly vulnerable to a slowdown in economic growth or to adverse economic shocks.[7]

Credit allocation provides some support to off-farm activities. While about 68 per cent of lending to the rural sector goes to agriculture, almost a third goes to non-farm activities: 9.5 per cent to industry, 7.6 per cent to construction and 14.9 per cent to services. However, loan bias toward agriculture is a major feature of the rural financial system in general. This bias reflects the reality that most people are still in agriculture and their choice is to invest in it. Moreover, the government also actively promoted improvement of agri-

Table 6.5: Weakening performance of Vietnam's financial system, end of June (%)

	1992	**1993**	**1994**	**1995**	**1996**	**1997**
Total Banking System						
Total overdues/capital	88.1	95.5	85.0	61.9	75.7	112.3
Total overdues/loans	13.7	11.1	6.0	7.8	9.3	15.4
Total overdues/total assets	6.0	6.6	5.5	4.4	5.5	8.9
Total capital/total assets	6.8	6.9	6.9	7.1	7.2	7.9
State-owned Commercial Banks						
Total overdues/capital	109.0	125.6	121.0	105.5	128.4	181.4
Total overdues/loans	13.7	11.6	10.2	8.9	11.0	16.4
Total overdues/total assets	6.0	6.9	6.3	5.2	6.4	13.0
Total capital/total assets	5.5	5.5	5.0	4.9	5.0	7.2

Source: World Bank 1997.

cultural production in the mid-1990s by pressuring banks to shift resources, which were at the time biased towards urban state-owned enterprises, to the agricultural sector. Even today, however, poor farmers have difficulty in accessing formal credit, especially medium- and long-term credit needed for investment in new types of production. If the banking system continues to behave this way, diversification into non-farm activities will be difficult to achieve.

One of the elements greatly contributing to the success of *Doi Moi* and stronger competitiveness in the goods market in Vietnam is that the government has removed almost all price subsidies. This has, however, not yet happened in Vietnam's credit market. The rural credit market is still controlled and exhibits many different levels of interest rate ceiling and subsidy that result in a significant degree of distortion. The VBP's lending rates are highly subsidised, at 0.7 per cent per month compared with the VBARD rate of 1.2 per cent and the PCFs' 1.5 per cent. In the informal sector, private moneylenders' rates are highest, at 8–10 per cent, although family and friends often lend without interest or by becoming *de facto* shareholders in the enterprise. The semiformal sector offers loans at medium rates ranging from 1.5 to 3.5 per cent per month.

Although the VBARD has as its major function the provision of funds to rural households, only about 32 per cent of them enjoy its services. The rest, especially the poor, hardly use VBARD because either it has no branch in their locality or transaction costs are too high (see below), while the bank, with its profit orientation, focuses on those who are richer and have collateral. Therefore, without the VBP, with its controlled rate of 0.7 per cent, the poor would not have access to funds from the formal sector at all. However, the VBP at present cannot mobilise savings from the public because the average interest rate in the countryside is higher than its lending rate,[8] nor does it reach the remotest areas. In 1996, for example, it planned to mobilise VND 300 billion as savings and achieved only VND ten million. In 1997, by contrast, most of its VND 433,349 billion of 'savings' actually came from the government budget (Nguyen 1998).

By imposing interest-rate ceilings – non-market-determined interest rates – for savings and loans the government is distorting the development of the rural financial sector. Interest rates, which are set low compared with market clearing rates (at one-half or one-third of comparable semiformal cost-covering rates) create excess demand for lending and force banks to ration credit. Since banks will only operate in areas where they can earn profits, they select those investments that are safest and reduce services in the very areas, remote regions and high-risk cases that the interest rate subsidy was supposed to help. Thus regional inequality in the availability of formal financial services is reinforced. There is clearly a contradiction between government demands that the banks act as commercial enterprises and its insistence on 'aiding the poor' through subsidised rates.

Because of the decision to lower the interest rate ceiling of all rural formal financial institutions and the controls over the spread between deposit and lending rates, banks are not able to set interest rates that will cover the cost of funds, operating costs and risk. Thus, competitiveness and expansion of services in the financial sector are severely limited. Rural households are less willing to put savings in banks while returns available elsewhere are much higher. The interest rate ceiling is already proving to be a constraint to the rapid growth of the PCF system.

Transaction costs are another barrier discouraging small borrowers from obtaining formal loans. Due to the excess demand for credit, borrowers try to bribe bank officers; otherwise it is hard to borrow money in time. To obtain loans they often have to wait or visit the bank several times and the opportunity costs incurred may be high for people who are busy or living far from the bank. Subsidised credit could therefore cause high transaction costs for borrowers. It is estimated that all costs incurred in bank borrowing are 9.7 per cent of the loan amount for the smallest borrowers but only 0.4 per cent for the largest borrowers (Tran 1998). In short, to enable rural diversification and especially off-farm activities to take place on a viable and sustainable base in the future, the elaboration of a strategy for medium- and long-term fund mobilisation must be viewed as an important and urgent task. Moreover, there should be less state intervention that distorted the financial sector but greater support for the relatively more efficient PCFs.

RELATIONS BETWEEN SOES AND PRIVATE ENTERPRISES

Rural sustainable growth will be based on sustained improvement in the incomes of the vast majority of rural households in Vietnam through diversified agricultural production and off-farm employment. As households move from agriculture to off-farm employment, many of them will not succeed in small business due to the nature of market competition and capital accumulation. There are winners and losers. Most people will not end up as owners

Table 6.6: Number of SOEs in agriculture and forestry

	1996	1997	1998	1999
Total number of SOEs	6,200	5,818	5,718	5,462
Of which:				
SOEs in agriculture and forestry	1,591	1,538	1,454	1,424

Source: Ministry of Finance.

of businesses in the long run, they will become the employees of more successful businesses. Opportunities therefore need to be provided for people to move from farming into better-paid wage employment where they can also develop their skills. The question here is not just how to develop more successful business in the rural areas but also how people can gain access to better employment opportunities. Thus, while rural finance may be the key to medium-term sustainability of household enterprises, education and training are important, as also is the development of investment in labour-intensive technologies. The latter can not only provide improved job opportunities but also feed small and medium enterprises (SMEs) through contracts, resources and information.

In that connection, there is evidence that SOEs, to some extent, have carried out rural diversification and industrialisation as demonstrated below. In the rural sector, farm households provide the bulk of agricultural output while agricultural processing and marketing activities are dominated by SOEs. Central and local governments own over 1,400 enterprises in the agricultural sector alone (Table 6.6). Although, the number of rural SOEs has declined since 1996, they still represent about a quarter of all SOEs in the country. In addition, according to the 1996–2000 Public Investment Programme, the total projected investment of VND 95.5 trillion in agriculture was going to be provided by a mixture of state investment (23 per cent), investment by SOEs (45 per cent), household investment (25 per cent) and FDI (7 per cent). This implies that SOEs are still expected to play the major role in rural investment.

SOEs in the agricultural sector provide off-farm employment in a variety of activities including the production and processing of sugar, rubber, and coffee and in artificial insemination and fertilisers. While these SOEs no longer receive direct subsidies, they receive indirect subsidies in various forms such as loans at concessional interest rates, debt forgiveness, and tax exemptions. For example, provincial fertiliser companies may receive interest rate subsidies on outstanding loans, exemptions from depreciation costs, subsidies on the cost of transporting fertiliser to remote areas, as well as subsidies to store higher levels of fertilisers to support the stabilisation fund. Other subsidies include trade restrictions that are used to protect local SOEs. The sugar industry, for example, is indirectly subsidised through local policies favouring conversion of paddy land to sugar cane and administrative restrictions on imported sugar. Through such support, SOEs in the rural sector help alleviate rural unemployment to a significant extent. Evidence can be found from sugar companies, cement blast furnaces, tunnel brick making, beer companies, state-owned farms and state forestry farms.

In addition, there are many business linkages between SOEs and the non-state SMEs in rural areas. The private sector in reality receives many of the benefits that go to SOEs in the form of capital, information, supply and marketing contracts and other resources obtained through connections with the SOE sector. Many SMEs are subcontractors for the SOEs or supply input and other services to them and more job opportunities and incomes to rural people are therefore indirectly offered by SOEs through the SME channel. SMEs are also growing in response to development in the SOE sector. From this standpoint, SOEs can be considered as major pillars of rural economy, to some extent leading the SME sector in rural industrialisation. Finally, SOEs remain a major source of revenue for the state, and this helps explain the assistance they receive from the government to develop these types of activity.

However, current studies suggest that not a few SOEs in sugar, rubber and beer make losses and are inefficient. In the sugar industry, for example, many refineries are uncompetitive due to their location in areas where insufficient cane is produced, resulting in underutilised capacity. According to the IMF, of the 50 most indebted SOEs from a sample of 1,044, food enterprises accounted for 24 per cent of the group's total debt (World Bank, 2000).

Support given to loss-making SOEs may result in either crowding in or crowding out of private sector SMEs. Despite the benefits passed on to the non-state sector mentioned above, in some areas it is clear that the private sector is discouraged from investing in areas where SOEs are dominant. Poor investment decisions (as in the case of sugar refining SOEs mentioned above) combined with protection reduce not only the incentives for SOEs to operate efficiently but also the potential development of linkages between the two sectors.

However, there have been some positive policy adjustments to facilitate private sector development. The government is aware that an increase in the levels of investment in the rural sector requires provision of an environment that is conducive to private sector investment. In recent years some SOEs have been equitised, to increase their capital base, privatised or liquidated. The government has also taken several steps to reduce unnecessary rules and improve the regulatory and legal system facing the non-state sector. It has simplified business registration procedures and regulations to make it easier for private businesses to get established and to reduce the scope of discretionary behaviour by officials. This action suggests that the government has recognised the importance of the private sector investment for creating jobs, particularly to balance declining investment from foreign sources.

There is evidence that SMEs are successful at absorbing rural labour, using labour-intensive technology that compensates for their lower productivity. The labour-capital ratio of non-state enterprises is about ten times that of SOEs, while value of output per worker in the former is roughly one-fifth that of the latter. In addition, a job created in a SME requires a capital investment of about US$800 compared to US$18,000 in a SOE (World Bank 1998). A shift in policy away from supporting SOEs for their own sake towards better targeting of public investment to maximise the development of linkages and employment growth is therefore desirable.

Rural Infrastructure

Roads, irrigation, power supply facilities, ports and telecommunications make up Vietnam's rural infrastructure, which is generally underdeveloped and in poor condition. The rural transport system is particularly weak in the mountainous and remote areas, limiting development of commercial crops and service provision. Irrigation is limited mainly to rice production (80 per cent of which is irrigated; only 20 per cent of industrial crops are irrigated), and rural electrification has a limited coverage. Due to decades of war and fiscal constraint, much of the other infrastructure has been damaged or has deteriorated because of lack of maintenance.

At present, the majority of rural Vietnamese do not have access to basic infrastructure services such as the national electricity grid, all-weather roads, irrigation, drainage and flood control facilities, clean drinking water, permanent markets. The poor and most remote have even less access. This situation exhibits clearly the great difficulties that Vietnam confronts on the road to transferring a large proportion of rural people to off-farm careers. Specific parts of the infrastructure are discussed below.

Electricity is considered one of the most crucial elements for Vietnam as it carries out industrialisation and modernisation of the rural areas. Today, almost all provinces and districts are connected to the national grid. However, connections below district level are not well developed. Only 62 per cent of the communes and 35 per cent of all households are connected (Table 6.7), while many rural households use small, fuel-powered generators or, in

Table 6.7: Connections to the national electricity grid (%)

	North	Centre	South	Total
Districts	92	79	100	91
Communes	62	52	73	62
Households	67	32	30	35

Source: World Bank 1998.

mountainous areas, micro hydroelectric generators. The amount of electricity supplied to these households is often only enough for one or two lights or a TV. Further electricity supply is therefore badly needed not only for production development but also for significant improvement in standards of living within the countryside.

The distribution networks are old, poorly maintained, overstretched and inefficient. Distribution losses range from 15 to 30 per cent. Prices of electricity are not the same from region to region and farmers have to pay more than urban residents. This situation prevents farmers from using machinery or, if they do use it, their costs are higher.

There are great variations in electricity charges between communes within a single district and even more between provinces. A kilowatt/hour of electricity costs, for instance, VND 550–650 in Ha Tay, VND 700 in Quang Binh, VND 1,200–1,500 in Ha Tinh, and in some locations it can be as high as VND 1,800–2,000. Higher prices charged to rural people effectively reduce the demand for electricity in those areas.

Vietnam has a well-developed road network of over 209,000 km, of which 7 per cent are national roads, 8 per cent provincial roads and the remainder district, commune and village roads. In terms of coverage, the network compares favourably to neighbouring countries. However, in terms of quality, Vietnam's road network counts among the worst. Only 42 per cent of national and provincial roads and about 4 per cent of the district and commune roads are paved. Almost half of the national road network is in very poor condition and one-quarter of the bridges need to be rehabilitated or replaced. In addition, more than 600 communes still do not have vehicle-accessible roads connecting them to district centres, 12 per cent of the rural population do not have access to motorised transport and more than 100,000 km of the local roads can only be used during the dry season.

The poor state of the roads not only imposes a high economic cost, wiping out the comparative advantage of Vietnam's products, but also prevents rural people from moving towards diversifying their income sources. The road conditions typically prevailing in Vietnam are estimated to increase vehicle operating costs by up to 80 per cent (World Bank 2000). Currently, although aid donors also provide infrastructure funding, progress in improving the nation's rural roads network has been slow and is a reflection of the resource constraints faced by the authorities, particularly local authorities.[9] Given this background it is not surprising that the rural areas are generally poorly endowed with transport infrastructure and services of an acceptable standard.

Sound infrastructure such as good roads, communications, power, water makes it feasible for producers to operate efficiently and cost effectively from rural areas rather than from a congested urban core. Thus the weak transport infrastructure is a major constraint on rural diversification and on closure of the urban–rural income gap. While development of rural infrastructure is largely associated with public investment policies, and despite a 25 percent increase announced in 1999, public funds for rural infrastructure remain limited. A further shift in central budget priorities is required, moving away from large-scale investments focused on already congested urban areas, towards development of wider and more effective networks that encourage rural diversification.

In addition to physical infrastructure needs, there are also the less tangible requirements of information about markets (demand, prices, quality requirements and competitors, for example) or the possibility of developing more forward linkages. In comparison to China at a similar stage of development, Vietnamese producers face greater competition in their own market, which causes difficulties in expanding rural enterprises. While early development of China's TVEs benefited from a vacuum in domestic markets for durable consumer goods (hence less competition), in Vietnam, goods produced by the urban private sector or imported from China and Thailand dominate these markets. In addition, low purchasing power restricts domestic demand and necessitates access to export markets if rural producers are to experience rising income levels.

Both farmers and processors frequently report that they lack the skills, information on customers' consumption patterns and tastes, and networks needed to acquire bargaining power and maximise their returns in a market economy. In the cashew industry, for example, a majority of processors acknowledge that they could raise export returns with a better understanding of customers' needs in packaging and quality and of competitors' performance. Instead they remain vulnerable to pressure from better-informed urban-based firms and middlemen, often selling at low prices while the larger firms reap most of the profits. Handicraft production units face similar difficulties. Producers rarely meet foreign buyers or sign contracts directly. Authorised trade intermediaries usually conduct this work and restrict information about prices and final destinations. Thus, development of business networks, by improving access to market information and marketing skills for rural entrepreneurs, would not only assist producers to follow market fluctuations and enable them to allocate resources more effectively but assist them to increase their bargaining power *vis-à-vis* suppliers and buyers. Information networks also increase the probability that success of rural enterprises in one area will in turn encourage new firms in nearby areas.

Education and Training

International studies showing that, other factors held constant, farmers with more education produce higher yields have been confirmed in the case of rice farming in Vietnam. Paddy yields were shown to be 7 per cent higher on farms headed by men or women who had completed three to four years of education than on farms headed by those with less education and 11 per cent higher where the household head had completed primary education (World Bank 1998). The remarkable increases in productivity both in industrial and service sectors over the last decade also indicate that education is important for helping Vietnam absorb and use effectively new technology channelled through FDI. Providing broad-based access to higher quality of rural education, and expanding informal and continuous education to rural people should form an integral component of the rural development strategy.

Basically, Vietnam has recognised the importance of education to economic development and has made good progress in providing broad-based access to education. Illiteracy is reported to be only 7 per cent, and net enrolment in primary education is estimated at 91 per cent. This performance is well above that of many countries with higher income levels. Nonetheless, the average duration of studies in Vietnam in 1998 was far less than in ASEAN and China in 1992. For rural Vietnam the figure was equivalent to the nationwide averages for China and Indonesia in 1970 and for Thailand and Malaysia in 1960 (Table 6.8).

Table 6.8: Years of study in Vietnam and other countries

Country	**Average Duration of Studies (years)**			
	1960	**1970**	**1980**	**1992**
China	2.8	5.4	7.3	7.8
Indonesia	4.0	5.5	7.9	9.0
Malaysia	5.5	7.1	8.6	9.5
Philippines	7.5	9.6	10.9	11.6
Sri Lanka	7.4	8.3	10.3	11.5
Thailand	5.8	6.1	8.2	8.7
Vietnam			**1992**	**1998**
– urban			7.1	8.0
– rural			5.0	5.7

Source: World Bank 2000.

Part of the reason for the short average duration of studies is the elitist Vietnamese education system that focuses on academic knowledge provided by the formal system, rather than on informal education given through short-term training programmes, vocational instruction programmes via television, and local community discussion groups. The latter are often more directly relevant to farmers and can increase their skills, eventually expanding significantly their chances of finding off-farm employment. While more vocationally orientated formal training can also be helpful for offering and upgrading skills and opening new job opportunities for people both in rural and urban zones, Vietnam has actually focused less on vocational and technical training compared with university education over the 1990s. While part of the burden has been taken up by the private sector, the shortage of relevant vocational training has not only limited the supply of skilled workers but also resulted in inefficient allocation of human resources. For instance, there are too many university graduates seeking jobs in cities but a great shortage of skilled workers in enterprises, particularly rural enterprises.

The unbalanced allocation of human resources indicates that the countryside is not of great appeal, partly because the rural sector is very poor with extremely limited diversification. Ironically this is another vicious circle: the less human resource allocation to improve the skills of rural population, the more limited rural diversification. Inappropriate government policies in educational development as well as other areas such as salary, promotion opportunities and working conditions have encouraged skilled people to work in the city rather than the countryside. Adjustment of the current educational structure can be seen as one of major tasks of the government as it designs a strategy for future rural development.

The reasons for low enrolment in vocational programmes lie, on the one hand, in the characteristics of the economy in which a majority of the rural population is largely reliant on agriculture and there are few rural enterprises employing skilled workers. This fact has discouraged young rural people from enrolling in technical training schools. On the other hand, the government has prioritised development of broad-based primary and secondary education throughout the country and higher education in the urban zones. Consequently, a limited amount of public funding is given to vocational and technical schools in terms of training facilities, classrooms and teachers. Small-scale and backward facilities limit the scope and slow down growth trends of technical worker training. As a result, the vocational sector's share of enrolments actually declined from 13.2 per cent in 1992 to 6.7 per cent in 1999 (World Bank 2000).

Education in the areas that are necessary for national development, such as agriculture and technical engineering, are not paid much attention. Many high school leavers are not interested in these fields, while graduates and skilled workers are not willing to work in their home villages. Therefore, many public servants in remote and mountainous areas have not finished primary school.

Access to different levels of schooling and the quality of schooling varies across regions. In general high drop-out rates in rural areas were due to inadequate availability of primary schooling. Over 90 per cent of pupils enrolled in primary school live in rural areas. Nonetheless, access to basic education in rural areas is significantly lower than urban zones. In many areas school density is low and children either walk long distances to school or attend schools that do not offer the complete cycle of primary schooling. This leads to high drop-out rates and repetition of grades, especially in the Mekong Delta, Central Highlands and Northern Uplands. In Yen Bai and Lao Cai provinces, of every hundred pupils who enter grade one, only 12 reach grade three, while in 1997 10 per cent of students repeated grades (World Bank 1998). Moreover, low salaries make it difficult to attract good teachers, classrooms shortage means that schools often have to operate double or even triple shifts, resulting in very low student contact hours.

Insufficient access and poor performance in rural areas are results of insufficient government funding and thus the education system is heavily reliant on household contributions to finance education. The shares of GDP and of the budget devoted to education were 3.5 per cent and 17.4 per cent respectively between 1993 and 1998, which were similar to other countries in the region. However, educational spending per head in Vietnam is much lower than other countries because of its low per capita GDP. There are no formal tuition fees for public primary education in Vietnam but, given the long tradition of voluntary contributions to education, the official fee policy plays a minor role in determining the full price that families face in sending their children to public schools. On average, households fund approximately 44 per cent of the total unit costs of primary schooling (World Bank 1998). Moreover, for primary schooling of equal quality, the financial burden on a rural family is twice that on an urban family. Moreover, costs rise at more advanced levels of education. Conversations with several rural families in Nam Dinh province revealed that if two children are attending either university or vocational school at the same time, the costs can absorb a large proportion of the family's savings.

Many developing countries have paid insufficient attention to investment in human capital for industrialisation. Eventually, the shortage of skilled workers becomes an important constraint on the expansion of non-agricultural industries. Thus, promotion of rural non-farm enterprises cannot be separated from improving educational standards of rural people, especially women and youth.

CONCLUSIONS

For over two decades Vietnam has been reforming its economy. The transformation that has occurred during this time has had remarkable success in initiating vigorous economic growth, reducing hunger and righting macro-economic imbalances. Agricultural reform, initiated in the early 1980s prior to the adoption of *Doi Moi*, yielded income growth in most delta areas and created positive externalities for industry, trade, finance and other services. The doubling of agricultural production over these two decades has made a significant contribution to economic development.

Rapid growth alone is, however, not sufficient to meet broader development objectives. What *Doi Moi* in general and the agricultural reform in particular have done so far, do not meet well the government's own stated objective of creating a more equitable society. Vietnam remains very much a dualistic economy, with the formal modern sector providing much of output growth but relatively few jobs. Growth in Vietnam has been tilted towards capital-intensive industry. The benefits of growth from such a pattern of development are unlikely to be as widespread or as sustainable as hoped for. In fact, such a pattern of growth is likely to favour the more skilled over the less skilled, the urban over the rural, and the owners of capital over those with labour as their main endowment. Therefore, unemployment and underemployment tend to increase, especially in rural areas. These, associated with inability to expand the cultivated land area and unbalanced growth biased in favour of cities, are the main factors keeping the most rural areas poor, backward, and undiversified.

Rural diversification – consisting of non-farm occupations and agricultural diversification are therefore seen as a primary mechanism to implement successfully the government's medium-term development objectives and drive the undiversified rural sector to a broader-based and labour-absorbing future. To create more employment opportunities through rural enterprise development for surplus labour, government policies could play important roles in reshaping institutional arrangements, lessening the intervention in financial sector which had negative effects on the development of the credit market, infrastructure investment, co-ordinating a balanced development strategy between the urban and rural economy, and education and training. Given the fiscal constraints placed on government in a low-income country, removal of current obstacles to rural diversification requires better targeting of public investments, especially in developing forward linkages for rural producers to reach final consumers (domestically and globally), as well as institutional and other forms of support. The challenges and constraints, if removed, will open up opportunities for a much larger proportion of the rural population to shift their careers to non-farm occupations and to increase their incomes.

AUTHOR'S NOTE

I would like to thank the editors of this volume for their substantial assistance in making revisions to this chapter. Needless to say, I retain responsibility for any remaining errors.

NOTES

1 The two terms 'non-farm' and 'off-farm' have the same meaning in comparison with 'farm' activities, but the former refers to the type of activity while the latter refers to its location.

2 By contrast, the population, according to the 1999 census, has been growing at 1.5 per cent and, in the cities, 3.5 per cent due to rural–urban migration (GSO 2001: 35).
3 Thailand has had a similar experience in this regard.
4 Details can be found in Mundle and van Arkadie (1997).
5 This pattern of changing consumption can be seen in Thailand, where annual per capita wheat consumption rose from 2 kg in the period 1961–65 to 8.1 kg in 1990–1992. In Indonesia over the same period, annual per capita wheat consumption grew from 1.3 to 12.5 kg (World Bank 1998).
6 Except in areas close to major cities (see Abrami and Henaff, Chapter 4 in this volume).
7 It should be noted, however, that these figures relate to the period of slowdown in the economy linked to the Asian crisis of 1997–98 and may have improved since then.
8 As Smith (this volume) shows, much saving in remote areas also takes the form of real assets such as livestock, gold and silver, which provide good protection against inflation.
9 Local road networks are usually half-funded by provincial and lower level government, with the other half, including millions of working days as well as financial contributions, coming from local people (UNDP 1996). They are constructed to low standards with high maintenance costs. Moreover, in an effort to ensure an equitable distribution of the available resources among provinces and districts, insufficient attention has been paid to the efficiency of the investment.

REFERENCES

Central Institute for Economic Management (CIEM) (1998) 'Vietnam's Economy in 1997, a Policy Analysis'. Hanoi, February.

General Statistical Office (GSO) (1999) *Vietnam Living Standards Survey 1997–1998.* Hanoi: Statistical Publishing House.

—— (2000) *Statistical Yearbook 1999.* Hanoi: Statistical Publishing House.

—— (2001) *Statistical Yearbook 2000.* Hanoi: Statistical Publishing House.

Johnson, A. (1998) 'Rural Finance'. Joint Ministry of Agriculture and Rural Development and World Bank Workshop, *Vision to Action: Rural Development Trends and Priority Issues*, Hanoi, 22 April.

Le Du Phong (2000) *Poverty Alleviation in Vietnam.* Hanoi: Statistical Publishing House.

McKenzie, John (1998) 'Rural Industrialisation'. Joint Ministry of Agriculture and Rural Development and World Bank Workshop, *Vision to Action: Rural Development Trends and Priority Issues*, Hanoi, 22 April.

Mundle, S. and B.Van Arkadie (1997) 'The Rural–Urban Transition in Vietnam: some Selected Issues'. Agriculture and Rural Development Strategies for Vietnam Workshop. Hanoi, 21–22 March.

Nguyen Manh Dung (1998) 'Vietnam Bank for the Poor, People's Credit Funds System and Rural Investment'. State Bank of Vietnam, Hanoi, January.

Saith, A. (1992) *The Rural Non-Farm Economy: Process and Policies*. Geneva: International Labour Organisation.

Tran. T.D. (1998) 'Borrower Transaction Cost, Segmented Market and Credit Rationing: A Study of the Rural Credit Market in Vietnam' PhD thesis, Australian National University, Canberra.

United Nations Development Program (UNDP) (1996) *Microfinance in Vietnam: A Collaborative Study based upon the Experiences of NGOs, UN Agencies and Bilateral Donors*. Hanoi: UNDP, May.

Vo Phuoc Tan (1998) 'Nhung de nghi phat trien nganh may xuat khau Vietnam' [Opportunities for Development of Export-led Garment Industry], unpublished.

World Bank (1997) 'Vietnam: Deepening Reform for Growth'. Report No.17031–VN, Washington, DC: World Bank.

—— (1998) 'Vietnam Advancing Rural Development from Vision to Action'. Report for the Consultative Group Meeting for Vietnam, 7–8 December, Hanoi.

—— (1999) *Attacking Poverty: Vietnam Development Report 2000*. Hanoi: World Bank.

—— (2000) *Vietnam Managing Public Resources Better. Public Expenditure Review*, vols 1 and 2. Hanoi: World Bank.

CHAPTER 7

Financial Markets in Vietnam's Northern Highlands

William Smith

The night mist has not yet lifted, but everyone has gone out to the fields.
The night mist has not yet lifted, but the credit officer is already on the road.
For the last few years, I have been doing credit work, doing credit work.
I bring the Government's money to the villages for everyone to borrow,
To rear more fat pigs, grow more rice and maize.
Though you are far away, I am still waiting for you;
the peach orchard is still promised its season of blossom.

From the song: 'I Do Credit Work'
(Nguyen Van Ty)

Vietnam's northern highlands are frequently characterised as remote and economically disadvantaged, suffering from limited market opportunities, weak infrastructure and severe environmental degradation. The ethnic minority groups that inhabit the northern mountains are perceived as culturally isolated, unused to markets and poorly educated. Similarly, financial markets are considered underdeveloped, even non-existent, in what is often portrayed as a highly subsistence-based economy. This image is intensified when the situation of the northern highlands is compared with the dynamic economic growth of urban and delta areas of northern Vietnam in the 1990s. The highlands constitute the backward hinterland of Vietnam's booming transition economy.

All of these traditional perceptions contain an element of unavoidable fact, evident in most of the economic statistics. However, closer examination of local financial markets can generate a picture of diversity and dynamism, which tends to be lost in the broader analyses of highland underdevelopment.

Though small scale and unsophisticated, financial markets do operate in some of the remotest parts of the region and in a wide variety of different sectors. There are small moneylenders in Dao villages, tontines in roadside Kinh villages, bank staff visiting remote commune markets, traders extending credit, tiny loans from families and friends. The objective of this chapter is to try to illustrate this diversity and dynamism.

An examination of financial markets in the northern highlands also helps to illuminate the varied and changing economy and society in which these markets operate. The features of local financial markets shadow to a great extent the features of local economy and society. It is also the objective of this chapter to try and trace some of these features.

Financial markets can provide such insights when analysed from a number of angles. It is useful to examine the range of *participants* in financial markets. The activities of state-owned banks and government programmes may reflect the role of the state in shaping the local economy. The role of formal, privately owned banks and co-operatives indicates the scale and strength of organised private capital within the economy and its effect on local society. An examination of informal moneylenders, shopkeepers, groups and savings clubs reveals the economic and social priorities of local people, which have not been met by government or financial institutions. A glimpse into financial arrangements within and between families and friends can illuminate something of the social fabric.

It is helpful to look closely at the range of financial *products* available. The prominence of different types of productive loan, consumption credit, insurance, deposit device, etc. can show the priorities of various participants in the market. What risks do households face and how do they address these risks? What are households' consumption priorities? What investment opportunities exist for expanding production? Are state banks promoting particular production practices through directed credit? The terms and prices of the various financial products available may also reflect the importance attached to these issues by various participants in the market.

The *scale and spread* of financial services and of various financial service providers can shed light on the health of the local economy, the degree of marketisation, cultural obstacles to the development of formal financial services, and the state's role in market regulation.

A snapshot of financial markets at a particular time constitutes a reflection of the society in which these markets operate. Analysis of the health of these markets will in turn cast some light on potential future developments within the local economy and society and the extent to which the developments achieved can be sustained.

Material in this chapter is taken from five provinces covered by the Vietnam–Sweden Mountain Rural Development Programme (MRDP). This was a bilateral rural development programme implemented through the Vietnamese Ministry of Agriculture and Rural Development in the provinces of Phu Tho, Tuyen Quang, Yen Bai, Ha Giang and Lao Cai. Much of the evidence is drawn from field work conducted by the author in Mu Cang Chai and Van Chan districts of Yen Bai province in November 1999 and in the Na Hang district of Tuyen Quang province in January 2000. Interviews were conducted in the communes shown in Table 7.1. The chapter also utilises

Table 7.1: Communes where interviews were conducted

Province	District	Commune	Population	Ethnic groups
Yen Bai	Mu Cang Chai	Ze Xu Phinh	1,567	H'Mong
	Van Chan	Nam Bung	2,808	Dao, Thai and Kinh*
		Nam Lanh (Nam Kip village)		Dao
Tuyen Quang	Na Hang	Da Vi	4,700	Tay, Dao and H'Mong

*Note: The Kinh are the majority ethnic Vietnamese.
Source: Smith (2000)

findings from other research work conducted in the five provinces, together with data from formal financial service providers. Its focus is on financial services used by rural households in those provinces.

The analysis will be structured from the perspective of farming households. It will start by examining the management of resources within the household and then spread out to look at family/village financial services, local commercial networks and finally the much larger formal state-owned financial intermediaries.

FIVE PROVINCES OF THE NORTHERN HIGHLANDS

The five provinces covered by the MRDP are situated in the far north of the country (Figure 7.1).. They are mountainous and remote. The population of

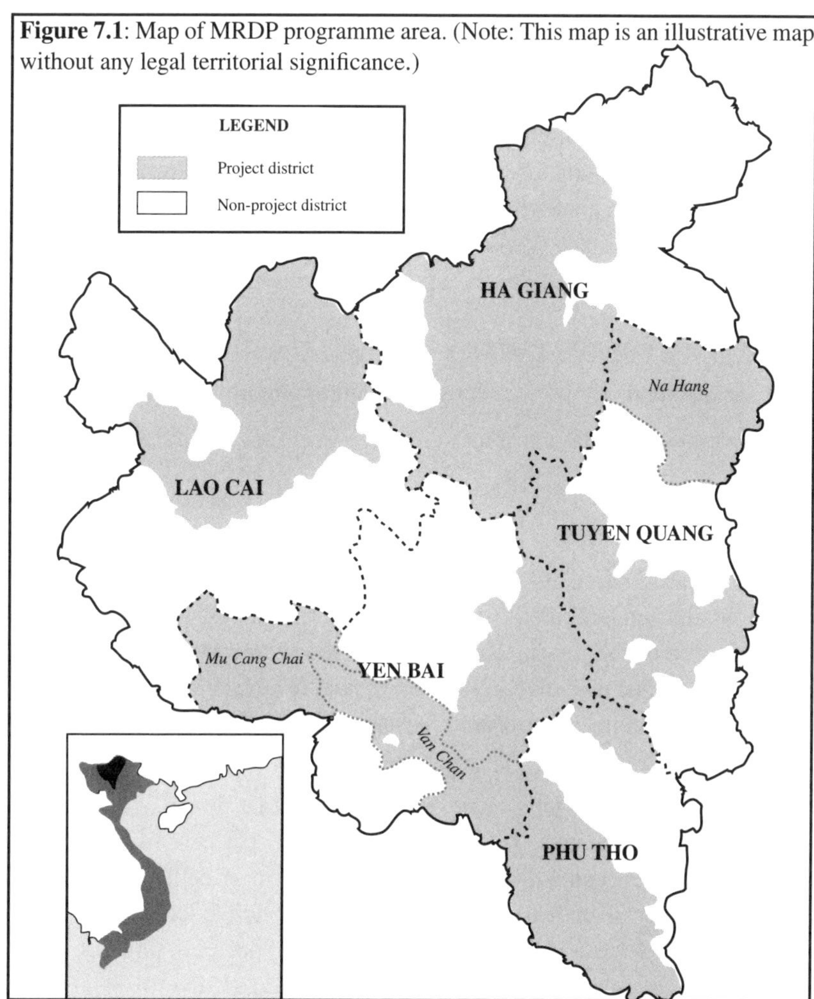

Figure 7.1: Map of MRDP programme area. (Note: This map is an illustrative map without any legal territorial significance.)

the five provinces amounted to 3.813 million in April 1999 (GSO 2000:7). This population is ethnically diverse. Figures from the 1999 census[1] indicate that the ethnic Vietnamese (Kinh) make up a majority of the population of the five provinces (53.4 per cent). The main ethnic minority groups include the Tay (16.2 per cent), the Dao (8.7 per cent), the H'Mong (7.5 per cent) and the Muong (4.7 per cent)

The population is predominantly rural, ranging from 80.4 per cent in Yen Bai up to 91.6 per cent in Ha Giang. Poverty is widespread. Monthly per capita income in 1996 ranged from just 141,040 dong in Tuyen Quang to 180,880 dong[2] in Phu Tho (then a part of Vinh Phu province) (GSO 1999).

Many ethnic minority households in the rural areas are dependent on upland cultivation of maize, hill rice and cassava. The area of irrigated paddy land is often limited. Livestock rearing, small trading and cash crops such as tea, sugarcane, fruit, cinnamon and others are also important sources of income. The region is characterised by wide diversity in terms of terrain, climate, cropping systems and market access.

MANAGING RESOURCES WITHIN THE FAMILY

In general, financial services are used to achieve one of four broad objectives:

- to access funds for investment when market opportunities arise;
- to accumulate capital, either for future investment or consumption purposes;
- to smooth out seasonal or irregular income flows;
- to hedge against risk.

Before describing some of the formal and informal financial services used by households in highland areas to achieve these objectives, it is necessary to describe some of the mechanisms that are used within households to meet some of these same objectives. A variety of simple mechanisms allow households to avoid recourse to external assistance or services:

Asset accumulation. It is particularly common for households to accumulate assets, especially cattle, gold or silver. In a survey of households in Tan Lap commune, Ha Giang province, 75 per cent of households claimed to be accumulating savings in the form of cattle and 11.2 per cent in silver (Tran Thi Que *et al.* 1998: 14). Such assets may be accumulated for a particular purpose or as a general buffer in times of emergencies. This mechanism has certain advantages in that the assets tend to maintain their value against inflation and tend to be relatively liquid. Households can sell cattle or silver quickly if in need of cash. However, accumulation of cattle carries risk – in the form of cattle disease or theft. Livestock is also a rather lumpy form of investment, which cannot be liquidated in part.

Cash saving at home. For reasons of security, interviewees are generally reluctant to admit holding large levels of cash savings at home. However, most households interviewed during field work conducted in Tuyen Quang and Yen Bai in November 1999–January 2000, acknowledged maintaining small emergency cash reserves. In Na Puc village, Da Vi commune, households acknowledged holding 20,000–300,000 dong in cash at home for emergencies. In Ze Xu Phinh commune, Mu Cang Chai district, it was claimed that richer households might keep up to 500,000 dong in cash at home at one time. This form of saving is relatively difficult, due to the pressing nature of expenditure claims within the household and security risks associated with storage at home.

Disaggregating expenditure. Rather than seeking out external financial services when faced with large items of expenditure, households often break up their expenditure requirements into smaller items in order to prepare gradually. Three examples were found during fieldwork in Da Vi commune (predominantly Tay ethnic group), Na Hang district.

A householder in Na Puc village (Tay ethnic group) explained that the construction of his house cost over 6 million dong in cash. However, this amount was spent gradually over the period 1996 to 1999. Timber was bought and transported to the site gradually over this period. At the time of construction, the family had to borrow only 1 million dong for a two-month period.

Poorer households in Da Vi commune sometimes used to hold what were known as 'dry funerals'. After an unexpected death in the family, households were immediately faced with the need to make the large-scale expenditure associated with organising a funeral. The family therefore conducted the burial with a very small, token ceremony, postponing the funeral proper until a time when they could meet the necessary expenses. During this time, the family was able to accumulate sufficient resources to organise the ceremony. This practice has now been outlawed in regulations issued by the Commune Fatherland Front as an attempt to reduce the amount spent on funerals.

In Khuoi Nan village (H'Mong ethnic group), the village manager described girls preparing their 'bottom drawer' in preparation for marriage from the age of 15 or 16 onwards. Typically, they start to accumulate blankets, pots and pans, thermos flasks, crockery, possibly a sewing machine or bicycle. These are all gifts that the bride's family must contribute at the time of the wedding but which would be impossible to purchase in one batch before the wedding.

In summary, it can be concluded that households demonstrate strong tendencies to save and accumulate in kind within the household. Accumulation most commonly takes place in the form of cattle, foodgrains, gold and silver. Households also maintain small reserves of cash at home. Saving takes place to deal with emergencies and in preparation for future consumption or investment.

RECIPROCAL SUPPORT WITHIN THE VILLAGE

When households face problems, which cannot be met within the household, common recourse is made to support mechanisms involving relatives and friends in the village. This support normally takes the form of small, non-interest bearing loans of paddy rice. The terms of these loans tend to be very flexible and can extend over long periods. One poor household interviewed in Khuoi Nan village, Da Vi commune claimed to owe relatives and neighbours a total of several hundred kilograms of paddy. This amount had built up over several seasons. Reciprocal support of this kind is very common, tends to be small scale and is used primarily to address problems of temporary food shortage. It demonstrates what appears to be a common and effective non-commercial mechanism for smoothing out irregular income flow.

Loans of this kind cannot be categorised as a financial service as no interest is charged and the lender's motivation is social rather than commercial. However, lenders do tend to keep records of outstanding debts and though loan terms may be flexible, such loans are not easily forgiven. Moreover, poor households' access to assistance of this kind may depend on fulfilment of a range of social obligations within the village. Wedding gifts and funeral contributions constitute a regular and heavy burden on poor households. The Khuoi Nan villager mentioned above who owed relatives several hundred kilograms of paddy complained of heavy obligations in terms of wedding gifts. When interviewed, he was in receipt of two wedding invitations, which were pinned to the central pillar of his house as a reminder of debts due.

In summary, it can be concluded that mutual assistance within extended families and villages contributes much towards the smoothing out of irregular and seasonal income distribution, particularly in terms of food. No nominal cost is associated with this assistance, except possible fulfilment of informal social obligations.

INFORMAL FINANCIAL SERVICES

When needs extend beyond the capacity of mutual assistance from relatives and friends, households in highland areas commonly appear to have access to informal moneylenders, credit from suppliers, tontines, etc. Figures for the northern highlands region from the 1997–98 Vietnam Living Standards Survey (GSO 1999b: 306) indicate that 56.81 per cent of households in the region had outstanding loans from the sources indicated in Table 7.2 at the time of the survey. Of these, a relatively high proportion of households are

Table 7.2: Borrowing sources, northern highlands

Sector	Source	% of households with outstanding loans
Informal	private moneylender	3.37
	relative	14.66
	other individual	11.25
	ROSCA, private bank, co-operative	4.50
Semi-formal	socio-economic development programme	6.18
Formal	Bank for the Poor	9.22
	Other government bank	24.99

Note: ROSCA is a Rotating Savings and Credit Association.
Source: GSO 1999b.

borrowing from informal sources. The survey results in Table 7.3 also show that 18.7 per cent of households are involved in lending money to others, primarily their relatives.

Table 7.3: Lending activities, northern highlands

Borrower category	% households lending to these borrower categories
Relatives	12.59
Friends	2.97
Neighbours	4.99
Other unrelated individuals	2.45
ROSCAs	0.00

Source: GSO 1999b.

Figures from a recent survey conducted in five highland villages, three of which lie in the five provinces covered in this chapter, also show a range of 21–77 per cent of households with outstanding loans of some kind (Le Trong Cuc and Rambo 2000) (Table 7.4). Most of these households are borrowing less than 2 million dong (approximately $138).

Cash loans are commonly available from market traders, small shopkeepers and richer households in the community. In some of the villages surveyed (Da Vi commune and Ze Xu Phinh commune, Mu Cang Chai district), cash loans were primarily available only outside the village in nearby market centres. In other villages (Nam Kip and Nam Bung villages in Van Chan district), cash loans are available in the village. Lenders are very careful in selecting creditworthy borrowers, and poor households may find it difficult to access even small sums from these sources.

Table 7.4: Per cent of households with outstanding loans (mio VND)

Village	Khe Nong	Thai Phin Tung	Tat	Ngoc Tan	Lang Thao
District	Con Cuong	Dong Van	Da Bac	Doan Hung	Doan Hung
Province	Nghe An	Ha Giang	Hoa Binh	Phu Tho	Phu Tho
Debt	%	%	%	%	%
0	70.0	60.0	78.6	22.5	30.0
< 0.5	15.0	12.5	19.0	15.0	17.5
0.5–1.0	10.0	7.5	2.4	17.5	15.0
1.0–2.0	0.0	20.0	0.0	30.0	10.0
>2.0	5.0	0.0	0.0	15.0	27.5
Total with loans	30.0	40.0	21.4	77.5	70.0

Source: Le Trong Cuc and Rambo 2000.

Loan sizes tend to be small and relatively short term. In a survey of borrowers in Tan Lap commune in Ha Giang, loans from private moneylenders were found to average 275,000 dong (approximately $19), compared with an average of 1,489,000 dong (about $103) for loans from government development programmes. Households in Ze Xu Phinh commune, Mu Cang Chai, can generally only access loans of up to 100,000 dong from market traders at Kim Crossroads.

Loans tend to be charged at relatively high rates of interest. According to results for the northern highlands area from the Vietnam Living Standards Survey 1998–99 (GSO 1999b: 323), interest rates on the private market average 2.72 per cent per month for one-year loans and 2.31 per cent per month for loans of two years or more. Respondents surveyed during field work quoted rates ranging from 2 to 7 per cent per month.

Loans appear to be taken for a wide range of different uses but consumption loans are common. One respondent in Nam Bung commune, Van Chan district, took a 1.5 million dong loan for three months to cover the costs of a kidney operation. He was charged 3 per cent per month. The village manager in Na Puc village, Da Vi commune, admitted lending out sums of up to 1 million dong for such purposes as tax payment or health care costs. One household in Da Vi acknowledged borrowing 1 million dong to pay some of the costs of constructing a new house.

The example of a Dao moneylender from Nam Kip village, Nam Lanh commune, illustrates well the sort of lending activities encountered. One 73-year-old Dao villager interviewed stated that he had accumulated savings of 4–5 million dong. He was too old to invest the money in agriculture and did not have major consumption requirements. He therefore decided to use his money to lend out to other households in the village. He usually lends sums of 100,000 to 1 million dong. The loan term is always short – only up to one year. Interest is paid by borrowers in advance at a rate of 5 per cent per month. Households borrow to finance weddings, funerals, house repairs and to meet medical costs. As a neighbour and friend of potential borrowers in the village, he is easily able to assess their repayment capacity before lending.

Borrowers appear to value the service he provides. One respondent who had borrowed from him said that 'borrowing with interest makes it easier to talk afterwards', indicating the social costs and obligations of borrowing from family and friends. No complaints were raised about the interest rate he charges.

In addition to loans extended by private moneylenders, households in highland areas are able to purchase many kinds of goods on credit. One meat seller interviewed in Nam Bung village, Van Chan district, claimed to have about 30 customers owing him as much as 2 million dong for goods received. Another respondent interviewed in the same village had bought materials on credit for building a rice-drying yard outside his house. The materials cost 500,000 dong, which he was able to pay in instalments.

Among Kinh villagers, participation in tontines or rotating savings and credit associations (ROSCAs) appears relatively common[3]. In a Kinh village of Nam Bung commune, Van Chan district, for example, villagers organised ROSCAs for the purchase of motorbikes and to meet wedding costs. The motorcycle ROSCAs could involve up to 30 people. ROSCAs were particularly common in the village among those with monthly salaries or pensions. However, no evidence has been found of tontines being organised in ethnic minority villages in the highlands. It would be interesting to investigate whether this apparent difference is determined by cultural, social or economic factors affecting savings behaviour.

Though very rare, evidence was also found of informal deposit taking in the highland areas. In Nam Kip village, Nan Lanh commune, it was reported that households use local tea traders as an informal savings service. Rather than receiving cash immediately on the sale of tea, households may deposit the money with the trader and request the cash later when a consumption need arises. A high degree of trust must clearly be established between the depositor and the deposit taker in such cases.

In summary, it can be concluded that households have access to informal financial services primarily for small-scale, short-term loans in cash or goods. These loans are often used to meet the need for larger consumption items, including weddings, funerals, medical costs etc. These services carry a high nominal interest-rate cost but, as they are generally available within the village or in nearby markets, involve low transaction costs for the borrower. These services are generally in short supply, particularly for poorer households unable to demonstrate their creditworthiness. Very few informal savings or insurance services are available.

SEMIFORMAL FINANCIAL SERVICES

A number of mass associations, government and international donor programmes also provide financial services in the highland areas. Typically, such semiformal financial services consist primarily of one to three year loans for investment in production. Loans for consumption purposes are seldom allowed under these programmes. Access to loans is sometimes conditional on a requirement for compulsory, non-withdrawable savings. None of these programmes offer voluntary deposit services.

Borrowers are often selected according to social criteria determined by government authorities and donors rather than market factors. For example, some of these programmes are focused only on women borrowers or on poorer households, as defined under local government categorisation. A frequent feature of such programmes is the promotion of group structures for lending. Group formation may be incorporated in an attempt to achieve a number of objectives:

- To reduce lending risk by requiring joint group liability for repayment;

- To increase outreach at a reasonable cost by delegating part of the loan administration and collection procedures to group leaders;
- To promote community development and social cohesion.

However, groups which are established to receive government or donor loans seldom develop internal momentum and strength and are often constrained by the limited literacy skills, organisational capacity and motivation of group leaders. Family and social ties between group leaders and members often make loan repayment difficult to enforce. Bookkeeping is often neglected. Weak group capacity, reliance on what are considered to be 'soft' donor funds and the direction of credit towards a targeted group of borrowers all contribute to poor repayment records in these programmes.

The Women's Union is one of the main semiformal providers of financial services in the highlands. Programmes operated by the Women's Union in two highland districts are summarised in Table 7.5. The services provided by such programmes tend to be concentrated in relatively small geographical areas. As with formal bank services, government and donor programmes (like those described in Table 7.5), they tend to lend for specific productive purposes designated by the programme.

FORMAL FINANCIAL SERVICES – PRIVATE AND CO-OPERATIVE

At the time of writing no private banks are operating in the northern highlands. The only formal non-state institutions providing financial services to households in the highlands are the People's Credit Funds (PCFs). These are co-operatively owned institutions that operate at the commune level. They have been formed since 1993 under a pilot programme monitored by the State Bank.

As of May 2000, only 46 PCFs had been established in the five provinces covered in this chapter (see Appendix 7.2), with over 28,000 members. Of these, over 66 per cent are concentrated in the more low-lying province of Phu Tho. PCFs tend to develop in less remote and more commercialised communes. Their establishment must be authorised by the local authorities and expansion of new People's Credit Funds is currently not being encouraged. PCFs are regulated by the provincial branch of the State Bank. They usually operate within the boundaries of a single commune, and local commune or co-operative leaders often play an important role in the gover-

Table 7.5: Women's Union credit activities in two districts

District	Programme	Description
Mu Cang Chai (Yen Bai)	Ethnic Minority Development Fund	• Loan fund of 45 million dong per commune in eight communes • One-year loans for livestock rearing • Interest 1.2% per month • Repayment of half principle after six months • Compulsory savings requirement • Problems met with interest and principal repayment
Na Hang (Tuyen Quang)	IFAD (International Fund for Agricultural Development)	• 1.4 billion dong on loan in 19 communes • Loans extended through groups • Interest 1.2% per month • Compulsory savings requirement • Other terms as with Vietnam Bank for the Poor loans (three years, lump sum principal repayment etc.)
	MRDP (Vietnam–Sweden Mountain Rural Development Programme)	• 802 million dong outstanding in three communes • One-year loans for productive investment • Interest 1% per month • 528 current borrowers • Lump sum repayment at year end • Maximum loan size, 2 million dong • Compulsory savings requirement

Source: Smith (2000)

nance structure. PCFs extend individual loans directly to their members. The State Bank allows a higher interest rate ceiling on lending by PCFs than on lending by the state-owned commercial banks. PCFs tend to offer shorter-term loans but may be flexible in terms of loan usage.

It is interesting to note that for PCFs in the five provinces as a whole, members' savings account for 71.5 per cent of total assets. Similar proportions have been achieved by PCFs in all of the five provinces. This success in savings mobilisation results from the convenience of a local service in the commune and the low resulting transaction costs to the depositor. In addition, savings deposited at a PCF enjoy a higher rate of return than deposits made at a bank. The achievements of the PCFs demonstrate both the strong potential for savings mobilisation and a healthy demand for savings services among local people, even in the highlands. However, their outreach at present is very limited in these areas.

FORMAL FINANCIAL SERVICES – STATE BANKS

The two major formal financial service providers operating in the highland areas are state owned: the Vietnam Bank of Agriculture and Rural Development (VBARD) and the Vietnam Bank for the Poor (VBP). The former is a large commercial bank, whose lending decisions are determined primarily by commercial considerations. The VBP is a policy bank, which began operations in 1996. As a policy bank, the VBP's mandate is to contribute to achievement of government policy on poverty reduction. Borrowers are selected according to social criteria issued by the government rather than any commercial criteria of the bank. The VBP is a separate financial entity but operates using the staff, buildings and equipment of VBARD.

VBARD has a wide branch network in each district of the five provinces. Several inter-commune branches have been established in most districts. By the end of December 1999, provincial branches had accumulated total assets of between US$11 and US$34 million as shown in Table 7.6.

In some provinces of the northern highlands, the VBP's lending activities are almost of comparable size to those of VBARD (Figure 7.2). In Lao Cai province, for example, the VBP's outstanding loan balance equates to 72 per cent of VBARD's outstanding loans .

Table 7.6: VBARD total assets, December 1999

Provincial VBARD branch	**Total assets: December end 1999 (VND)**	**Total assets – US$ equivalent**
Ha Giang	159,343,988,000	11,357,376
Phu Tho	482,264,546,000	34,373,809
Tuyen Quang	232,617,070,000	16,579,976
Yen Bai	242,736,171,000	17,301,224
Lao Cai	212,362,810,000	15,136,337

Source: VBARD and VBP financial reports provided by VBP headquarters.

Figure 7.2: VBP–VBARD Outstanding loans, December 1999 (bn dong)

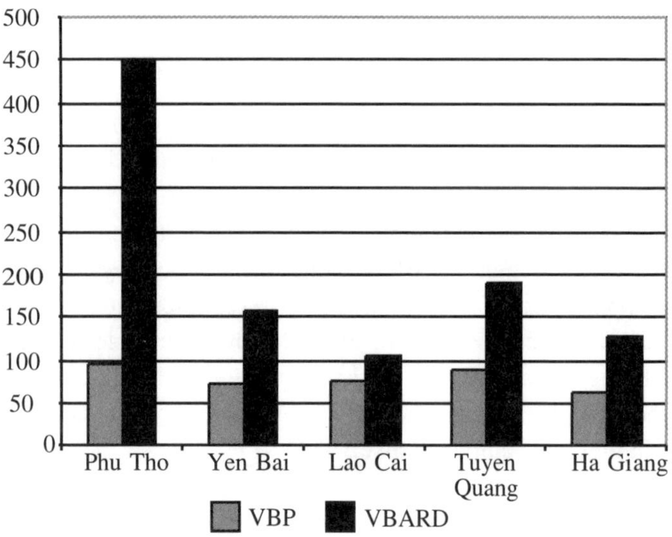

Source: VBARD and VBP financial reports provided by VBP headquarters.

Savings services

Very few rural households in the highlands use VBARD deposit services. The chairman of Nam Bung commune, Van Chan district, estimated that only around ten households in the whole commune held savings accounts at the district bank branch. Likewise, the director of Na Hang district VBARD branch estimated that on average his bank serviced only around five savings accounts per rural commune. VBARD's minimum deposit requirement of 50,000 dong effectively prevents small, regular deposits. Long distances between villages and bank branches also result in customer transaction costs that are exorbitantly high for small deposits. This situation contrasts strongly with the savings mobilisation record of the People's Credit Funds which, situated at the commune level, are more accessible to potential savers.

VBARD has, however, been strong in mobilising urban deposits and the five provincial branches were able to fund from 39 to 89 per cent of their total assets from savings deposits at the end of December 1999 (Figure 7.3).

The VBP has mobilised minimal deposits, ranging from 0.06 per cent of total assets in the Ha Giang provincial branch to just 3.67 per cent in Lao Cai

Figure 7.3: VBARD - Structure of liabilities - December 1999

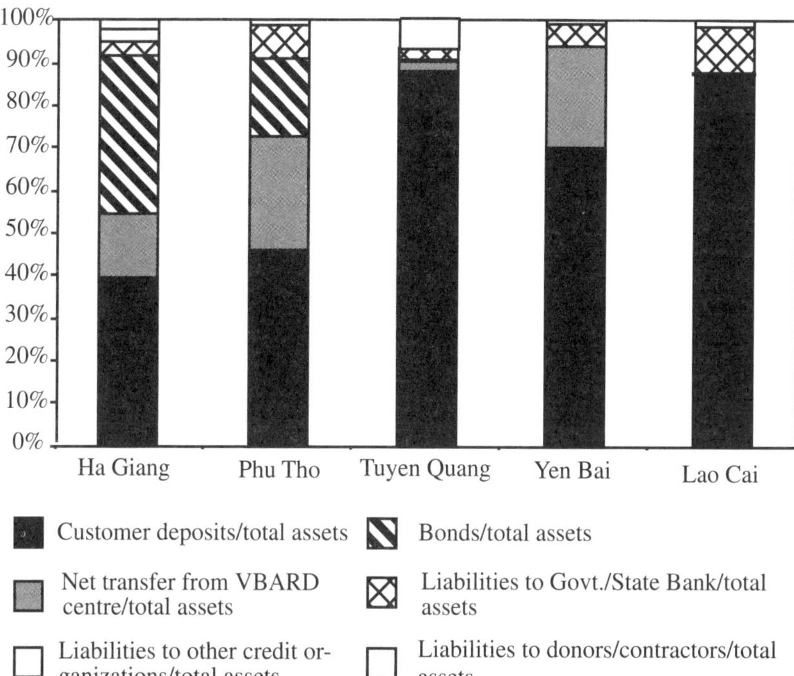

Source: VBARD and VBP financial reports provided by VBP headquarters.

province (December 1999). The VBP remains overwhelmingly dependent on government budget sources for its funds. As VBP lending rates are fixed by the government at artificially low levels, it is impossible for the VBP to mobilise funds in the open market.

In summary, it is clear that formal savings services are highly undeveloped in the rural highlands. State banks rely on the mobilisation of urban savings and on state provision of credit funds. As a result of government imposed constraints on lending interest rates, it is just not cost effective for the commercial banks to invest in rural savings mobilisation in highland areas. Establishing local commune branches, frequent deposit collection services or mobile bank units in the highlands is too expensive, given the banks' external constraints on their income.

Lending services
In some highland districts, the Vietnam Bank of Agriculture and Rural Development's lending activities are relatively strong. Na Hang district in Tuyen Quang is an example. In the remote commune of Da Vi, VBARD has outstanding loans of 180 million dong (January 2000). In other remote parts of the highlands, however, VBARD lending is very limited. In the Mu Cang Chai district of Yen Bai province, for example, VBARD only lends to customers in the district town and has no activities in the rural communes.

In the five provinces overall, short-term loans accounted for 50.7 per cent of total loans outstanding to households and economic organisations in December 1999, compared with 43.7 per cent medium-term loans and 3.5 per cent long-term loans. Most VBARD loans in Da Vi commune were one-year loans of up to 3 million dong. Borrowing is restricted to productive investment purposes – primarily livestock rearing in the case of Da Vi. Interest charged on VBARD loans at that time was 1 per cent per month. In Da Vi commune, bank staff make regular weekly visits to the commune market in order to approve and disburse loans, as well as collect repayments.

VBARD lending activities in the highlands have suffered from a number of constraints, some internal and some external. Perhaps the most important constraint is the interest rate ceiling determined by the government. Lending in remote highland areas is inherently more costly than lending in the lowlands. Travel by credit staff, establishment of local commune branches or the purchase and operation of mobile banking units are all costly. However, despite its status as a 'commercial' bank, VBARD is not free to set its own pricing structure. It cannot set interest rates to reflect these costs or, indeed, the higher risks of lending in an unstable economic environment. Rather it is subject to specific government intervention to 'protect' borrowers. VBARD lending rates in the remotest Zone 3[4] communes are subject to a statutory 30 per cent reduction, while rates in the middle-ranking Zone 2 communes have been subject to a 15 per cent reduction since April 2000. This apparent 'protection' of borrowers in fact acts as a negative incentive for the expansion of lending activities by commercial banks in these areas, as expansion will only result in greater losses.

In addition, VBARD lending in the highlands is constrained by government intervention in favour of state-owned enterprises. Loans to state-owned enterprises accounted for over half the outstanding balance of VBARD's short-term loans in two of the five provinces in December 1999 (Lao Cai and Tuyen Quang). In the five provinces as a whole, 38.5 per cent of short-term loans were outstanding to state owned enterprises, compared with 45.5 per cent to households, 6.9 per cent to private businesses, 0.04 per cent to co-operatives and 9.1 per cent to 'other' sectors (Figure 7.4). This preference for lending to state-owned enterprises reduces funds available for lending to rural households.

Figure 7.4: VBARD Short-term loans, December 1999

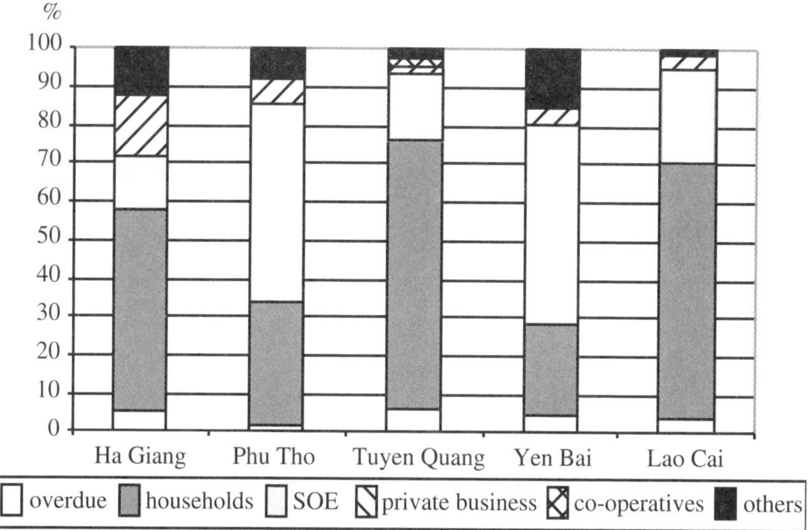

Source: VBARD and VBP financial reports provided by VBP headquarters.

A number of internal weaknesses have also checked the growth of VBARD's lending activities in the highland areas. The banks have gained little success in experimenting with alternatives to traditional collateral guarantees for loans. For asset-poor farmers, VBARD's collateral requirements constitute a major barrier to access. However, alternative guarantees like joint group liability or risk-reducing strategies like principal repayment in instalments have not been utilised by VBARD. One of the reasons for this relatively conservative attitude towards innovations from the 'microfinance' industry has been the high cost associated with such technologies. Again, interest rate controls have made it difficult for VBARD to experiment with group lending and other risk reducing technologies.

One further constraint has been VBARD's unwillingness to move outside of lending for production purposes. Despite the widespread and pressing consumption needs of highland households outlined above, VBARD has been reticent to move into these areas, preferring to invest only in areas which it considers to be more productive. In practice, demand for investment in these sectors is often limited.

The Vietnam Bank for the Poor, on the other hand, has been relatively active in lending to rural households even in the remotest communes. In three typical highland communes, VBP outstanding loans averaged from 183,500 dong to 328,700 dong (that is, about $13-23) per household (Table 7.7). As a

Table 7.7: VBP lending in 3 communes

Commune	Outstanding loan balance (million dong)	Average outstanding loan per household in commune (dong)
Ze Xu Phinh	40	183,500
Nam Bung	167	328,700
Da Vi	250	318,100

Source: Smith (2000).

result of government determination to pursue its poverty alleviation objectives, the VBP's outstanding loan balance in all of the five provinces has increased rapidly each year since the bank's first year of operation in 1996 (Figure 7.5).VBP borrowers are selected by the bank from lists of eligible poor households drawn up by commune-level Hunger Eradication and Poverty Reduction Committees. These lists are based on income criteria issued by the Ministry of Labour, Invalids and Social Affairs. The VBP generally extends medium-term, three-year loans. At the end of December 1999, medium-term loans accounted for 93.3 per cent to 99.1 per cent of loans outstanding to economic organisations and households in four of the five provinces. Only in Tuyen Quang province have short-term loans predominated (75.7 per cent of total outstanding balance). Loans are extended for investment in production only – primarily livestock rearing. In Da Vi commune, for example, households have been awarded fixed 3 million dong loans for the purchase of buffalo, repayable in a single lump sum at the end of the loan term.

For poor, asset-less households, these 3 million dong loans are relatively large. As discussed above, loans on the private market tend to be much smaller. While access to large, low-cost loans may be welcomed initially, the final repayment demand can cause grave difficulties for poor borrowers. In the H'Mong commune of Ze Xu Phinh (Mu Cang Chai district of Yen Bai), it

Figure 7.5: VBP outstanding loans 1996–99 [bn dong)

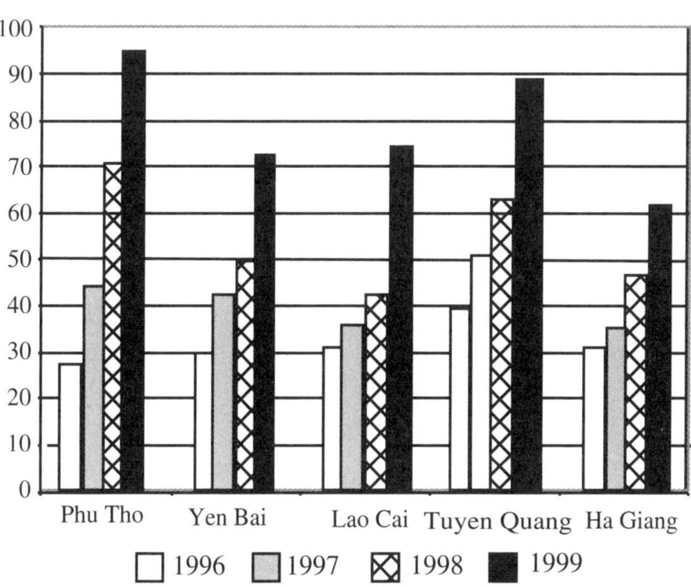

Source: VBARD and VBP financial reports provided by VBP headquarters.

was reported that virtually all VBP loans had had to be rescheduled. Repayment difficulties were also reported in Na Hang district. This is a commonly quoted phenomenon with VBP loans.

In some cases, VBP lending has been directed towards specific production uses. In the Na Hang district of Tuyen Quang province, for example, the VBP is required by the local authorities to co-operate with the District Agricultural Inputs Department to make short-term crop input loans. Borrowers receive fertiliser and seeds to the value of around 30,000–40,000 dong, with repayment due in cash after the harvest. These loans are tied closely to government attempts to promote the adoption of high-yield maize varieties. Cases were found of compulsory borrowing and continued lending to households, which had not repaid similar previous loans. This has resulted in serious repayment problems, with many borrowers receiving loans for four or five successive crops without repaying the principal from the previous loan.

The expansion of VBP activities over the past five years has only been possible as a result of significant state subsidy. VBP interest rates are fixed by the government and are very low. At the end of 2000, VBP borrowers were being charged 0.7 per cent per month (0.6 per cent in remote, Zone 3 communes) when the base rate for state commercial banks stood at 0.75 per cent and VBARD short-term lending rates to customers were around 1 per cent per month. The cost to the state budget of interest rate subsidy to the VBP in highland areas is very high. Dr Nguyen Dai Lai has estimated that 'the total value of preferential interest for the northern highlands[5] on an annual average reaches up to 160 billion dong per year – equivalent to the total annual agricultural tax levy of Thai Binh province'. (Nguyen Dai Lai 2000: 35–36) In addition, VBP's costs are also subsidised through privileged access to VBARD's buildings, equipment and staff.

In summary, there has been expansion in formal lending services of state-owned banks in the northern highlands – particularly through the Vietnam Bank for the Poor. This increase in coverage has occurred at high cost to the Vietnamese state budget and reflects a strong government commitment to development in the highland areas.

However, state intervention to promote these subsidised lending services has also had a stunting effect on the development of more sustainable, market-based financial services. In particular, state intervention through interest rate controls has prevented commercial banks from expanding their lending activities into areas, which are inherently higher cost and higher risk. In addition, interest rate controls have resulted in the stunting of savings mobilisation activities in rural areas. The highlands have remained underserved as a result. Direction of credit towards state-owned enterprises and 'productive' sectors with insufficient market potential leads to repayment difficulties. Direction of credit towards government-prescribed target groups results in credit overload of poor, assetless households.

Such problems are not fully reflected in VBARD or VBP published figures for overdue and uncollectable loans (Appendices 7.3–7.6). The five provincial VBP branches quoted figures for uncollectable loans at from 0.21 per cent to 4.05 per cent of total loans outstanding in December 1999. However, repayment difficulties are easily hidden by frequent loan extension, rescheduling and roll-over and, as noted above, there is much circumstantial evidence of repayment problems.

The negative effect of government intervention on the health of the formal financial service sector in the highlands is perhaps most clearly demonstrated by the income and expenditure figures quoted by VBARD provincial branches. Even without making provision for loan loss, only one of the five provincial branches achieved a surplus of income over expenditure in 1999 (Figure 7.6).

Figure 7.6: VBARD income and expenditure surplus/deficit, 1999 (m. dong)

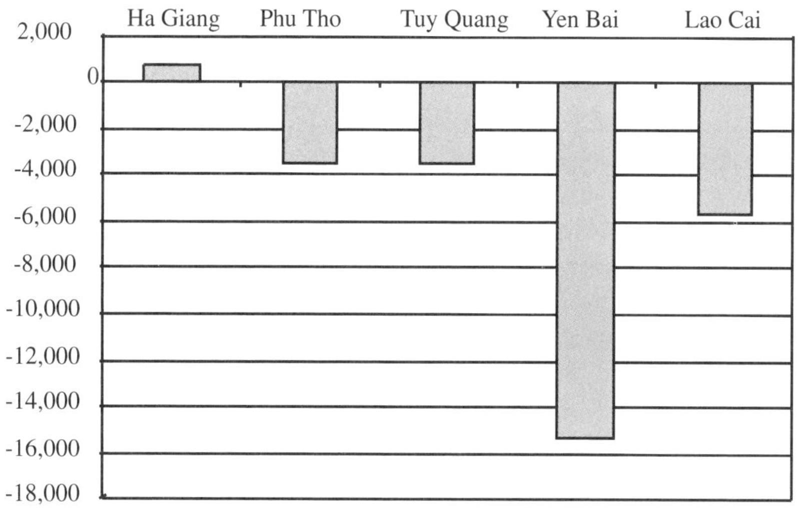

Source: VBARD and VBP financial reports provided by VBP headquarters.

For the five provincial branches as a whole, expenditure exceeded income by 27.2 billion dong during 1999. Though state intervention may be designed to protect borrowers' interests, it is clear that the resulting weakness of the banking system can have only a detrimental effect on the local economy.

CONCLUSION

Rural households in Vietnam's northern highlands face a surprisingly wide range of financial service needs. Though neither wealthy nor highly integrated with the market economy, households face expenditure requirements for food, health care, education, tax, social ceremonies and obligations, housing, transportation and production. Many of these needs are met through tight household management and economy and, for smaller emergency needs, through mutual assistance within the family or village.

Formal sector financial services are available only to meet a very limited range of household needs – primarily credit for productive investment. demand for savings services and consumption credit is met partly by the informal and co-operative sectors, but, in general, these services are very limited and unable to meet existing demand. This imbalance results from a well meaning but paternalist government policy towards financial services, which seeks to direct credit towards certain 'productive' sectors and towards particular market players. In order to achieve this aim, considerable government expenditure has been made to subsidise the price of credit extended by state-owned banks.

This paternalist policy reflects the often-repeated truism that the highlands are economically backward and its people culturally and educationally disadvantaged. It gives rise to the conception of credit as the need to 'bring the government's money to the villages for everyone to borrow. To rear more fat pigs, grow more rice and maize' (Nguyen Van Ty from the song *I do credit work*). Paradoxically, it is this paternalistic concern which itself contributes in some part to continued underdevelopment in the highlands. The state seeks to replace market stimuli with its own definition of which people, areas and activities require investment. By trying to protect borrowers with subsidised interest rates, the state deprives them of a vibrant financial services sector, which can adapt to meet market demand. Constrained by government intervention, the formal sector remains unprofitable and dependent on subsidy from the state budget. This policy choice is politically motivated and its long-term financial sustainability is in question. Only perhaps when state policies on financial services shift further towards a more trusting attitude to real market conditions in the northern highlands can the 'peach orchard' expect its real 'season of blossom'.

APPENDICES

Appendix 7.1: 1999 census 3 per cent sample information on ethnic breakdown of the five provinces (%)

Ethnicity	Lao Cai	Yen Bai	Phu Tho	Ha Giang	Tuyen Quang	Total
Kinh	40.21	50.65	85.55	13.99	43.18	53.45
Tay	15.22	21.87	0.21	32.12	27.29	16.25
Dao	11.28	11.84	0.14	15.00	13.71	8.71
Hmong (Meo)	18.43	4.89	–	21.22	2.48	7.54
Muong	0.08	0.51	13.99	0.07	0.02	4.74
Nung	3.87	2.56	0.02	12.58	1.16	3.26
Thai	4.55	6.55	0.02	–	–	1.88
San Chay (Cao Lan)	0.02	1.00	0.05	0.05	8.91	1.78
San Diu	–	–	–	–	2.20	0.39
Giay	1.12	0.09	–	1.20	–	0.38
Hoa (Han)	0.08	0.03	0.02	0.93	0.99	0.35
Phu La	1.84	–	–	0.18	–	0.32
La Chi	–	–	–	1.93	–	0.31
Ha Nhi	1.78	–	–	–	–	0.28
Lao	1.26	–	–	–	–	0.20
Bo Y	0.25	–	–	0.56	–	0.13
Lo Lo	–	–	–	0.13	–	0.02
Pa Then	–	–	–	–	0.05	0.01
Pu Peo	–	–	–	0.04	–	0.01
Kho-me	–	–	–	–	0.01	–
Co Lao	–	–	–	0.02	–	–
Kho-mu	–	0.01	–	–	–	–
Ba-na	–	–	–	–	–	–
E-de	–	–	–	–	–	–
NR	–	–	–	–	–	–
Tho	–	–	–	–	–	–
Co-tu	–	–	–	–	–	–
Lu	–	–	–	–	–	–
Ngai	–	–	–	–	–	–

Appendix 7.2a: People's credit funds in the five provinces (m VND)

Province	Phu Tho	Yen Bai	Ha Giang	Lao Cai	Total
No. of PCFs	28	13	4	1	46
Members	18,922	7,070	2,140	339	28,471
Total assets	45,607	16,962	4,636	807	68,012
Statutory capital	2,675	1,470	415	120	4,680
Savings deposits	31,660	12,899	3,468	629	48,656
External loans	6,312	765	400	0	7,477
Other sources	4,960	1,828	353	58	7,199
Outstanding loans	41,345	15,027	4,260	695	61,327
Overdue loans	1,411	290	42	0	1,743
Profit/loss	716	62	139	25	942

Appendix 7.2b: People's credit funds in the five provinces

Province	Phu Tho	Yen Bai	Ha Giang	Lao Cai	Total
Av. members per PCF (no.)	676	544	535	339	619
Savings/total assets (%)	69.4	76.0	74.8	77.9	71.5
External loans/total assets (%)	13.8	4.5	8.6	0.0	11.0
Av. statutory capital per PCF (m VND)	95.54	113.08	103.75	120	101.74
Statutory capital/total assets (%)	5.9	8.7	9.0	14.9	6.9
Overdue loans/loans outstanding (%)	3.4	1.9	1.0	0.0	2.8
Loans outstanding/total assets (%)	90.7	88.6	91.9	86.1	90.2
Av. profit/loss per PCF (m VND)	25.571	4.769	34.75	25	20.478

Appendix 7.3: Overdue and uncollectable loans with Vietnam Bank of Agriculture and Rural Development and Vietnam Bank for the Poor, 31 December 1999 (billion dong)

	Ha Giang	**Phu Tho**	**Tuyen Quang**	**Yen Bai**	**Lao Cai**
Total outstanding loans	125.98	449.76	189.12	158.06	104.00
• of which loans to households/economic organisations	109.01	311.91	93.36	111.07	85.71
Short term loans	66.44	127.77	58.72	73.03	34.89
• of which in term/extended	63.16	125.62	55.31	69.33	33.60
• of which households	35.19	41.11	41.40	16.92	23.31
• of which SOE	9.08	66.14	11.28	38.42	8.58
• of which private business	10.61	8.88	0.50	2.54	1.35
• of which co-operatives	0.00	0.00	0.14	0.00	0.00
• of which other	8.27	9.50	1.99	11.46	0.35
Medium term loans	42.57	149.29	34.65	33.63	50.82
• of which in term/extended	40.99	147.36	33.85	32.89	50.07
• of which households	33.20	113.97	12.91	19.11	25.39
• of which SOE	0.90	25.83	0.03	0.09	1.34
• of which private business	0.00	0.13	0.15	0.00	0.06
• of which other	6.89	7.43	20.76	13.70	23.28

Appendix 7.3: Overdue and uncollectable loans with Vietnam Bank of Agriculture and Rural Development and Vietnam Bank for the Poor, 31 December 1999 (billion dong) *(continued)*

	Ha Giang	Phu Tho	Tuyen Quang	Yen Bai	Lao Cai
Long term loans	0.00	20.44	0.00	4.42	0.00
• of which in term/extended	0.00	20.44	0.00	4.42	0.00
• of which SOE	0.00	20.44	0.00	0.00	0.00
• of which other	0.00	0.00	0.00	4.42	0.00
Foreign exchange loans	0.00	14.41	0.00	0.00	0.00
Liabilities					
• Customer deposits	62.7	222.0	206.8	170.4	183.9
• Bonds	24.4	129.0	3.7	61.2	1.4
• Liabilities to Govt./State Bank	4.7	39.8	5.6	10.0	23.8
• Liabilities to other credit organisations	4.0	2.5	17.7	11.0	1.5
• Liabilities to donors/contractors	0.4	0.0	0.0	1.1	1.0

Source: VBARD and VBP financial reports provided by VBP headquarters.

Appendix 7.4: VBARD uncollectable and overdue loans, December 1999 (%)

	Uncollectable loans/ total loans outstanding	Overdue loans/total loans outstanding	
		Short-term loans	Medium-term loans
Ha Giang	0.71	4.94	3.72
Phu Tho	1.92	1.68	1.29
Tuyen Quang	1.58	5.79	2.30
Yen Bai	2.72	5.06	2.17
Lao Cai	2.79	3.69	1.47

Source: VBARD and VBP financial reports provided by VBP headquarters

Appendix 7.5: Total outstanding loans, year end 1996–99 (billion dong)

	Phu Tho	Yen Bai	Lao Cai	Tuyen Quang	Ha Giang
1996	27.36	29.94	31.13	39.61	31.14
1997	44.36	42.41	35.85	50.98	35.50
1998	70.52	49.72	42.29	62.95	46.55
1999	94.64	72.85	74.62	88.81	61.78

Source: VBARD and VBP financial reports provided by VBP headquarters

Appendix 7.6:VBP uncollectable and overdue loans, December 1999 (%)

	Uncollectable loans/ total loans outstanding	Medium-termloans: Overdue loans/total loans outstanding
Ha Giang	0.21	1.34
Phu Tho	0.9	0.52
Tuyen Quang	0.75	6.21
Yen Bai	4.05	1.04
Lao Cai	1.13	0.52

Source: VBARD and VBP financial reports provided by VBP headquarters

NOTES

1 See data from 1999 census 3 per cent sample in Appendix 7.1.

2 These figures represent about US$13 and US$16 using the average 11,033 dong/USD nominal exchange rate in 1996 (Institute of Economics 2001: 80).

3 Rotating Savings and Credit Associations (ROSCAs) involve regular (daily, monthly, seasonal) contributions of an agreed sum of money by a group of people. On each occasion on which contributions are made, one member of the group receives the full pool of money. Members of the group either take agreed turns, pull names out of a hat or bid for access to the pool. ROSCAs exist for a limited time period, depending on regularity of contribution and number of participants.

4 The Committee for Ethnic Minorities and Mountainous Areas (CEMMA) categorises communes and villages into three zones based on five criteria: natural resources, infrastructure, social factors, production conditions and living standards. Zone 1 includes 'areas beginning to develop', Zone 2 contains 'relatively stable areas' and Zone 3 is made up of 'areas with difficulties'.

5 The northern highlands region here includes 15 provinces in north-west and north-east Vietnam.

REFERENCES

CECARDE (1999) *Rural Credits in Vietnam: a Case Study in Tuyen Quang and Thanh Hoa.* Hanoi: CECARDE, April.

GSO (1999a) *Results of the Socio-Economic Survey of Households 1994–1997.* Hanoi: Statistical Publishing House.

—— (1999b) *Vietnam Living Standards Survey 1997–1998.* Hanoi: General Statistical Office, August.

—— (2000) *Statistical Yearbook 1999.* Hanoi: Statistical Publishing House.

Le Trong Cuc and A. Terry Rambo (eds) (2000) 'Bright Peaks, Dark Valleys: a comparative analysis of environmental and social conditions and development trends in five communities in Vietnam's northern mountain region'. Centre for Natural Resources and Environmental Studies (CRES), November, Vietnam National University, Hanoi.

Nguyen Dai Lai (2000) 'Bank credit policies for socio-economic development in northern mountain provinces'. *Banking Review,* no.12.

Smith, William (2000), 'Financial services in highland areas: results and proposal', MRDP January.

Tran Thi Que *et al.* (1998) 'Microfinance Market Research', MRDP, May.

CHAPTER 8

Institutional Challenges for Sustainable Development in Vietnam: The Case of the Coal Mining Sector

Bach Tan Sinh

> One thing that has become clear over the last decade is that even though sustainable development has created joint global discourse on environmental politics, we cannot assume that this will in itself produce better outcomes. Behind all the consensus are different frames of reference that inspire the way in which different cultures take up the challenges implicit in sustainable development. Such differences in cultural frames of reference now lead to new sort of conflict in environmental politics.
>
> (Hajer and Fischer 1999: 7)

INTRODUCTION

Until recently, research concerning institutional change in Vietnam has mainly focused on the role of state and business sectors as the two major social domains in shaping the development of Vietnam which can be argued as being exclusively state centric and elite driven.[1] The aims of this chapter are three fold. First, it examines the nature and dynamic interaction between not only the two social domains but also between them and the third social domain – civil society. Second, it examines the way in which they influence the development of Vietnam, in the context of the transformation from a centrally planned to a market-orientated economy and economic crisis in the region. Using sustainable development as the lens through which the quest for a sustainable development and the politics of sustainable development in Vietnam can be carried out at the discourse and operational levels, the chapter attempts to contribute to the understanding of the roles played by the three social domains, and especially the tensions among them. Third, it identifies the institutional challenges Vietnam has been facing in its effort to pursue a sustainable development path. Partly due to the inherent limit of the sustainable development concept in itself – its failure to question the existing institutions that produced the crisis in the first place – the chapter suggests some institutional restructuring that appears to be necessary.

The chapter first sets out the institutional context in which sustainable development as a project is to be implemented. A conceptual framework of cultural approach to environment and development is introduced to examine the nature and tension among the three major social domains in interpreting and carrying out sustainable development in Vietnam at three levels – the discursive/cosmological, technological/material and operational/organisational. The coal-mining sector is selected to illustrate the tensions among the three groups of institutions. The chapter discusses the institutional challenges Vietnam faces in its attempt to achieve economic growth and at the same time to protect the environment in the coal-mining sector. It does not, however, attempt to provide a set of solutions to overcome these institutional challenges. Instead it argues that bringing the cultural dimension to environment and development as a meaningful approach is helpful for understanding the dynamics of environmental and development politics surrounding the concept of sustainable development.

THE INSTITUTIONAL CONTEXT OF SUSTAINABLE DEVELOPMENT IN VIETNAM

The concept of development has undergone significant change during the last two decades. Original concepts of development defined in primarily economic terms, e.g. GNP and per capita growth, have become increasingly inadequate for the complexity of national aspirations. In reality, the definition of development is highly ideological and will remain so for the foreseeable future (Derman and Whiteford 1985). Capitalist and eurocentric developmentalism presents 'development as the process that creates the industrial world: industrialised, urbanised, democratic and capitalist' (Adams 1992: 4). It suggests that developing countries develop through different stages on 'a linear path towards modernisation' (Chilcote 1984: 10), or, in the words of Verhelst (1987: 10), go 'through various growth stages, which W.W. Rostow described with an optimism equalled only by his ethnocentrism'. This ideology has come to define and dominate development thinking both within and outside the countries of the 'Third World' (Aseniero 1985). The development defined by Adams is most interesting to consider at the time when Vietnam is in the process of transforming into a more market-orientated society in which the central government no longer decides development policy and programmes at all levels. For Adams, development is 'a product of power relations, of power of states, using capital, technology and knowledge, to alter the culture and society of particular groups of people'. Therefore, development is 'about control, of nature and of people' and creates 'losers as well as winners' (Adams 1992: 83–84).

In Vietnam, until now, the decision-making process associated with mainstream development planning has been highly centralised and compartmentalised, stemming from a legacy of the former centrally planned economy. Development plans are mainly dominated by the government and recently by the newly emerging economic actors. A set of civic or non-governmental actors is still at the early stage of formation and plays only a minor role in shaping the development path of Vietnam. Public participation in planning is viewed as unnecessary and time-consuming and there is little room for involvement of the public in scrutinising and affecting governmental decision-making.[2]

Before examining the social transformation of the development process in Vietnam through the case of coal-mining sector, the following institutional contexts need to be taken into consideration. First, there has been a transition from a centrally planned to a market-orientated economy. The former centrally planned economy, sometimes called the 'traditional socialist economy', was one in which the government attempted to impose central planning as the main means of controlling the economic development process. This economy was, as Beresford and Fraser argue, 'in spite of its alleged capacity to engage in "rationally planned" use of resources, capable of generating a very high level of environmental damage'. Its key feature was the emphasis given to growth of produced output value due to the economic backwardness of the socialist countries relative to the capitalist world and a desire to prove the superiority of socialism (Beresford and Fraser 1992: 10).[3]

The market-orientated economy form of socialism, on the other hand, is one in which 'economic levers (e.g. the price mechanism, taxation) are used to plan the economy by setting certain key parameters and allocating individual enterprises freedom to make their own investment, production and marketing decisions' (Beresford and Fraser 1992: 3). While the former centrally planned economy left behind certain sorts of environmental problems, the market-orientated economy will create other sorts due to the failure of the market to cover externalities. In other words, environmental costs are not included in the market price of a commodity or service (Lemons and Brown 1997: 55–58).

Second, there has been a gradual decentralisation of decision-making power from the central to local levels. The argument for decentralising decision-making power to local authorities in the market economy is that they are in a better position to understand their local conditions and to formulate and implement economic development in their locality, including land-use planning, provision of education, health, housing and welfare services. On the other hand, the side effect of the relative autonomy of regional bureaucracies can be the difficulty of implementing central government decisions. This factor needs to be taken into account in the process of decentralising decision-making power in Vietnam. Concentration of power in the hands of local authorities can result in the establishment of independent empires that are impervious to central control (Beresford and Fraser 1992; Vasavakul 1999). For example, some provinces in Vietnam signed over logging concessions to Japanese, Thai and overseas Chinese companies in order to develop their local economy. Another example is that of NAFORIMEX, a state-owned enterprise that engaged in the export of animal products, violating the Law on Conservation of Endangered Species.[4]

Third, there is a legacy of an ideology which involves the domination of nature by man. This legacy has resulted in recent government development policy supporting resource-intensive industries like oil and gas, mining, food processing and processing of raw materials for industrial use. While this policy can help Vietnam to reduce poverty and raise living standards, industrial development is also likely to bring with it direct and indirect adverse impacts on natural resources and environmental quality.[5] Gandhi once warned of the way developing countries industrialise following the Western model:

> God forbid that India should ever take industrialism after the manner of the West. The economic imperialism of a single tiny island kingdom is today keeping the world in chains. If any entire nation of 300 million took to similar economic exploitation, it would strip the world bare like locusts.[6]

The dominant attitudes towards nature stem from the following beliefs and assumptions. First, people are fundamentally different from all other creatures on earth, over which they have domination. Second, people are masters of their own destiny; they can choose their goals and learn to do whatever is necessary to achieve them. Third, the world is vast, and thus provides unlimited opportunities for humans. Fourth, the history of humanity is one of progress; for every problem there is a solution, and thus progress need never cease.[7] The roots of this attitude in Vietnam can be traced back to the concept of a 'triple revolution' – in the forces and relations of production, culture and science and technology – adopted by the Third Party Congress in 1960. Science and technology were considered as direct productive forces that should contribute to enhance economic growth. Little attention was given at that time to the role of science and technology in controlling or ameliorating the impact of production on the environment, or to the social and environmental effects of technologies that are not domestically generated but transferred from abroad (Beresford and Fraser. 1992: 10).[8]

Last but not least, Vietnam is under the pressure to 'catch up'[9] with other countries in the region at all costs, especially the environmental cost (Vo Quy 1997; Nguyen The Nghia 1997). The type of development Vietnam follows is not much different from the mainstream ideology of development, which suggested, as Adams put it:

> Countries developed through different stages, on a linear path toward modernisation and progress down that path could be measured in terms of the growth of the economy, or some economic abstraction such as per capita gross domestic product. 'Development' means the projects and policies, the infrastructure, flows of capital and transfer of technology which were supposed to make this imitation possible. (Adams 1992: 5)

Economic development in this way is 'sustained by economic ideology rather than resources. Looked at in this way GNP is a measure of decay (of food, clothing, gadgets and gasoline) and the bigger the economic system the more it decays and the more that has to be produced simply to maintain it. Most developed countries are geared to resource utilisation rather than resource conservation' (Redclift 1984: 21–22).

The environment cannot be viewed in isolation or separation from the macroeconomic development model that a country chooses or is forced to pursue. While Vietnam used to follow Malhotra's third model – state-dominated and -controlled 'socialism' – it is moving toward a modified version of the second model – state-led and -controlled capitalism or high-speed economic growth model (Malhotra 1998). In the context of globalisation and the increase of private flows to Southeast Asia, the future trends in the region are clearly in favour of private investment in infrastructure, since governments can no longer fund all that is needed. This trend will have major negative impacts on natural resources because the private sector is less likely to internalise environmental costs in its cost-benefit analysis. It is also less likely to be held accountable to directly affected communities or to be open to public scrutiny. Government is also likely to concentrate on giving it more competitive incentives and to pay less attention to compliance with existing laws and regulations (Malhotra 1998).

The competition of Vietnam with other countries in the region became more intense since the economic and financial crisis at the end of 1997. Economic growth, measured in terms of GNP, decreased from 8.9 per cent in 1997 to 5.8 per cent in 1998 and 4 per cent in 1999. Foreign investment fell in 1998 by more than half its level of the previous year (from US$2 billion to US$800 million) (Beresford, Chapter 3 this volume) since most of foreign investors come from countries in the region. Vietnam has had to compensate for shortages of foreign exchange through even more rapacious resource extraction policies. In order to attract foreign investors to return, the normal assessment procedures applied to development projects are likely to be simplified. For example, a recent decision of the Ministry of Planning and Investment allowed FDI projects that export 80 per cent of their output or more, are committed to industrial parks or export processing zones and are worth at least $5 million, to receive licences within one day without submitting feasibility studies as before.[10]

The nature of development in Vietnam will depend on which are the main social and political forces deciding what type of development Vietnam is going to follow. Development is a political process and in that process decision-making rationality is often derived primarily from considerations of political power, not from the information generated by assessment studies (Henry 1990).

CONCEPTUAL FRAMEWORK TO STUDY SUSTAINABLE DEVELOPMENT IN VIETNAM: A CULTURAL APPROACH TO ENVIRONMENT AND DEVELOPMENT

Development plans and programmes are often the result of resolving or asserting conflicting development interests of various groups of actors representing three main social domains or constituencies: (1) government, (2) business and (3) civil society (Jamison and Baark 1990).[11] Depending on their institutional background and epistemological orientation, these different groups of actors acquire and interpret different notions of development, carrying implications for their own political actions over the development process. These different actors with conflicting interests constitute dynamic interactions that affect the political decision-making processes within which development plans are formulated and shaped.

In order to understand the social transformation process from traditional development (during the 1960s and 1970s) to sustainable development, promoted during the 1980s and 1990s, and its implication for cultural tensions and conflicts among the three groups of actors involved in this process, I use the conceptual framework developed by Jamison and Baark (1990) and Elzinga and Jamison (1995) to study the cultural dimensions of science and technology policy. In addition, I draw on the concept developed by Jamison *et al.* (1990) and Eyerman and Jamison (1991) in their study of three dimensions of cognitive praxis in environmental movements in Sweden, Denmark and the Netherlands. This conceptual framework has been developed to examine the cultural tensions between the three social domains, at three levels, in the process toward sustainable development in Vietnam (see Figure 8.1).

Concerning the cultural dimensions of science and technology policy, Jamison and Baark (1990) have distinguished three types. of 'policy culture', which are classified as the bureaucratic, economic and academic. They have argued that 'while in practice they often become intertwined in the process

Figure 8.1: The conceptual framework: cultural tensions between different social domains

	Domains		
Dimensions	**Government**	**Business**	**Civil Society**
Cosmological or discursive	sustainable economic growth	sustainable business growth	sustainable livelihood and community development
Technological or material	impact assessment	cleaner production/ clean technology	access to and control over resources
Organisational or operational	networking with formal/administrative establishments	corporatist/ company management	public participation and community involvement

Source: Adapted from Jamison *et al.* (1990) and Eyerman and Jamison (1991)

of policy-making, for analytical purposes it is useful to separate them as 'ideal types'. They exist primarily as interest lobbies, or institutional networks, and as such exercise significant influence over practical policy-making (Jamison and Baark 1990: 32). Elzinga and Jamison (1995) recently expanded this analytical framework by adding a fourth domain, namely the public or civic domain. For Elzinga and Jamison, these four policy cultures 'coexist within each society, competing for resources and influence, and seeking to steer science and technology in particular directions'. Each policy culture has 'its own perception of policy, including doctrinal assumptions, ideological preference, and ideals of science, and a different set of relationships with the holders of political and economic power'. Although the concept of policy culture is not directly related to the conceptual framework, it is useful in providing a model for studying the cultural dimensions of three social domains.

The concept of the dimensions of knowledge interest (cosmological, technological and organisational) developed by Jamison and Eyerman to study the cognitive praxis of the environmental movement is used to present the three levels (discursive, technological/material and organisational) in which the tensions among the three social domains occur. At the cosmological or discursive level, the worldview of the social domains toward development and environment and their interrelationships can be found in specific texts, programmes, books, articles, etc. At the material or technological level, one can find the substance of the debate at the discursive level, for example in different kinds of technology, production and consumption. And at the organisational level, one can find the ways in which the ideas discussed at the cosmological level are translated into practical activities at the technological level.

The cosmological or discursive dimension

Cultural tensions between different social domains occurring during the transformation to sustainable development can be seen at three levels. On the cosmological or discursive level, the domains are distinguished on the basis of different basic worldview assumptions or beliefs concerning development, environment and their interrelationships, and different interpretations of the new doctrine of sustainability. Since the issuing of the NPESD (National Plan for Environment and Sustainable Development) at the end 1991 and especially after the Rio Earth Summit in June 1992, the concept of sustainable development was widely accepted in Vietnam by government, business and society but interpreted in different ways. For the government and business, sustainable development has often been interpreted as sustainable economic growth and sustainable industrial growth, respectively.

In Vietnam, the basic assumption of mainstream developmentalism held by government, business and a great part of the scientific establishment is in line with the anthropocentric approach to sustainability. It follows the Western development paradigm based on international free trade, maximisation of output and expansion of individual economies, local and national, measured in terms of GNP. The 'pro-growth' school argues that 'the best way to provide for future generations is to exploit resources, not conserve them. Market forces and human ingenuity will always take care of shortages by providing solutions which will leave us better off than we were before' (Parnwell and Bryant 1996). This perspective puts faith in the market mechanism and the advancement and transfer of technology (MOSTE and NISTPASS 1996), and in the human reaction to environmental pressures to create the circumstances for change. The government has to secure conditions for continued economic growth.[12] The orthodoxy still gives economic growth the highest priority on the development agenda. The growth approach and free-market environmentalism have been promoted by state and business (Dao The Tuan 1992; Nguyen Thi Hien 1998).

Looking at the National Development Strategy to the Year 2020 presented at the Eighth National Congress of the Vietnamese Communist Party in December 1996, one can see the focus of the strategy on issues 'relating to the socio-economic and political development of the country, but not the concern for sustainable development' (MPI and UNDP 1997: 27). In Vietnam such a document is considered the most important strategic document in directing the country's future development. In the main body of this document (Part 3), entitled 'Directions for Development in Major Sectors' with ten chapters, nothing relating to environmental protection or sustainable development was addressed.

The document thus paid attention to the economy, culture, defence, and security, but did not mention the environmental challenges facing Vietnam. It stated that:

> The objective of industrialisation and modernisation is to develop Vietnam as an industrialised country characterised by a modern technical and material infrastructure, and appropriate economic structure, a progressive production system, high material and spiritual living standard, stable defence and security, well-off people, a strong country and equal and civilised society. ... By the

> year 2020 we should try our best to turn Vietnam into an industrialised country. (MPI and UNDP 1997: 27)

The issues explicitly highlighted in the document are important, but to improve living standard and conditions, the country's main development strategy must embrace the concept of sustainable development and emphasise the integration of environmental concerns into socio-economic decision-making at all levels. A newly emerging civic domain, represented by NGOs and some critical scientists has, however, raised concern over the impacts of development. In her article 'The role of culture for development', published in the newspaper *Van Hoa* [Culture], Nguyen Thi Hien, a scientist, criticised the development policy of government:

> While Britain turned the place where Shakespeare was born to a tourism centre attracting million of tourists each year... In Vietnam, because of short-term profits, mountains which were considered as historical places were exploited to produce cement. If this kind of exploitation geared just for profits is not controlled, we will have to pay a high price for the profits gained today. (Nguyen Thi Hien 1998 [author's translation])

Tension between government/business and civil society can also be seen in competing sustainabilities in development activities and the idea of promoting 'green' industry. For example, promotion of the 'green' renewable Hoa Binh Hydropower Plant by the government and business undermines the sustainable livelihoods of those who must be resettled and the radical change of the ecosystem on which their livelihood depends (Nhat Ninh 1991; Hirsch *et al.*1992; Bui Dinh Thanh 1997). Nhat Ninh in his articles published in the newspaper *Nhan Dan* [The People] addressed the negative impacts and the risks of modern science and technology to society, particularly the impact of large-scale technological development projects:

> Scientists, technologists, even managers and politicians were too optimistic about the results achieved by modern science and technology, wanted to apply them quickly in production to meet socio-economic objectives. For example, the construction of hydro- and thermo-electric power stations was a necessary requirement of the society and an economic goal to be achieved. The Song Da Hydropower Plant and Pha Lai Thermopower Plant have generated electricity for the northern region, and other similar projects are under the construction to meet the demand

> of production and consumption. But while these goals were achieved, others were not – we have electricity but the environment is degraded and polluted, and people's livelihoods were not dealt with properly. (Nhat Ninh 1991 [author's translation])

Another example is the critique raised by Thai Van Trung, a French-trained forestry specialist of the construction of a golf course and recreation area near Ho Chi Minh City. He was considered by some as the 'leader of Vietnam's nascent green movement'. Signatures from many leading scientists were collected to oppose these new changes of landscape by foreign investment projects (Hiebert 1992).

Other competing sustainabilities concern the increasingly prevalent practice of fish and shrimp farming. At one stage aquaculture represented a panacea for dealing with the massive over-exploitation of marine and riverine resources. However, it has quickly become apparent that aquaculture has brought with it a host of other ecological and economic problems, which ultimately threaten the sustainability of this industry and the ecosystems (especially mangrove forests) which it affects.

The concern with the alliance between the bureaucratic and economic domains in controlling development and the need for a countervailing force to protect the interest of the public in a market economy was voiced by Nguyen Khac Vien. Being trained and holding a PhD degree from France in the 1940s, Vien was a well known intellectual of the Communist Party of Vietnam (CPV) and a very 'hard core' communist. For decades he was a mainstay of the CPV foreign propaganda apparatus. In an open letter to Nguyen Huu Tho, President of the Fatherland Front in 1991, Vien raised the problem of the need to manage society in the emerging market economy in Vietnam. First he expressed his opinion about the nature of a market economy, in saying that:

> The private economy will develop; the international companies will invest. That is the irresistible trend. It will stimulate the progress of science and technology, and make it possible for a number of people to develop their capacities. Capitalism inside and outside the country will join hands to exploit resources and to use labour. To serve that kind of economy there will be a machine with three blocs: (1) one to manage the economy; (2) one to govern (administrative and public security); and (3) one to manage culture and ideology (control of the means of information and the media).

> Since it is a market economy based on profit, it is useless to talk about ethics. Since it is a bureaucratic machine, it is equally idle to make ethics its guiding principle. (Nguyen Khac Vien 1991: 5)

As a consequence of this economy, Vien was aware of the conflict of interest in bureaucratic agencies and the alliances built between groups of actors representing their own interests and asked for a countervailing power to defend the interest of the public:

> Faced with an economic, administrative, and cultural machine which is national, and which at the same time has international ties *(a high ranking cadre in that machine will consider himself a Vietnamese, as well as a man of Mitsubishi, Toyota, or Philips), the people must at all costs set up a People's Democratic Front as a countervailing force to defend* [emphasis added]: (1) freedom and democracy; (2) social justice (the worker must be paid an adequate wage; inequality between rich and poor must not be excessive, education and health care must be guaranteed; culture must be protected); (3) the environment; and (4) peace.
>
> This front does not advocate armed struggle, but it must use all forms of democratic struggle, and above all it must absolutely demand and secure: (1) freedom of expression and opinion; (2) freedom of association… and freedom from the constraints of the above-mentioned machine. (Nguyen Khac Vien 1991)

THE TECHNOLOGICAL OR MATERIAL DIMENSION

If sustainability as a new doctrine formed the terms for debate at the cosmological/discursive level, it was the practices in pursuit of the respective goals set up at the cosmological level that provided the debate with its substance. In terms of technological measures the three domains are characterised by different ways to achieve sustainability.

For the groups of actors representing the bureaucratic domain, impact assessment is the mechanism for integrating social, economic and environmental concerns into economic development planning and thereby achieving sustainable economic growth. During the 1990s the notion of economic development was mainly discussed in terms of modernisation and industrialisation, as expressed in the Socio-Economic Development Strategy 1991–2000 adopted by the Seventh National Party Congress in 1991. Toward this end, science and technology, particularly technology transfer were considered the driving forces (Nguyen Dinh Tu 1995; Vu Dinh Cu 1995; Dang Ngoc Dinh 1998).

While most people have strong faith in the role played by science and technology for socio-economic development and environmental protection in the course of modernising and industrialising Vietnam, there have been other voices demanding a need to assess technology impacts. Debates concerning what types of technologies Vietnam would need to acquire from abroad have been articulated in a number of journal articles, notably the *Communist Review*, a platform of the Communist Party of Vietnam.

While people from government agencies have taken the lead in discussing the types of technology needed for industrialising and modernising the country, there has been very little debate on this issue among business people. It was environmental scientists at the universities carrying out research on industrial pollution who talked about the need of the government to encourage development of clean technologies. For example, Dinh Van Sam, director of the Centre for Environmental Science and Technology within the Hanoi University of Technology, commented, at a ceremony celebrating the donation of 2,000 copies of the 'Cleaner Production' poster (sponsored by Texaco), that the government should pay more attention to cleaner production, especially in the industrial sector, and environmental protection (Trong Tin 1997). One reason why such debates were not much found among business people was a lack of motivation to make profits through technological innovation, especially in the state-owned enterprises. This problem has been researched in a number of studies at the Institute for Science Management and the National Institute for Science and Technology Forecasting and Strategic Studies under the MOSTE.[13]

Access to and control over the resources for a sustainable livelihood is another aspect of the technological debate conducted by civil society. In their long history, the farmers in the Red River Delta have developed the VAC (*vuon, ao, chuong*) system comprising home garden (V), fishpond (A) and livestock breeding facilities (C). It is a closed recycling system whereby the waste of one element of the system can be used as the input for other elements. For example, the fruit and vegetables planted in the garden supply food for people but also feed pigs and fish. Household and livestock waste is used to fertilise the soil and to feed the fish. The VAC system has proved to be a productive and environmentally friendly living system in which farmers can manage and control all resources in the system. VAC has become popular and has led to several studies of models of natural resource management at the household level in the lowlands. VAC is a traditional technology, accumulated over generations and provides an alternative to input-intensive production using a large amount of chemical fertilisers by rationally utilising locally available resources with very little waste.

The organisational dimension

Between theory and practice, the cosmological and the technological dimensions, there is the organisational dimension. The organisational dimension reflects different strategies and organisational initiatives to translate the concepts debated at the cosmological level into practical activities at the technological level.

For the first group of actors, those representing the bureaucratic domain, tensions occur within the governmental agencies responsible for environment and development regarding their way of realising the concept of sustainable economic growth in plans and programmes. The NPESD adopted by the government in 1991 resulted in the establishment of a national system of environmental administration with MOSTE/NEA at the national level and its affiliated DOSTE in all 61 provinces,[14] and a legal system comprising the Law on Environmental Protection and a number of regulations. However, until recently, the governmental agencies representing environmental concerns and interests have been considered rather weak and have often come into conflict with production-orientated agencies traditionally associated with economic growth programmes. For example, the requirement of having an EIA appraisal before granting an investment licence has usually been ignored or avoided by development agencies and project proponents. In addition, the two planning processes (economic development and environmental protection) have been carried out in separate streams, each following its own procedure in its own framework with little interaction or integration.[15]

The attempt to overcome this institutional tension was initiated by the Ministry of Planning and Investment (MPI) by the establishment of a so-called National Sustainable Development Network, in the framework of the Vietnam Capacity 21 Project. The Network consisted of representatives from various agencies co-ordinated by MPI and MOSTE. The network was composed not only of government officials but also of researchers from universities and institutes, as well as of business organisations. During the implementation of the Vietnam Capacity 21 Project during 1995–98, a number of activities were carried out. For example, two major research programmes (Environmental

Economics and Sustainable Development Planning) were conducted to identify the institutional barriers to the integration of environment and development in Vietnam. Another effort was to organise training courses on environmental screening for development planners who play a very important role in identifying the potential environmental impacts of development projects at the beginning of the appraisal procedures, before requesting submission of EIA studies to the environmental agencies.

For business groups, an attempt to set up the Vietnam Business Council for Sustainable Development was initiated by the WWF and UNDP and implemented in the framework of the Vietnam Capacity 21 Project with the participation of the MPI, MOSTE and the Vietnam Chamber of Commerce and Industry (VCCI).[16] At the same time, UNIDO has also been involved in creating a Sustainable Industrial Development Network in the region including Vietnam and China. Although these two networks are not yet in place, there is a clear indication of the need for a network that could translate the idea of sustainable industrial development into actions carried out by business.

While the groups of actors from the bureaucratic and business domains want to prove their role in formulating and implementing sustainable development in Vietnam, the third group of actors, representing the civic domain, has its own way of being involved in carrying out sustainable development. The first network in this group is the Vietnam Association for Conservation of Nature and Environment (VACNE). VACNE can be considered a semi-non-governmental organisation as it was set up on 26 November 1988 according to the Decision of the Prime Minister 299/CT. Its main functions are (1) to provide consultancy and appraisal of development activities concerning environmental impacts; (2) to be involved in education and in increasing environmental awareness; and (3) to contribute to setting up civil movements for environmental protection. It is directed by a board consisting mainly of people from government administration and research institutions. VACNE's chairman is Le Quy An, a former vice-minister of MOSTE, and Nguyen Ngoc Sinh, General Director of the NEA, is its general secretary. Because of the composition of the VACNE's board and its tight relations to MOSTE/NEA, its role as an independent organisation is rather limited.

Another network, the VAC Association, established as a result of the VAC movement, took the form of a community involvement as a different way to pursue sustainable development independently of state control and direction. The association was created in 1990 and quickly developed all over the country. It was mobilised by an NGO to disseminate knowledge regarding best-practice agriculture, achieving waste minimisation at the household level and without using chemicals.

One dimension of controlling the livelihood of citizens is closely linked to the aspect of sustainable development, namely the role of ordinary citizens as participants in a process of defining sustainable development. To be able to participate in this debate, one fundamental requirement is the 'right to know'. The principles and tools of the right to know were recognised and officially endorsed at the UNCED meeting in Rio de Janeiro in 1992. In Vietnam this principle has not been widely applied, except in Ho Chi Minh City, but has proved a very powerful tool for creating public pressure on the business community. The DOSTE of Ho Chi Minh City, with technical assistance from UNIDO, has been able to conduct pollution surveys of a majority of the industrial enterprises in the city, resulting in the compilation of a black list of 50 polluting industries. This list has been made public. On the other hand, the reports on the state of the environment in Vietnam prepared by the NEA and submitted to the National Assembly every year have not been available to ordinary citizens who want to know more about the environmental situation of sectors and industries in their localities. Until now there has been no legal requirement ensuring the right of access by citizens to information regarding the state of the environment at any government environmental agency.

CASE STUDY OF COAL MINING

Coal mining in the national and local economies and its historical development

Coal mining, mainly concentrated in Hong Gai-Bai Chay and Cam Pha of Quang Ninh province is considered one of the most important economic sectors in terms of contributing to Vietnam's foreign exchange earning capacity. In 1998, 11.2 millions tonnes of coal were produced and 10.5 millions sold, for VND 2.8 trillion (roughly $202 million). Of this amount, Vietnam exported 3 million tonnes, with Japan being its largest importer at 1.4 million tonnes, followed by West European countries with 540,000 tonnes (JCOAL 16 June 2000). Quang Ninh province contributes 90 per cent of the total coal production of Vietnam and 100 per cent of the volume exported. The coal reserves of Vietnam have been estimated at 2,345 million tonnes of anthracite, all in Quang Ninh Province, 78 million tonnes of semi-anthracite, 38 million of coking coal, 96 million tonnes of thermal coal and 306 million tonnes of lignite (Bach Tan Sinh 1998).

The history of coal mining in Vietnam can be traced back to the nineteenth century when France discovered coal there for the first time. Here, however, we are concerned only with the *doi moi* period, reflecting the most important changes regarding development and environmental protection in the operation of the coal-mining sector. The development of the sector can be divided into four periods:

- *First period (1987–89):* this period is characterised by the expansion of output under the former centrally planned economy, in which the government gave a high priority to achievement of its goal of 10 million tonnes annually. However, this very ambitious goal was never met; only 4-6 million tonnes were achieved. Since 1989 and the transition to a market-orientated economy, the demand for coal has decreased sharply, pushing the sector into a crisis.
- *Second period (1990–94):* the sector continued in crisis for different reasons, including market reduction, shortage of investment capital and increasing illegal coal mining outside government control in the mining area of Quang Ninh.[17]
- *Third period (1995–97):* recovery and export-orientated expansion of production capacity with support of loans from transnational banks and joint ventures. The establishment, in January 1995, of the new Vietnam Coal Corporation (VINACOAL), aimed at concentrating coal-mining business under state ownership, marked the start of this rehabilitation period. Production increased each year, reaching 10.7 million tonnes in 1997, an unprecedented figure in the history of coal mining in Vietnam. VINACOAL projected to increase its annual production to about 11 millions tonnes in 2000 (10.9 million was achieved), 12 million tonnes in 2002 and 21 million tonnes by 2020 (Nguyen Chi Quang *et al.* 1998; GSO 2001: 326).[18]
- *Fourth period (from 1998 onward):* over-production leads to temporary mine closures under the impacts of financial crisis in the region. From the end of 1997 the Asian crisis gradually affected the coal business in Vietnam because the major importing country was Japan and important joint venture partners, such as Japan and Indonesia, come from within the region (US Department of Commerce 1998). Although there was already a stockpile 2 million tonnes of coal at the end of 1997, VINACOAL continued to increase production and formed joint ventures with foreign companies to create new coal mining capacity due to its debt repayment obligation to transnational banks. The 'unexpected' surplus stockpile of 4 millions tonnes reported by VINACOAL on 4 June 1999 required the

suspension of coal production and 'temporary' pit closures, mainly in state-owned mines, until the end of year, threatening the jobs and livelihood of nearly 86,000 miners in Quang Ninh (Greenfield 1999).

State, Business and Civil Society in Shaping Development of Coal Mining

Applying the conceptual framework described above, this section examines dynamic interactions and occasional tensions among the three social domains in shaping the way coal mining developed in Vietnam and discusses the implications for institutional changes to ensure a sustainable development of the sector. The state has the two main functions, namely to ensure the conditions for continued accumulation of capital of the nation and to secure its legitimacy in the society through maintaining viable conditions for this accumulation, part of which involves minimising environmental degradation associated with the accumulation process. These two functions are potentially in conflict with each other.[19] This section examines the responsiveness of the state to both the immediate need of capital accumulation and the longer-term concern (legitimation process) with impacts, including the social and environmental impacts, of the accumulation process in Vietnamese coal mining. The state-specific responses must be located within the economic context of global capitalist accumulation and the recent economic crisis in the region.

Vietnam's recent economic development relies heavily on state-owned enterprises (SOEs) (Beresford, Chapter 3 this volume; Vasavakul 1999), considered the leading economic sector and accounting for about 60 per cent of the country's industrial output and 42 per cent of the GDP. The sector also absorbs 60–65 per cent of available credit (Asia Intelligence Update 1999). Almost all joint-venture investment involving foreign firms has been with the SOEs. Medium-sized domestic private firms with 25–100 employees are scarce and account for only 1 per cent of GDP (US Department of Commerce 1998). In the mid-1990s the government reorganised some large state-owned firms into general corporations in 16–18 sectors such as coal, cement, petroleum product, steel, sugar, fertiliser, rice, telecommunications, aviation, financial services, importing, distribution and others. These SOEs tend to be capital intensive and produce few new jobs. In 1999 the government decided to turn Vietnam's 91 state corporations, particularly the 17 under the direct control of central government, into strong business conglomerates. Their subsidiary enterprises will be restructured and equitised, but state and the Communist Party control of the parent companies will be increased (Asia Intelligence Update 1999).

Another characteristic of Vietnam's development strategy is that it is based on heavy use of foreign investment, which has shown signs of faltering (Beresford, Chapter 3 this volume). For example, to maintain a GDP growth rate in the 9–10 per cent range for the five-year period 1996–2000, the government planned to invest US$ 42 billion, of which half was to come from foreign sources (US$14 billion from FDI and US$7 billion from official development assistance). The remaining US$21 billion was to come from domestic sources (US Department of Commerce 1998).

A clear example of the attempt by government to enhance capacity for capital accumulation in the coal-mining sector was the establishment of VINACOAL, which began operations in January 1995.[20] The establishment of VINACOAL indicated the government's desire to create a number of economically strong and independent corporations following the model of the South Korean *chaebol* (giant industrial conglomerates). The functions and mandates of this kind of corporation were stipulated in Decision No. 91/TTg, enacted 7 March 1994 by the prime minister, concerning the experimental establishment of business groups, referred to by the name 'Corporations 91'. These were to be set up in certain strategic industries including power, coal, oil and gas.[21]

It is interesting to see how much power these corporations have been given by the government, reflecting its strong interest in strengthening the business sector with the aim of being able to compete not only in Vietnam but in the global market.[22] In line with Decision No. 91, the groups of corporations are under the management of a Board of Management but independent in economic accounting from the ministries that administer the sector, in this case the Ministry of Industry. They are accountable only to the prime minister. The Board of Management is responsible for management, utilisation and allocation of resources within the corporation and for deciding its development strategy, business solutions, as well as approving administrative arrangements within the corporation.

As part of its strategy of industrialisation by the year 2020, the government has provided assistance to VINACOAL in expanding production capacity and accumulating capital. The sector has been ensured access to foreign capital through loans from transnational banks, official development assistance (ODA) and joint ventures. In 1997, VINACOAL borrowed $30 million from six overseas banks in a consortium led by US-based Citicorp at 8 per cent interest over five years. VINACOAL has also received bilateral technical aid and loans through the Japan International Cooperation Agency (JICA) to support the interests of Japanese trading companies and heavy industry, since Japan is the largest importer of anthracite from Vietnam. The combination of technical assistance and soft loans led to the acquisition by Sumitomo Corporation of a long-term contract with VINACOAL's Hong Gai Company to export coal to Japan. Through this contract Sumitomo was able to establish control over more than half of Vietnam's coal export to Japan. In addition, VINACOAL formed joint ventures with foreign mining companies from Canada and Japan (Greenfield 1999). In 1998 a Japan–Vietnam Joint Coal Exploration–Red River Delta Project was formed between Japanese Coal (JCOAL) and VINACOAL for a period of five years (1999–2003). Another joint-venture project between VINACOAL and CAVICO International Ltd. from Canada was set up with a total investment of US$22.4 million to exploit the Nui Beo coal mine for a period of 28 years. It plans to extract and export 29 million tonnes of coal during this period (Greenfield 1999). The access to foreign capital in turn drives VINACOAL to pursue an export-orientated over-production strategy to repay its debt.

In 1997 the government approved, in Prime Minister's Decision No.98/TTg, VINACOAL's revised medium- and long-term Master Development Strategy for 2010 and 2020. The previous version of the strategy, which was prepared in the context of the centrally planned economy and before the establishment of VINACOAL, had not reflected the new conditions. The revised version of the strategy was therefore formulated based on an opened market economy and projected market demand, from both domestic and international clients, with two scenarios (basic and high). Table 8.1 shows the projection of total coal production over the next 20 years (MPI/UNDP 1997a).

While the government aims to secure the conditions for capital accumulation in coal mining, by recentralisation under VINACOAL, provision of access to finance and approval of the long-term development strategy of the sector, it also has to protect its legitimacy in such affairs as employment and environmental protection. In June 1999, VINACOAL announced that it had a stockpile of 4 million tonnes and therefore had to suspend coal production and temporarily close mines on a rotating basis until the end of the year. As a result, the jobs of 86,000 miners and the livelihoods of about 250,000 miners and their dependants in Quang Ninh province were threatened.[23] The small and medium mines were the first target of production stoppage and miners on short-term contracts immediately lost their jobs (Greenfield 1999; Spaeth 1999). However, the production stoppage at the state-owned mines under VINACOAL did not apply to mines operating under joint venture or

Table 8.1: Coal production demand forecast, 1997–2020

Year)	**Basic scenario (m. tonnes)**	**High scenario (m. tonnes)**
1997	10,312	
1998	10,618	
1999	11,046	
2000	11,734	12,500
2005	13,725	15,000
2010	18,000	19,500
2015	20,000	22,000
2020	21,500	26,000

Source: VINACOAL Master Development Strategy for 2010 and 2020.

production contracts with foreign capital. In effect this stoppage and the possibility of the permanent closure of several state-owned mines would have given foreign mining companies operating in Vietnam a larger share of the coal export market, and eventually the domestic market (Greenfield 1999).

Facing potential social instability associated with the loss of several thousands jobs, the government instructed VINACOAL to re-employ over 50,000 laid-off miners on shorter workdays instead of suspending mining operations. Moreover, to increase the domestic demand for coal, it approved the plan to build Pha Lai Thermal Power Plant No. 2, with a generation capacity of 600 MW, and Uong Bi Thermal Power Plant, with 300 MW. These two plants will create a more stable market for domestic coal mines, especially for low-quality coal. New investment and bidding plans for two further projects (Na Duong and Cao Ngan) were also approved. VINACOAL has also carried out feasibility studies for Cam Pha coal-fired power plant near the Cua Ong Coal mine, Son Dong in Bac Giang province, An Hoa in Quang Nam province and the Tien Dung plant near the Chu Dong Tu coal mine in Hung Yen province (*Vietnam News* 1999b). Other measures applied to help the mining sector out of economic difficulties included requesting those ministries consuming a large amount of coal to accumulate more reserves, sending redundant workers to work overseas, investing more from the state budget in building infrastructure in mining centres, debt rescheduling and changes to deduction of equipment amortisation (*Vietnam News* 1999a) .

Coal mining usually brings with it major environmental impacts, especially as the sector has almost doubled its production capacity in recent years. In Quang Ninh province, coal mining comes into conflict with other economic sectors such as tourism, agriculture/forestry and natural conservation. Ha Long Bay, located alongside the main mining centres, was designated a World Heritage site by Unesco in 1994 and is a major tourist destination in Vietnam.[24] The government has been aware of these impacts and demanded that VINACOAL incorporate environmental considerations into its Master Development Strategy. Furthermore, the provincial government (the Quang Ninh People's Committee) was also requested by the prime minister to integrate both the coal development plan and environmental concerns into its Socio-Economic Development Strategy for 2010 and 2020. However, due to the lack of institutional capacity in dealing with strategic environmental impact assessments, the environment aspects were not appropriately addressed in either VINACOAL's strategy or the province's socio-economic plan (MPI/UNDP 1997a).

After the Law on Environmental Protection (LEP) was passed in 1994, there has been an institutional set-up in place to deal with environmental protection in the whole country. An environmental administrative system was established with the Ministry of Science, Technology and Environment (MOSTE) and its arm the National Environmental Agency (NEA) at the national level and, at the provincial level DOSTEs were created. The function of DOSTEs are to assist provincial governments to enforce the LEP locally, including appraisal and monitoring of environmental impact assessments of development projects in the province. Given the limited capacity of DOSTEs in general (O'Rourke 2002) and Quang Ninh DOSTE in particular, especially its Environmental Management Unit which employs only 4 persons, it is a challenge for the Quang Ninh DOSTE to fulfil its assigned tasks.[25]

Role of business in ecological modernisation in coal mining

Since adoption of the NPESD in 1991, the concept of sustainable development has been widely accepted by the government as the alternative to the previous development path. More recently, the concept of 'greening industry', or 'ecological modernisation', has entered the country and been taken up in some industries, notably in coal mining, as a way of running business in an environmentally friendly manner. At the discourse level, one can find the idea of ecological modernisation in coal mining in a study conducted jointly by the Ministry of Planning and Investment and VINACOAL that addressed the attempt of the government and the corporation to incorporate environmental concerns into the coal development plan. The study argued that production can be changed in such a way that environmental externalities can be internalised. Ecological modernisation is attractive to the industry because it allows business restructuring through building environmental criteria into the existing business system according to the belief that business can make money from investing in environmental protection (MPI 1998).

The idea of ecological modernisation was thus reflected in the way VINACOAL defined sustainable development of the sector. Borrowing the definition from *Our Common Future*, VINACOAL injected the concept of sustainable development into its strategic development statement:

> For Vietnam's coal-mining sector, sustainable development means *not only maintaining the highest profits, but ensuring a clean, unpolluted environment*. Therefore, sustainable development of the coal-mining industry is defined as below:
>
> Sustainable development of the coal-mining sector is not only designed to *answer the present demand for coal without compromising the ability of future generations to meet their needs, but is also concerned with the ability to release pollution of the environment from coal exploitation and consumption.* (Nguyen Chi Quang *et al.*1998: 3 [emphasis added, author's translation])

For VINACOAL, it is possible to apply a 'positive-sum game'[26], or 'win-win' approach, to its business. Pollution is a matter of inefficiency, so what is needed is to apply better and cleaner technologies to improve the effective use of production inputs and to integrate environmental management that prevents or minimises pollution (MPI/UNDP 1997a).

At the operational/organisation level, where ecological modernisation is intended to be implemented as a technical tool to achieve more environmentally sensitive coal mining, there appears to exist a number of technological and institutional barriers in Vietnam, even though a 'weak version' of ecological modernisation is being applied. Weak ecological modernisation is considered by Hajer as a 'techno-corporatist' strategy, which treats the issues in technical terms and seeks a managerial structure for their implementation (Hajer 1995). Further, it has been characterised by Christoff as an emphasis on technological solutions to environmental problems and by a technological/corporatist style of policy-making monopolised by a scientific, economic, and political elite working in close co-operation with each other (Christoff 1996).

An examination of VINACOAL's environmental protection strategy can show the above-mentioned barriers VINACOAL faces in pursuing its ecological modernisation. The first fundamental question is: why is VINACOAL interested in environmental protection at all? For Nguyen Chi Quang, assistant to the general director of VINACOAL in charge of the environment and, at the same time, director of its Centre for Environmental Technology, the reasons are:

> In the past, environmental issues used to be seen as 'a heavy load or burden' or 'ethical issue'. With the trend of global development and increasing environmental awareness, the coal sector as well as VINACOAL are aware of the need to protect the environment for the following reasons. First, to comply with the Law on Environmental Protection to avoid costs, fines and charges for violation. Second, there is a need for companies to save natural resources by reducing material and energy, thereby saving the budget. Third, the competition of VINACOAL's products in domestic and international markets requires the corporation to adopt environmental standards to enhance competitiveness. Fourth, it is increasingly recognised that a good relationship with the local community is important for a company to be successful in the local market as well as in long-term operation. And finally, it is vital to improve the environmental performance of the company through environmental education of its employees. (MPI/UNDP 1997a: 65)

Although VINACOAL is aware of the need to comply with laws and regulations, it is interesting to investigate whether the corporation goes beyond compliance to develop the market potential and opportunities for innovation with an environmental strategy. A company is environmentally orientated if it has integrated environmental issues into its overall strategy and organised environmental protection in an appropriate way. To meet this requirement, it is necessary to integrate environmental protection into the goal structure of the corporation. For Williams *et al.* (1993), using different sets of goals, it is reasonable to assume that the most important objective (or 'vision') of a company is survival – that is, strengthening its resources and capabilities to meet the requirements of changing business and to gain a competitive edge. At the next level are strategic goals (or 'missions'), which include profit and market objectives as well as basic objectives. The latter are objectives, such as social benefits and a new factor – environmental protection (see Figure 8.2) that a corporation has to fulfil and include in its mission in order to ensure long-term survival.

Figure 8.2: Goal structure of a corporation

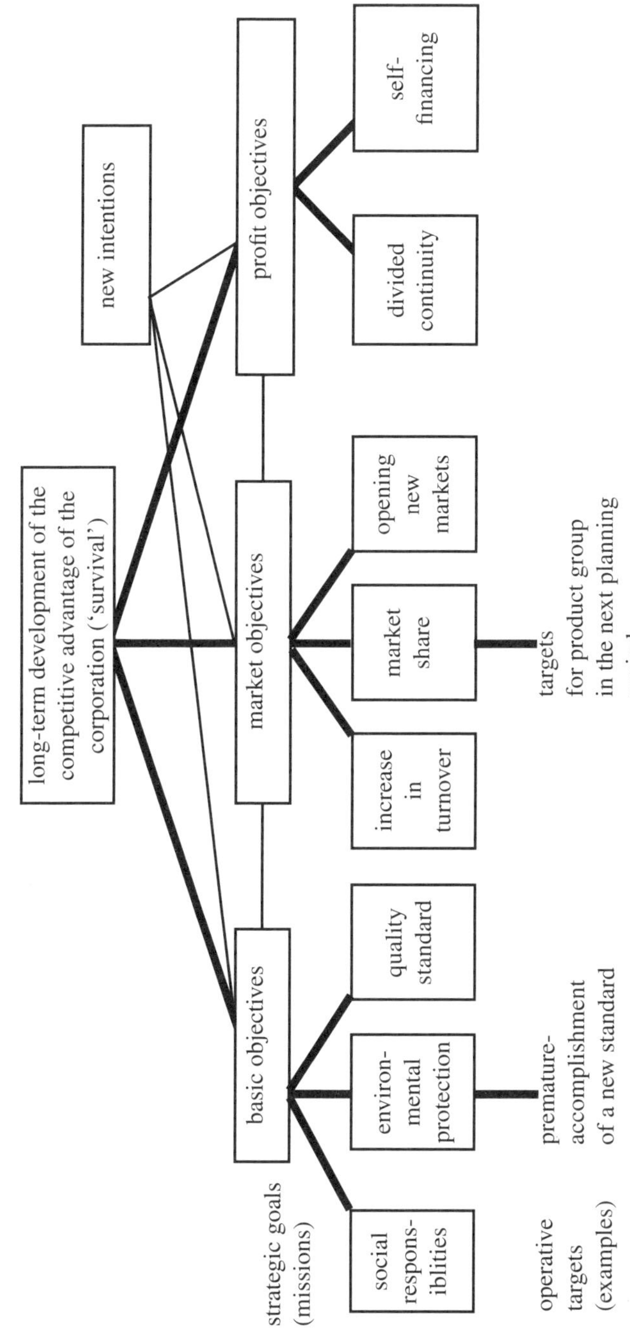

Source: Steger (1993)

Steger (1993) offers a framework to assess the four generic strategies – offensive, defensive, innovative and indifferent – in co-ordinating or minimising conflicts between goals. This framework can be applied in order to understand the new environmental pressure experienced by VINACOAL. According to this framework, the type of strategy is determined according to two conditions: the company's potential for market opportunities resulting from an environmental protection stance, and the level of environmental risk inherent in the company's activities (see Figure 8.3). Of the four strategies, the defensive strategy is probably the most appropriate for the coal-mining sector in Vietnam due to the following factors.

First, there is no relevant market opportunity in being environmentally orientated.[27] It is therefore rational merely to comply with environmental legislation. In addition to coal mining, this attitude is also typical of the fossil-fuel-based, electricity-generating industry. Second, because of high environmental risks, such as air pollution, the company will be a primary target of environment regulation.[28] The coal-mining areas are located in one of the most environmentally sensitive zones of the country, the Unesco-designated World Heritage area of Ha Long Bay. Because of the environmental impacts of coal-mining activities on the landscape, forests and coastline, and especially on the livelihoods of local people, the mining companies faced years of criticism for their destructive economic operations. Furthermore, investments in the production process with end-of-pipe technologies, for example, wastewater treatment, dust pollution control and reclamation techniques for mining over-burden lead to considerable increases in production costs as external effects – in this case environmental costs – that are internalised into the company's financial picture.

In practice, following the defensive strategy reveals many difficulties for VINACOAL: the first is coping with the legacy left over from inefficient production with less attention to the environment under the former centrally planned economy. The net yield of coal exploitation was about 70 per cent, with the remaining 30 per cent discarded with soil and rocks (MPI/UNDP 1997b).

Second, out-of-date technologies mostly imported from the former Soviet Union during the 1960s and 1970s are still used in mining. These technologies cause increasing dust pollution, CO_2 emission and water pollution, due to the discharge of poorly treated wastewater, as well as significant losses of coal. The mixing of coal with soil makes reforestation difficult in areas where overburden has been deposited. In addition, the innovation of techno-

Figure 8.3: Strategies based on market opportunities and environmental risks

Market opportunities through environmental protection		
large	offensive	innovative
small	indifferent	defensive
	small	large
	Corporate environmental risks	

Source: Steger (1993)

logy and equipment has been low in the coal-mining sector. The ratio of technological innovation is about 5–7 per cent of investment in open-pit mining and 28 per cent in underground mining (MPI/UNDP 1997b).

Third, low prices in the domestic market force the coal companies to adopt short-term strategies, mining the easiest and richest lodes, and prevent them from internalising external costs, such as social and environmental costs. Domestic sales recover only about 60 per cent of the production costs, even before allowing for capital depreciation, due to the low productivity (MPI/UNDP 1997a), thus encouraging the purchase of output from illegal mining. For example, Hong Gai Coal Company, one of the largest state-owned mines regularly purchased coal from the illegal coal miners, making up a third of its stated output. Illegal or 'bandit' coal miners are unskilled rural workers displaced from the countryside and child labourers and retired miners forced back into work by inadequate pensions. Bandit mines usually involve little expenditure on infrastructure, use simple mining techniques, are unsafe, exploit cheap labour and are uninsured (Greenfield 1999).

An issue of concern relates to conflicts of interest occurring within VINACOAL since its Management Board operates both as the owner of the business and as the sector management agency.[29] As a business, operating according to the profit motive, the board could allow its member companies to exploit natural resources without taking into account measures for environmental protection. In principle, however, as the sector management agency, the board should require all businesses under its jurisdiction to abide by national environmental standards and laws. Conflict of interest makes the latter less likely to happen. This process of providing the economic actors with more power reflects a new trend of forming alliances between groups of actors representing the bureaucratic domain in charge of economic development and those from the business domain. It is difficult, therefore, for the Ministry of Industry, and especially for the environmental agencies such as the Ministry of Science, Technology and Environment, to enforce tighter control over the industry concerned (MPI/UNDP 1997b). The example of VINACOAL's Environmental Fund illustrates this issue. To date, VINACOAL has had full authority to use the fund without informing either MOSTE or the Quang Ninh DOSTE about how it has actually spent the money or whether it has been used for its designated purpose.

The process of moving VINACOAL towards market-orientation has revealed the difficulty that arises sometimes in relying on the market to protect the environment. The pressure to generate profits turns the environment into an 'externality' that is not expressed in the market price. To date, the coal industry pays no environmental taxes, fees or charges, though it does pay a low natural resource tax. Recently, VINACOAL experimented with a tax and natural resource accounting system in co-operation with the University of Michigan to incorporate the full cost of production into the price. The whole idea of implementing coal resource accounting is to increase the utilisation of coal and reflects the instrumental rationality conception of efficient use of resources, environment management and planning. In addition, VINACOAL's proposal to set aside 1 per cent of its production costs for an environment fund is an attempt to correct this distortion. This fund will provide grants to different mining companies for pollution control activities. It is a specific application of the 'polluter pays' principle, in the sense that coal producers will have to internalise the environmental damages associated with their mining activities (either reducing profitability or raising costs to consumers which may result in lost markets). Some pilot projects financed by the fund will be implemented by a UNDP supported project, 'Environmental Protection in Open-pit Mining in Quang Ninh Province'. At the time of writing, the other ministries involved, such as the Ministry of Finance and the Ministry of Science, Technology and Environment had not yet approved the proposal.

There is a gap between VINACOAL's claim to be a good environmental corporate citizen at the discourse level and what it actually has implemented in its ecological modernisation, even in the weak version at the operational level. In this regard, Dryzek rightly argued that

> Ecological modernisation is not something that can be accomplished by business managers and engineers voluntarily and independently on their own products and processes. It

> requires much in the way of political commitment, to the enlightened long term rather the narrow-minded short term, and to a holistic analysis of economic and environmental processes rather than piecemeal focus on particular environmental abuses...Ecological modernisation involves commitments on the part of the entire society, not just industry. These commitments include foresight, attacking problems at their origins, holism, greater valuation of scarce nature, and the precautionary principle. (Dryzek 1997: 143)

The role of civil society: public participation in development planning of the coal mining sector

Until now, the debate and the actual implementation of sustainable development and ecological modernisation, at the discourse and operational level respectively, have been mainly dominated by two of the social domains – the government and business.[30]

Their dominance has left little place for the third social domain (civil society) to be involved in forming a so-called cultural critique of mainstream development. The term 'cultural critique' refers to 'the various utterances within environmental discourse that problematise existing arrangements and suggest alternative ways of living with nature' (Hajer and Fischer 1999: 7). However, very recently a small number of new institutions in Vietnam, for example journalists, writers, scientists and local community organisations, have become involved in the development and environmental discourse to challenge the usual practices of government and business and suggest alternatives.

The environmental degradation associated with coal mining, especially in Quang Ninh, has received attention from the public through the mass media, including national and local newspapers and TV programmes. Notably, the social (including health and safety) and environmental problems caused by illegal coal mining have been covered by a number of articles published since the early 1990s in national newspapers, such as *Labour and Society* and *Culture*, and in the Quang Ninh local newspaper.[31] The film *The Life of Mrs Luu*', telling the story of a woman fighting for survival in an illegal coal-mining society, was shown on national television.

Apart from journalists, who first brought this issue to light in the media, there have been scientists who have also actively participated in the debate over the way the coal business has operated. In July 1998, members of the National Association of Historians and the Centre of Historical Monument

Conservation were openly critical of the expansion of coal mining operations in an area designated by the government as a national historical site. In an open letter to the chairman of the Quang Ninh People's Committee, Tran Quoc Vuong, a well-known professor of history at Hanoi National University, pointed to the role of Yen Tu as the centre of Vietnamese Buddhism.

> Our colleagues and I may think in a short-term way that the economic loss of the coal mining you are exploiting now is regrettable since our country is still poor and needs more natural resources. But this country is as Nguyen Trai once stated 'a country with a rich cultural tradition' and we are now preparing to celebrate the 1,000th anniversary of the capital, Thang Long-Hanoi, and the 300th anniversary of Sai Gon-Ho Chi Minh City. That means the government and people highly respect culture and consider it to be an endogenous factor for development as the former general secretary of the Party Do Muoi once said, or in the words of Unesco, culture is the driving force of development. Yet, the problem of illegal mining in Yen Tu has not been solved. And now, being informed of the recent decision made by the People' Committee to open two mines in this area, we do worry very much. We know, according to the Constitution of Vietnam, that we as ordinary citizens are masters of the country through the political system of the government. Therefore I would like to express my sincere opinion and hope that you as the chairman of the People's Committee and other concerned agencies in Quang Ninh pay attention to this problem. If because of economic benefits, historical and cultural places are destroyed, you all will have to take the responsibility for your decisions for the present and future generations. (Tran Quoc Vuong 1998 [author's translation])

This open letter was published in the newspaper *Culture* and widely distributed. As a result, the People's Committee together with VINACOAL, had to organise a press conference to respond to the critique.

It is interesting to see in this case how actors representing the interests of the bureaucratic domain (local government) were in line with the economic actors from the corporation representing the interest of the central government. (This is not always the case, as illustrated in the paragraph below on the Ha Long City Coal Washing Plant.) It was representatives of the intelligentsia who spoke out on the citizens' behalf against a kind of development, which paid more attention to economic benefit then to keeping cultural traditions alive. Scientists are rarely involved in this type of debate in Vietnam. One explanation is that science and technology systems in Vietnam are part of the government apparatus, which is why scientists usually serve the bureaucratic system instead of serving a social critical function in investigating the impacts of science and technology as they often do in the West.

While a 'cultural critique' of mainstream development thinking has been begun by intellectual actors at the discourse level, action and resistance by local communities has taken place at the operational level. When conventional development, in terms of economic growth, threatens the environmental conditions on which their life is based, communities will resist. For them, searching for sustainable livelihood in this sense means searching for decentralised, rather than accumulation-centred, forms of society (Sachs 1999). It also means there is a need to protect local initiatives and create new institutional arrangements, e.g. the right to know (consulting the public), decentralisation of decision-making and the right of self-determination (Hajer 1996). These new institutions will ensure local participation and provide ways of expressing local concern in decision-making.

The opposition of the community of Halong City to the Coal Washing Plant was a clear example of this kind of critique by a local community against the imposition of a development project by business – VINACOAL – and the exclusion of local concerns from the planning process.[32] In 1990 a new Coal Washing Plant was proposed by the Hong Gai Coal Company as a joint venture project with an Australian counterpart – the Material Coal Handling Pty Ltd (MCH). The new plant would provide increased washing capacity to meet increased demand for coal exports. It was to be funded by a loan from the Australian Export Finance and Insurance Corporation (EFIC) with an annual interest rate of 8.13 per cent after five years. The total cost of the project was US$11.5 million. The goal was to replace the old coal washing plant built during the French colonial period in the early 1900s and located, at that time, outside of the centre of the Halong City. Nowadays, however, the city has expanded and the original site is right in its heart. This location causes environmental problems, mainly from dust created by the transport of coal from nearby mines to the washing plant. The new project was approved by the central government in 1992, and construction of the foundation started, but was stopped during implementation because of strong opposition from the local community in Halong City.

The resistance of the communities, of which workers employed in the coal industry accounted for more than 50 per cent, was mobilised by the local city government. A petition with 14,000 signatures was collected and sent to the Quang Ninh Province People's Committee, asking the Council of Ministers (now the government) as well as the National Assembly to stop the project. The local community was able to demand a number of visits to the project site by the concerned governmental agencies to try to resolve this conflict. Finally, after many visits and meetings with the company, a visit from the prime minister resulted in the decision to move the project to a site about 8 km from the city centre, at a cost to the company of US$1 million already spent on construction of the new foundation. The company could have avoided the whole problem if the local community and concerned local government agencies had been involved in the decision-making process from the start. Although an EIA report was made and appraised by the central environmental authority in Hanoi – the NEA – the local environmental authority in Quang Ninh province was neither informed nor consulted about the nature of the project.

The discussion presented in the previous two subsections reflects what Hajer called an 'institutional learning' perspective on sustainable development and ecological modernisation (Hajer 1996; Hajer and Fischer 1999). According to this perspective, the existing institutions, including governmental agencies and the business community can change their way of doing business by internalising environmental costs and incorporating environmental considerations in development planning and business management. They have in fact set up new forms of management to deal with relevant issues, such as appraisal of environmental impact studies by MOSTE and VINACOAL's integrated environmental management plan. The political meaning of development and the implications of the environmental 'problematic' are predetermined in the ongoing debate on sustainable development and ecological modernisation among these institutions. The existing institutions, as the 'institutional learning' perspective suggested, 'could learn, had learned and would be able to reinvent themselves so as to become co-producers of a new sort of development that would be more environmentally sustainable' (Hajer and Fischer 1999). But this perspective failed to address the 'cultural critique' – the institutional limitations of the existing institutions.

Unlike the 'institutional learning' perspective, the 'technology critique' (Hajer 1996) and 'cultural critique' (Hajer and Fischer 1999) of sustainable development and ecological modernisation illustrated in this subsection, though in their infant phase demand new socio-political arrangements. Such arrangements need to support a more democratic social choice centred on civil society rather than just on the state and business.

CONCLUSION

As in other countries, the concept of sustainable development has provided the 'generative metaphor', or story line, around which different key economic and environmental interests of the three major social domains – state, business and civil society – could converge in Vietnam. As such, it initially proved to be a very functional concept for setting out a common way of talking about the complementary relationship between environment and development. Essentially, the concept suggested that we 'can have it all', both further economic growth and a cleaner environment (Dryzek 1997). Yet the conceptual basis of sustainable development has been weak from the outset (Foucault 1991) and failed either to produce the sort of institutional restructuring that appears to be necessary or to question the existing institutions that produced the environmental crisis in the first place. Sustainable development has served as a vehicle for a form of 'eco-managerialism' and facilitated elements of ecological modernisation (Hajer and Fischer 1999).

This chapter has demonstrated that the common institutional discourses and cultural practices of sustainable development have been carried out by state and business according to conventional modes of production and in ways in which the social order is implicated in environmental politics. The state has faced a contradiction between ensuring conditions for continued capital accumulation and its legitimacy in order to secure economic growth and at the same time minimise accompanying environmental impacts. Business, under the ecological modernisation project, claimed to be able to reconcile the environmental problems with the search to maximise profits. The alliance between state and business determines the issues to be discussed in debates about environment and development and pre-defines directions for solutions. Among others, these include co-ordinated management with all necessary institutional arrangements such as policy planning, impact assessment, integrated environmental management and environmental accounting. As such, sustainable development as an institutional approach to environmental degradation fails to question the existing institutions implicated in producing the environmental crisis in the first place. Vietnamese civil society, represented by critics such as journalists, writers, scientists and civic groups has, on the other hand, begun to formulate a 'cultural critique' of the present nature of development in Vietnam. By raising critical voices and expressing resistance, these civil actors contribute to the effort of finding alternative futures. The balance of power between the three social domains will allow Vietnamese society to respond and cope with the rapid changing and uncertain environment in the region and to redefine the development pattern of Vietnam in the future. In the context of the present economic crisis in the region, the following message is particularly relevant: 'it cannot be business as usual. The crisis has underscored the need for more transparent, rule-based institutions – institutions which are not just a club of governments and elites, but which engage national and regional civil societies' (Acharya 1999: 23).

AUTHOR'S NOTE

This chapter was originally written during the author's visit to the Energy and Resources Group, University of California, Berkeley from October 1999 to July 2000 as a Fulbright Post-doctoral Visiting Scholar. The author would like to express his sincere thanks for the generous support of the Fulbright Program.

NOTES

1 For the argument that the studies on Vietnamese politics have tended to conflate the Communist Party with the state and therefore failed to analyse adequately the evolution of the Vietnamese political system, see Vasavakul 1999.

2 A recent review of literature on environmental impact assessment (EIA) and environmental planning by (Doberstein 1998) has well presented the social, political and institutional context of development planning and the way in which such a context affects efforts to implement environmental planning process such as EIA. The problems discussed by Doberstein for developing countries are very similar to those facing Vietnam.

3 This point was presented in detail by Manser (1993) who discusses the irrational utilisation of natural resources caused by the central planning process in the former East European socialist countries such as Czechoslovakia, Poland, Hungary and East Germany.

4 Elizabeth Kemf, 'Tears and Logging in Indochina', *New Scientist*, no. 1675, 29 July 1989: 47 and Vern Weitzel, 'Vietnam's Primates in Strife',

Vietnam Today, no. 52, February 1990: 10, cited in Beresford and Fraser (1992: 14).

5 It is a common belief among developing countries that they have to make a choice between industrialisation and environmental protection. These countries have often succeeded in attracting investment precisely because they have a great toleration of pollution and environmental hazards. Put differently, development has to be traded off against environmental protection. However, as Yearley showed, this conviction appears to be changing and the belief is emerging that ecological concern is central to the politics and practice of development in developing countries (Yearley 1994: 164–165).

6 *The Ecologist*, cited in Shiva (1991: 17).

7 Catton, W.R. and R.E. Dunlap, (1980) A new ecological paradigm for postexuberant sociology. *American Behavioural Scientist* 24: 15-47, cited in Jacob (1994).

8 For a more detailed discussion on the relationship between the idea of 'triple revolution' in Vietnam, the concept of scientific revolution in the west and its implications for science and technology policy in Vietnam, see Bach Tan Sinh (1993).

9 The term 'catch up' came originally from Rostow (1990). According to Rostow, the development model is based on a unilinear view of history, according to which the modern West is at once the goal to be reached and the example to be followed. This conception stems from the somewhat simplistic perspective of evolutionism.

10 It is interesting to know that the list of industrial products allowed to be produced in the industrial parks and export processing zone include among others NPK fertiliser, detergents, paints, lead and acid storage batteries that are not environmentally safe.

11 There is no single, static definition of civil society. The term has a long and continually evolving, if not contestable, conceptual history (Wapner 1998). For the early formulation following Hegel, civil society was defined as 'that arena of social engagement which exists above the individual yet below the state' and 'a complex network of economic, social, and cultural practices based on friendship, family, the market, and voluntary affiliation (Wapner 1998: 510). The concept includes the economy within its domain. Later formulations, notably those offered by Gramsci and Parsons, introduced a three-part model that differentiates civil society from both the state and the economy (Parsons 1971; Gramsci 1971). The

latter concept is in line with the framework used here, which classifies society into three sectors – government, business and civil society.

Different versions of the concept of civil society are proposed by Kaldor including: (1) *societas civilis*; (2) bourgeois society (*Bürgerliche Gesellschaft*); (3) the neo-liberal version; (4) the activist version; and (5) the post-modern version. (Kaldor 2000). In the Vietnamese context, civil society consists of institutions or components which grow out as 'self organisation outside formal political circles, … expand space in which individual citizens can influence the condition in which they live both directly through self organisation and through pressure on the State' [and] 'provide a substitute for many of the functions performed by the state ... and the function in the field of welfare which the state can no longer afford to perform' (Kaldor 2000).

12 This point will be discussed at length in the next session on the role of government in coal-mining sector.

13 See Vu Cao Dam (1989)) and Bach Tan Sinh (1991).

14 MOSTE is the Ministry of Science, Technology and Environment. Each province has a related DOSTE (Department of Science, Technology and Environment). NEA is the National Environmental Agency. A detailed description on the network of environmental agencies, especially for EIA, is presented in (Bach Tan Sinh 1998: chapter 5).

15 This point is addressed at length in (Bach Tan Sinh 1998:Chapters 4 and 5).

16 For a detailed discussion on this point, see Bach Tan Sinh (1998: Chapter 6).

17 For more description on this problem, see Bach Tan Sinh (1998).

18 For a detailed forecast with the low and high scenarios see Table 8.1.

19 The issue related to crisis between two functions of the capitalist state – accumulation and legitimacy was examined first by Habermas (1975) in the 1960s and recently by a number of authors whose writings were collected by O'Connor (1994): for example, James O'Connor, John S. Dryzek and Colin Hay.

20 See Decision No. 563 of the Prime Minister, October 1994; Government Decree No. 13, 17 January 1995.

21 The Vietnam Oil and Gas Corporation (PETROVIETNAM) was set up according to the Decree No. 38/CP. enacted 30 May 1995; Electricity of Vietnam Corporation (EVN) was established according to the Decree No. 14/CP, enacted 27 January 1995.

22 Along this line, see Beresford (Chapter 3 this volume).

23 For a detailed discussion of the impacts on miners and their families see (Greenfield 1999; Spaeth 1999; Greenfield 1998; Minh Tam 1994).

24 For a further description of environmental conflicts between coal mining and other economic sectors and the environmental impacts created by coal mining, see Bach Tan Sinh (1998: chapter 7).

25 For a detailed discussion, see Bach Tan Sinh (1998, chapter 7).

26 That is, that desired development of material welfare is intrinsically compatible with the protection of the environment (Hajer 1995).

27 Interview with Nguyen Chi Quang, director of the Environment and Technology Centre, VINACOAL, August 1998.

28 On this point see Bach Tan Sinh (1998: Chapter 7).

29 Before VINACOAL became one of the Corporations 91, the MOI was responsible for formulating and submitting the coal-mining sector plan. Although the MOI still has a regulatory function over all business activities in the industrial sector, it has no further planning function in relation to VINACOAL. See also the section on 'The Rise of State-Business Interests' in Vasavakul (1999).

30 For a lengthy discussion on this point see Bach Tan Sinh (1998: Chapters 4, 5 and 6).

31 See Huynh Thai (1992); To Ngoc Hien (1994); Minh Tam (1994); Do Hoang (1994); To Phan/Ngo Mai Phong (1996).

32 For a more detailed discussion, see Bach Tan Sinh (1998: Chapter 7).

REFERENCES

Acharya, Amitav (1999) 'Realism, Institutionalism and the Asian Economic Crisis'. *Contemporary Southeast Asia*, vol. 21, no. 1, April, pp. 1–29.

Adams, W. M. (1992) *Green Development: Environment and Sustainability in the Third World*. London and New York: Routledge.

Aseniero, G.A *et al.* (1985) 'Reflection on developmentalism: from development to transformation'. In Samir Amin, *et al. Development as Social Transformation: Reflection on the Global Problematique*. Singapore: United Nations University Press; pp. 48–85.

Asia Intelligence Update (1999) 'Hesitant to Reform: Vietnam Warned it may be Left Behind'. 5 March, at: http://www.stratfor.com/asia/aiuarchive/b990305.html

Bach Tan Sinh (1991) 'The Impact Assessment of the New Management Mechanism of Macro-economy on Scientific and Technological Activities in Economic Sectors'. Report submitted to the Council of Ministers, March 1991.

—— (1993) 'Science and Technology Policy in Vietnam: Historical Aspect'. Masters Thesis, Research Policy Institute, University of Lund, Sweden.

—— (1998) 'Sustainable development in Vietnam: Institutional challenges for integration of environment and development'. PhD Thesis, Aalborg University, Aalborg, Denmark.

Beresford, Melanie and Lyn Fraser (1992) 'Political Economy of the Environment in Vietnam'. *Journal of Contemporary Asia*, vol. 22, no. 1.

Bui Dinh Thanh (1997) 'Mot so suy nghi ve moi quan he giua tang truong kinh te va phat trien xa hoi' ['Some thoughts on the relationship between economic growth and social development today'], *Tap chi Cong san* [*Communist Review*], February.

Chilcote, R. H. (1984) *Theories of Development and Underdevelopment*. Boulder CO: Westview Press.

Christoff, Peter (1996) 'Ecological Modernization, Ecological Modernities'. *Environmental Politics*, no. 5.

Dang Ngoc Dinh (1998) 'Ve dinh huong chien luoc khoa hoc va cong nghe' [About the directions of science and technology strategy of our country]. *Tap chi Cong san* [Communist Review], February.

Dao The Tuan (1992) 'Tang truong kinh te va cong bang xa hoi' [Economic growth and social equality], *Tap chi Cong san* [Communist Review], September.

Derman, W. and S. Whiteford (eds) (1985) *Social Impact Analysis and Development Planning in the Third World*. Boulder, CO: Westview Press.

Doberstein, B. (1998) 'Environmental Impact Assessment Capacity Building in Vietnam: The Role and Influence of Development Aid Programme'. Paper presented at the International Association for Impact Assessment (IAIA) Annual Conference, Christchurch, New Zealand, April.

Do Hoang (1994) 'Quang Ninh sap xep lai lao dong' [Rearrangement of the labour force in Quang Ninh], *Lao Dong Xa Hoi* [Labour and Society] 27 October–2 November.

Dryzek, John S. (1997) *The Politics of Earth: Environmental Discourse*. Oxford: Oxford University Press.

Elzinga, A. and A. Jamison (1995) 'Changing Policy Agendas in Science and Technology'. In S. Jasanoff *et al.* (eds), *Handbook of Science and Technology Studies*. Thousand Oaks, London, New Delhi: Sage.

Eyerman, R. and A. Jamison (1991) *Social Movements: A Cognitive Approach.* Cambridge: Polity Press.

Foucault, M. (1991) 'Governmentality' In G. Burchell, C. Gordon and P. Miller (eds), *The Foucault Effect: Studies in Governmentality.* Chicago: University of Chicago Press.

Gramsci , A. (1971) *Prison Notebooks.* New York: International Publishers.

Greenfield, Gerard (1998) 'Miners and the Market in Vietnam'. *New Politics,* no.25, Summer, pp. 38–45.

—— (1999) 'Vietnam: The Collapse of Nationalised Coal Production. Mass Lay-Offs of Miners in the Face of "Temporary" Pit Closures'. *International Viewpoint,* September.

GSO (General Statistical Office) (2001) *Statistical Yearbook 2000.* Hanoi: Statistical Publishers.

Habermas, J. (1975) *Legitimation Crisis.* London: Heinemann.

Hajer, Maarten A. (1995) *The Politics of Environmental Discourse: Ecological Modernisation and the Policy Process.* Oxford: Clarendon Press.

—— (1996) 'Ecological Modernization as Cultural Politics'. In S. Lash, B. Szerszynski and B. Wynne (eds), *Risk, Environment and Modernity: towards a New Ecology.* London: Sage, pp. 246–268.

Hajer, Maarten A. and Frank Fischer (1999) 'Introduction, Beyond Global Discourse: The Rediscovery of Culture in Environmental Politics'. In Frank Fischer and Maarten A. Hajer (eds), *Living with Nature: Environmental Politics as Cultural Discourse.* Oxford: Oxford University Press, pp. 1–20.

Henry, R. (1990) 'Implementing Social Impact Assessment in Developing Countries: A Comparative Approach to the Structural Problems'. *Environmental Impact Assessment Review,* no. 10, pp. 91–101.

Hiebert, M. (1992) 'Green fees' *Far Eastern Economic Review,* 20 August.

Hirsch, P. *et al.* (1992) 'Social and Environmental Implications of Resource Development in Vietnam: The Case of Hoa Binh Reservoir'. *Occasional Papers,* no. 17, Research Institute for Asia and the Pacific, University of Sydney.

Huynh Thai (1992) 'Than Lau' [Illegal coal], *Van Nghe* [Literature and Art], 19 September, pp.15–16.

Information and Resource Centre (1991) *Vietnam Commentary,* Singapore, March–April.

Jacob, M. (1994) 'Sustainable Development and Deep Ecology: An Analysis of Competing Traditions'. *Environmental Management*, vol. 18, no. 4.

Jamison, A. and Baark, E. (1990) 'Technological Innovation and Environmental Concern: Contending Policy Models in China and Vietnam'. *Discussion Papers*, no. 1987, Research Policy Institute, University of Lund.

Jamison, A., Eyerman, R., and Cramer, J. (1990) *The Making of the New Environmental Consciousness: A Comparative Study of the Environmental Movements in Sweden, Denmark and the Netherlands.* Edinburgh: Edinburgh University Press.

Japan–Vietnam Joint Coal Exploration–Red River Delta Project (n.d.) at www.jcoal.or.jp/e/Presen/Takakuwa/tsld022.htm

JCOAL (1999) *JCOAL topics*, no. 17, 11 January, at www.jcoal.or.jp/e/topics_E17.html

Kaldor, Mary (2000) 'For the Global Civil Society Almanac'. *Brainstorming*, 4–5 February.

Lemons, J. and Brown, D. (eds) (1997) *Sustainable Development: Science, Ethics and Public Policy*. Dordrecht, Boston and London: Kluwer Academic Publishers.

Malhotra, K. (1998) 'The Political Economy and Natural Resource Conflict in the Lower Mekong Sub-Region'. Paper presented at the Consultative Conference, Promoting Dialogue on the Natural Resources of the Lower Mekong, Chulalongkorn University Social Research Institute, Bangkok, 23–25 August.

Manser, Roger (1993) 'The squandered divided: The free market and the environment in Eastern Europe'. Unpublished.

Minh Tam (1994) 'The Fate of Miners. *Labour and Society*, 5–11 August, pp. 1–8.

MPI (1998) *Environmental Assessment and Sustainable Development of Coal Mining Sector in Vietnam: A Case Study of Coal Mining in Quang Ninh Province*. Hanoi: MPI.

MPI and UNDP (1997) 'An Analysis of National Environmental Plans in Vietnam'. Hanoi: Vietnam Capacity 21 Project.

MPI/UNDP (1997a) 'Integrating Environment and Economic Policy in Vietnam'. Hanoi: Vietnam Capacity 21 Project.

—— (1997b) 'Planning Tools for Environmental Assessment of Economic Development Policies and Programmes'. Hanoi: Vietnam Capacity 21 Project.

Nguyen Chi Quang *et al.* (1998) 'Environmental Assessment and Sustainable Development of Coal Mining Sector in Vietnam: A Case Study of Coal Mining in Quang Ninh Province'. Hanoi: VINACOAL.

Nguyen Dinh Tu (1995) 'Chuyen giao cong nghe: yeu to quan trong phuc vu cong nghiep hoa va hien dai hoa' [Technology transfer: an important factor to promote industrialisation and modernisation], *Tap chi Cong san* [Communist Review], January.

Nguyen Khac Vien (1991) *Vietnam Commentary*. Singapore: Information and Resource Centre, March–April.

Nguyen The Nghia (1997) 'Nhung van de cap bach ve xa hoi, van hoa va nhan van trong qua trinh cong nghiep hoa hien dai hoa' [Urgent social, cultural and human issues in the course of industrialisation and modernisation], Tap chi Cong san [Communist Review], September.

Nguyen Thi Hien (1998) 'Vai tro cua van hoa trong phat trien' [The role of culture in development], *Van Hoa* [Culture], Hanoi, 19 August.

Nhat Ninh (1991) 'Trao doi ve nhung mat trai cua khoa hoc va cong nghe hien dai' [Debate on the Negative Sides of Modern Science and Technology], *Nhan Dan* [The People], 13 November.

O'Connor, Martin (ed.) (1994) *Is Capitalism Sustainable?* New York and London: The Guildford Press.

O'Rourke, Dara (2002) 'Motivating a Conflicted Environmental State: Community-Driven Regulation in Vietnam'. In A.P.J. Mol and F.H. Buttel (eds), *The Environmental State under Pressure*. London: Elsevier/JAI.

Parnwell, M. J. G. and Bryant, R. L. (1996) *Environmental Change in South-East Asia: People, Politics and Sustainable Development*. London and New York: Routledge.

Parsons, T. (1971) *The System of Modern Societies*. Englewood Cliffs, NJ: Prentice-Hall.

Quang Ninh (1994) 'Khoi phu lai trat tu trong khai thac than va lao dong' [To restore order in coal exploitation] *Lao Dong* [Labour] Hanoi, 14 July.

Redclift, Michael (1984) *Development and the Environmental Crisis: Red or Green Alternatives?* London and New York: Methuen.

Rostow, W.W. (1990) *The State of Economic Growth: A Non-Communist Manifesto,* Third edn. Cambridge, New York: Cambridge University Press.

Sachs, Wolfgang (1999) 'Sustainable Development and the Crisis of Nature: On the Political Anatomy of an Oxymoron'. In Frank Fischer and Maarten A. Hajer (eds), *Living with Nature: Environmental Politics as Cultural Discourse*. Oxford: Oxford University Press, pp. 153–185.

Shiva, Vandana (1991) *Ecology and the Politics of Survival: Conflicts over Natural Resources in India.* New Delhi: Sage/United National University Press.

Spaeth, Anthony (1999) 'Vietnam's newly laid-off coal miners are struggling to cope with life's challenges outside the shaft: climbing out of a deep, dark hole' *Time Asia*, vol. 154, no. 4, 2 August.

Steger, U. (1993) 'The Greening of the Board Room: How German Companies are dealing with Environmental Issues'. In K. Fischer and J. Schot, (eds), *Environmental Strategies for Industry: International Perspectives on Research Needs and Policy Implication.* London: Island Press.

To Ngoc Hien (1994) 'Ban ve chong kha thac than tho phi' [Talking again about 'bandit' coal mines]. *Bao Quang Ninh* [Quang Ninh newspaper]. Quang Ninh; May 17.

To Phan and Ngo Mai Phong (1996) 'Ben kia cua mua ban than tho phi o Quang Ninh' [The down side of illegal coal trade in Quang Ninh]. *Lao Dong* [Labour], Hanoi.

Tran Quoc Vuong (1998) 'Thu ngo gui Chu tich Uy ban Nha dan Tinh Quang Ninh' [Open Letter to the Chairman of Quang Ninh People's Committee], *Van Hoa* [Culture], Hanoi 12 August.

Trong Tin (1997) 'Vietnam needs cleaner production'. *Vietnam News*, 21 July.

US Department of Commerce (1998) 'Vietnam: Economic Trends' 10 July, at http://strategis.ic.gc.ca/SSG/da92038e.html

Vasavakul, Thaveeporn (1999) 'Vietnam: Sectors, Classes, and the Transformation of a Leninist State'. In W. James Morley (ed.), *Driven by Growth: Political Change in the Asia-Pacific Region*, revised edn, Armonk, NY and London: Columbia University Press, pp. 59-82.

Verhelst, T. C. (1987) *No Life without Roots: Culture and Development.* London and Atlantic Highlands, NJ: Zed Books.

Vietnam News (1999a) 'Coal mines ordered to scale back – government moves to protect Quang Ninh miners' jobs'. 6 July at http://vietnamnews.vnagency.com.vn/1999–07/05/Stories/05.html

—— (1999b) 'VINACOAL plans for new power plants', 11 August at vietnamnews.vnagency.com.vn/1999-08/10/stories/03.html

Vo Quy (1997) 'Environmental Issue in Vietnam', in H. Mecker, and Vu Phi Hoang (eds), *Environmental Policy and Management in Vietnam.* Berlin: Public Administration Promotion Centre, pp. 5–30.

Vu Cao Dam (1989) 'Improvement of Policy Measures for Stimulating Technological Innovation in the Macro-economic Management System'. Hanoi: Institute for Science Management.

Vu Dinh Cu (1995) 'Khoa hoc va cong nghe, luc luong san xuat chinh' [Science and technology, the major forces of production], *Tap chi Cong san* [Communist Review], September.

Wapner, P. (1998) 'Politics Beyond the State: Environmental Activism and World Civic Politics'. In J. Dryzek, and D. Schlosberg, (eds), *Debating the Earth: Environmental Politics Reader.* Oxford: Oxford University Press.

Williams, H. E., Medhurst, J. and Drew, K. (1993) 'Corporate Strategies for a Sustainable Future'. In Fischer, K. and Schot, J. (eds), *Environmental Strategies for Industry: International Perspectives on Research Needs and Policy Implication*. London: Island Press.

Yearley (1994) 'Social Movement and Environmental Change'. In M. Redclift and T. Benton (eds), *Social Theory and the Global Environment.* London and New York: Routledge.

Index